DEVELOPING STATES, SHAPING CITIZENSHIP

AFRICAN PERSPECTIVES
Kelly Askew and Anne Pitcher
Series Editors

Developing States, Shaping Citizenship

Service Delivery and Political Participation in Zambia

Erin Accampo Hern

University of Michigan Press
Ann Arbor

Published in the United States of America by the
University of Michigan Press
Manufactured in the United States of America
Printed on acid-free paper
First published May 2019

A CIP catalog record for this book is available from the British Library.

Library of Congress Cataloging-in-Publication Data

Names: Hern, Erin Accampo, 1987– author.
Title: Developing states, shaping citizenship : service delivery and political participation in
    Zambia / Erin Accampo Hern.
Description: Ann Arbor : University of Michigan Press, 2019. | Series: African perspectives
    series |
Identifiers: LCCN 2018053130 (print) | LCCN 2019000413 (ebook) | ISBN 9780472125258
    (E-book) | ISBN 9780472074143 (hardcover : alk. paper) | ISBN 9780472054145 (pbk. : alk.
    paper)
Subjects: LCSH: Political participation—Zambia. | Zambia—Politics and government—1991–
Classification: LCC JQ2881 (ebook) | LCC JQ2881 .H47   2019 (print) |
    DDC 323.042096894—dc23
LC record available at https://lccn.loc.gov/2018053130

Publication of this volume has been partially funded by the African Studies Center,
University of Michigan.

Cover photo by Erin Accampo Hern.

For my mother, who taught me to write like an academic;

my father, who reminded me to write for those who are not;

and Tom, who met me because of this project
   and stayed with me despite it.

CONTENTS

Digital materials related to this title can be found on the Fulcrum platform via the following citable URL: https://doi.org/10.3998/mpub.9989603

ACKNOWLEDGMENTS

This book would not have been possible without the immense generosity and support of many people and organizations. I am grateful to Nic van de Walle, Mary Katzenstein, and Tom Pepinsky at Cornell University for their feedback as I designed and executed the first version of the project on which this book is based and wrote version after version of the results. Their suggestions, along with Suzanne Mettler's, were instrumental in guiding the ultimate shape of this book. This research never would have occurred without Muna Ndulo encouraging me to go to Zambia and helping me find my footing for my first trip. I am thankful to Cornell University Graduate School for funding that initial research trip to Lusaka in 2012 and to Cornell's Department of Government for enabling a follow-up trip in 2014. Most of this research took place under the auspices of a nine-month Fulbright grant. An additional research trip in 2016 was funded through various sources from the College of Idaho, including the Faculty Growth and Development Committee and Academic Affairs. That trip dramatically deepened the depth of analysis I was able to conduct.

I am indebted to Marja Hinfelaar and Jessica Achberger at the Southern African Institute for Policy and Research (SAIPAR) in Lusaka for all manner of support, both academic and personal, from facilitating research contacts, providing office space, discussing ideas, giving unending emotional support, and literally putting a roof over my head when I had nowhere else to go; I cannot imagine having completed this research without them. I am also grateful to SAIPAR for institutional support, to the Zambian Governance Foundation for providing me office space and professional connections, and to the staff of the National Archives of Zambia for making my work there both pleasant and efficient. Several research workshops organized by SAIPAR gave me opportunities to present early versions of my work to an interdisciplinary group of Zambia specialists, who provided invaluable feedback from multiple disciplinary perspectives. I thank the staff at the United National Independence Party Archives for their warm reception, and I thank Mr.

Munshya for patiently humoring my countless requests for documents from those archives.

I cannot offer enough gratitude to the people who helped me get oriented and recruit research assistants at each of my field sites: Namo Chuma and Justin Njobvu of Environment Africa in Livingstone, Ifeoma Anene of Restless Development in Kabwe, and Philip Phiri and John Kalusa of Caritas in Solwezi. At each site, I relied heavily on the local knowledge and energy of my research assistants: Yvonne, Jacob, and Gift in Livingstone; Chimwemwe, Loveness, Irene, and Robert in Kabwe; and Lewis, Precious, Mackenzie, and Holmes in Solwezi. During later trips, Agnes in Kabwe and Hope in Livingstone provided instrumental support as translators. In 2016, Cameron Arnzen and Ruth Nakalyowa accompanied me as undergraduate research assistants, conducting excellent research that dramatically increased the amount of work I was able to complete. I would be remiss not to mention all those who helped me find my way around the country: Dylan and David, Alli and Elissa, Maureen and Ivo, Alan and Alan, Nina and Simon, and Rory.

I thank the institutional review boards at both Cornell and the College of Idaho for their oversight and support, as well as the thousands of Zambians who patiently spoke with me or my research assistants for this project. All consent for this project was obtained orally, and all general interview and survey subjects were anonymized. Where the text refers to their responses specifically, they are numbered. Most public figures or institution representatives who I interviewed consented to their names being used; those few who preferred to remain anonymous are cited as such.

The road from fieldwork to dissertation to book is long, and my work has benefited from the feedback of numerous people who commented on various iterations of the content now included in this book. I thank Lauren Honig, Natalie Wenzell Letsa, Elizabeth Sperber, Adam Harris, Rachel Behler, Michael Wahman, Alex Curritt, and Jennifer Brass for providing feedback and suggestions about everything from secondary literature to appropriate strategies for statistical estimation. Input from anonymous reviewers (of both the book manuscript and a few pieces adapted for journals) has helped me to sharpen and strengthen my arguments. Tom Mowle provided invaluable assistance in reorganizing and clarifying my writing. Lauren MacLean provided comments and feedback on various pieces of this project and acted as an advocate and mentor. I thank Anne Pitcher, Ellen Bauerle, Kelly Askew, and others at the University of Michigan Press for believing in the project and deciding to publish it.

Finally, I am grateful to Tom Callaghy for making sure I got to Africa in the first place and to Tom Cronjé for rescuing me when everything went wrong. I appreciate my mother, Elinor, for understanding better than anyone what this process has been like, and my father, Bob, for helping me keep it all in perspective.

TABLES

CHAPTER 1

Understanding Political Participation in Africa's New Democracies

THINGS ARE CHANGING, BUT THEY ARE ALWAYS THE SAME

When I arrived in Lusaka in July 2012, the city was still awash in electric energy from Zambia's presidential elections nearly one year earlier. "Things are changing," my taxi driver told me as he dodged potholes along the Great East Road. "Now that Sata is in power," he explained, "things are going to be different."

In September 2011, Zambians elected Michael Sata of the Patriotic Front (PF) as their president, ending 20 years of uninterrupted rule by the Movement for Multiparty Democracy (MMD). In the world of political science, this peaceful alternation of power moved Zambia from the category of "unconsolidated" to "consolidated" democracy. For many Zambians, this shift was an indication that perhaps their democracy was functional after all. Zambia's 1991 return to multiparty democracy was part of the third wave of democracy that swept across the African continent, unseating long-standing rulers and opening the political sphere. But in Zambia, as in many other new African democracies, excitement turned to skepticism, as the MMD manipulated electoral rules, rigged elections, and consolidated power around a strong presidency (Bratton and Posner 1999). Sata, a member of the MMD when it won power, became disillusioned with the party and started his own—the PF—in 2001, unsuccessfully running for president in 2001, 2006, and 2008 before finally winning in 2011. His victory was a symbol of a new political era for Zambia, one in which opposition parties can win presidential elections.

One year later, in July 2013, I returned to Zambia and was (perhaps naively) surprised at how much the mood had changed. The enthusiasm and jubilation that had been pervasive in 2012 had already morphed into resignation. "Nothing has changed," my taxi driver told me this time. This sentiment was repeated to me in many forms over the course of the next year. "It doesn't matter who is in power," one survey respondent lamented, adding, "It is always the same."

This sense of resignation is not unique to Zambia, nor are the cycles of euphoria and disappointment that have characterized African polities broadly since the end of colonization.[1] The African state has been the subject of many adjectives: weak, vampiric, predatory, neopatrimonial (respectively, Jackson and Rosberg 1982; Frimpong-Ansah 1991; Fatton 1992; Bratton and van de Walle 1997). Africa's democracies have similarly received attention for their deficits, termed choiceless, virtual, shadow, and dominated by "politics of the belly" (respectively, Mkandawire 1999; Joseph 1999; Reno 1996; Bayart 1993). Even Botswana, regularly regarded as a beacon for liberal democracy and economic development, has recently been criticized for the way its dominant ruling party limits the possibilities for political competition.[2] In general, scholars suggest that there is something different about African democracies, and characterizing the nature of these democracies is a cottage industry of sorts.

Yet, flawed as they may be, many African polities have regular political competition, with some degree of electoral choice. While turnout rates may fluctuate, Africans vote, contact their officials, organize into voluntary associations, and demonstrate to express their political opinions. Just as the nature of African democracies seems to diverge from the Western standard, predictive models of political participation have not fared particularly well at explaining African turnout.[3] Voting behavior, in particular, has attracted a bevy of explanations. The importance of patronage networks, ethnicity-based mobilization, and distributive politics each provide some explanation for the ways in which African parties mobilize voters. These explanations tend to give primacy to material motivations for political participation, the expectation that voting the "right" people into power will result in some kind of material benefit—be it through low-level patronage distribution, public goods allocated on the basis of ethnicity, or targeted distribution of state resources (see, e.g., Bratton, Bhavnani, and Chen 2012). In many African democracies, however, the government only has access to limited resources, and patronage networks tend to be concentrated among the elites (van de Walle 2012, 113–19). Many Africans, especially those further from major cities, are rarely positioned to benefit from government-distributed goods. In this context, where the costs of participation are comparatively high and the benefits are dubious, what explains ongoing political engagement and participation?

My argument in the present study is that the degree to which citizens of low-capacity African democracies engage in politics depends partly on their personal experiences with the state through service provision. While the promise of political participation is access to state resources—through patronage or public goods provision—government officials have a limited ability to fulfill these promises. As such, governments and politicians must make decisions about where to target limited state resources, creating variation in the presence of the state (and particularly of state service provision). My argument hinges on the idea that citizens' past experiences with service provision educate them as to what they might expect in the future—whether the government is likely to target them for resource distribution, make a half-hearted effort to extend services, ignore them, or even make things worse. These experiences send citizens powerful signals about the possible utility of political participation. When governments make decisions about how and where to extend state capacity, they are not just constructing the state; they are constructing citizens as well.

This approach to explaining political participation privileges material motivations over nonmaterial ones. Sense of civic duty, the importance of exercising political rights that have been newly won, and the emotional satisfaction of making symbolic gestures are all important motivators of political participation that do not figure in my argument. I do not deny that such nonmaterial motivations for political participation can be powerful and, under the right circumstances, may overwhelm the material ones. Material and nonmaterial motivations are not mutually exclusive; depending on the circumstances, they may be either mutually reinforcing or countervailing. However, my focus in the present study is on the material motivations that influence citizens' political activity, with the understanding that material concerns are not the only motivator for political action.

This chapter's elaboration of my argument begins with a discussion of the dominant approaches to African politics and political behavior. Assessing the strengths and weaknesses of these approaches provides the context for my argument, which is theoretically based in the literature on policy feedback. This chapter then explains the policy feedback approach and its application in Zambia's case, as well as this study's research design and the plan of this book.

POLITICS AND POLITICAL PARTICIPATION
IN AFRICA'S NEW DEMOCRACIES

At the end of the 1980s, with the fall of the Soviet Union, the third wave of democracy crashed over the African continent. Over a few short years, Crawford Young estimates that no fewer than 39 constitutions had been completely revised or redrafted, paving the way for multiparty democracy (2012, 26). The euphoria that followed this rapid and dramatic transition was short-lived, however, as many countries that had taken steps toward political liberalization exhibited a return to autocratic tendencies. Analysis of political participation and elite-level political processes indicates that democratization did not lead to the same political outcomes as it had in the older, more established democracies of the West. This divergence has occurred partly because the legitimating logic of these regimes reflects patrimonial ideals, which shape incentives for both political elites and voters differently than the bureaucratic-rational ideals of democracy. Attempts to appraise the nature of African democracies have tended to revolve around three questions. First, to whom is the state beholden? Second, who is positioned to benefit from state resources? Finally, how do these realities affect party formation and voter behavior?

To Whom the State Is Beholden

Concerns about the nature of African states emerged shortly after the euphoria of independence dissipated. After the 1960s, during which a massive expansion of the state's role in the economy characterized so many African countries, observers highlighted how such market involvement created plentiful opportunities for corruption sponsored by the state. Such corruption gutted government-run sectors, and wealth remained concentrated in the former colonies' urban cores, despite socialist rhetoric promising shared development in rural areas. Examination of African states in the 1970s and 1980s focused heavily on the predatory nature of elites and the influence of interest groups, each driving policy-making that undermined the goals of shared development and participatory democracy (Bates [1981] 2014; Frimpong-Ansah 1991). This economic mismanagement coincided with the abandonment of multiparty democracy in favor of centralization of power and autocracy, often in the form of one-party states. Initially, moves toward autocracy in African states were justified with the logic that achieving national unity and shared development would require silencing dissenting voices (Young 2012, 138–39). However, as early African states moved from the euphoric postindependence period into the economic decline of the 1970s, these explanations rang false, and scholars highlighted the ability of the few to benefit from state involvement in the economy.

By the 1980s, nearly all scholarship of African political economy noted that the political and economic spheres had been captured, in one way or another, by elites. Some critics alleged that the government lacked autonomy and was manipulated by interest groups and elite machinations at the expense of the broader citizenry (e.g., Bates [1981] 2014). In examinations of the ways in which elites were able to manipulate access to state resources for the purposes of personal enrichment or cultivating patronage networks, the African state was, at various times, described as a vampire, predatory, a lame leviathan, or comprising decentralized despotism (respectively, Frimpong-Ansah 1991; Fatton 1992; Callaghy 1984; Mamdani 1996). Bayart (1993) famously described the African state as a rhizome, penetrating the nooks and crannies of society while operating according to "politics of the belly," whereby agents of the state employed various tactics of corruption in order to "eat" at the expense of the rest of the population. Other critics pointed to the ways in which state authorities could "systemically appropriate public resources for their own uses," which generally constituted a combination of rent-seeking and maintaining elite patronage networks (van de Walle 2001, 52; see also Bratton and van de Walle 1997). Many country-specific case studies examined the particular manifestations of such broader trends, pointing to the way patrimonialism was eroding both economic potential and democratic processes in African states.[4]

In the late 1980s and early 1990s, as the third wave of democracy brought the return of multiparty democracy to most of the African continent, hope that the transition would change the logic of African politics was short-lived. While a few countries managed to consolidate high-quality democracies, most African countries were in a state of "semidemocracy," characterized by a neopatrimonial logic, by which incumbents adapted and manipulated the rules of the game in order to pursue the familiar pattern of capturing state resources to maintain patronage networks (Young 2012, 195; see also Joseph 1999). While the return of multiparty politics has not altered the underlying logic of African political systems, some scholars have argued that it has changed the methods by which political leaders are able to retain power. With the return of multiparty democracy, universal suffrage, and political competition (however farcical), African political parties generally lack the resources to engage in mass patronage and have resorted to prebends instead, ultimately limiting the scope of who is able to gain access to such resources (van de Walle 2012). Incumbents maintain control in multiparty systems precisely through this access to state resources, which allows them to cultivate loyalty and create elite coalitions oriented toward preserving their hold on power (Arriola 2013). The result is that clientelism has increasingly come to benefit a narrow band of elites—those to whom the state is beholden (van de Walle, Ball, and Ramachandran 2003).[5]

Many contemporary African publics thus reflect the logic outlined by Peter Ekeh's insightful thoughts on Africa's "two publics," in which the "civic public," including the instruments of government administration, is amoral and subsumed by the logic of the "primordial public," which prioritizes the distribution of resources on the basis of personal relationships (1975, 92; see also Terray 1986). Neopatrimonialism—a system in which power flows through patrimonial relationships though legal-rational institutions exist—creates a political structure in which the state is beholden to the political elite. Some scholars have suggested that neopatrimonialism is not necessarily predatory, but others indicate that it constitutes the "reverse of power institutionalization," creating a state that is the personal tool of the elite (Bach and Gazibou 2012; see also Chabal and Daloz 1999). Indeed, critics have pointed out that the concentration of state resources among elites erodes the very legitimacy of patrimonialism, because it bypasses those most in need (Smith 2007; Bayart, Ellis, and Hibou [1999] 2009). While the precise nature of the relationship between the trappings of the state and the exercise of elite power provides fodder for ongoing debate, few scholars would argue against the idea that African polities are often characterized by elite capture, and the elites generally maintain their power by carefully cultivating patronage (or prebendalist) networks.

Who Benefits from the State?

A peculiar feature of African politics is that while the vast majority of patronage resources are concentrated, in the form of prebends, among elite networks, the promise of access to state resources remains a critical component of maintaining broad-based political support, particularly in states with electoral politics. Most African political parties lack the resources to engage in systematic mass patronage, but instances of parties courting voters with material goods are common (van de Walle 2003). In some cases, parties distribute resources directly through clientelist relationships, to cultivate loyalty among base voters (Wantchekon 2003) or to woo swing voters (Weghorst and Lindberg 2013). Parties may also distribute low-value material goods as a campaign strategy, suggesting to voters that they stand to benefit should the party in question remain in (or gain) office (see, e.g., Rakner 2001 on the MMD in Zambia).

Because of the limited resources to which parties have access, overlapping scholarship on ethnic and distributive politics seeks to understand where parties and governments target state resources through individual clientelist relationships or provision of club goods. The literature on these trends suggests, however, that these processes are highly dependent on context. Recent works have shown that the incumbent party attempts to electrify swing voter districts in Ghana (Nugent 2001; Briggs 2012), while the Kenyan government diverts aid resources to its base of core supporters (Briggs 2014). When states are in the midst of fiscal crises, extension of land rights can be a powerful way to build electoral coalitions (Boone 2009). In Mali, extension of services is distinctly political: public goods provision is better in communes that have a higher degree of political competition, suggesting that elites must improve service provision to signal that supporters will gain some access to state resources (Gottlieb 2015).

In countries where political parties have ethnically homogeneous support bases, distributive politics takes on distinctly ethnic characteristics. Yet the degree to which resource distribution follows political (or ethnic) logic is ultimately uncertain. While studies have indicated that rulers' coethnics across multiple countries have better health and infant mortality outcomes than non-coethnics (Franck and Rainer 2012) and that Kenyans who share ethnicity with government officials experience more infrastructure development (Burgess et al. 2015), the pattern of resource distribution is far from certain. Conducting a thorough examination of the literature and performing their own tests, Kramon and Posner (2013) demonstrate that the relationship between ethnic identity, coethnicity, and public resource distribution in African countries depends entirely on the resource in question. Furthermore, coethnics sometimes get the raw end of the deal if incumbents believe they can "get away with" worse treatment of their base (Kasara 2007). This uncertain climate creates a conundrum for voters but can explain some patterns of voter behavior.

How Do Distributive and Ethnic Politics Influence Voter Behavior?

If elites are gatekeepers for state resources and if access to these resources depends on individual or community relationships with politicians and political parties, it follows that voters will throw their support behind the candidate or party that is most likely to deliver resources. In many African countries, voters draw these conclusions based on ethnic identity. Indeed, much scholarship on distributive politics blends into scholarship on ethnic politics, as the logic behind voter incentives under distributive or ethnic politics is similar.

Even in circumstances under which ethnic or racial identity is particularly charged, as in South Africa, scholarship has indicated that identity-based preferences for political candidates do not reflect jingoism or distinct policy differences; rather, race or ethnicity serve as heuristics for voters regarding the likelihood that they will receive material benefits from a certain candidate (Ferree 2006). Others have demonstrated that ethnic and racial identities become more salient around elections, reflecting the politicization of identity and underscoring why voters vote based on such identity characteristics: as a means to the end of greater access to state resources (Eifert, Miguel, and Posner 2010; Michelitch 2015). The extensive body of literature on ethnicity in African politics need not be repeated here; the important lesson is that ethnicity becomes embedded in distributive politics as a way for voters to maximize their likelihood of receiving state benefits in an uncertain environment. A study of the 2008 Ghanaian presidential election provides evidence of this utilitarian calculus: Ghanaians will vote for non-coethnics when they live in a region dominated by that ethnic group, following the rationale that they will benefit from any nonexcludable community-level public goods provision (Ichino and Nathan 2013).

The broad conclusion that follows from this exposition is that when Africans go to the polls, they vote for the candidate that is most likely to deliver material resources to their community or to them personally. Often, ethnic heuristics guide this choice. While Africans also take past performance into account in determining whether to support the incumbent, personal calculations still (on average) play a large role.[6] Missing from this conclusion—and from many accounts of African voter behavior—is ideology or other nonmaterial motivations for political participation. However, there are a number of reasons to expect that African voters would face substantial challenges to voting based on ideological preference. Even if an African voter had a sophisticated and well-developed set of ideological preferences, political parties in many African countries operate in such a way as to make such preferences irrelevant in the political sphere. African democracies tend to exemplify two opposing trends: either high levels of party volatility and excessive competition or dominant party systems in which there is practically no competition.

Regarding excessive competition, the high level of party volatility in many new African democracies has detrimental effects on the quality of democracy (Kuenzi and Lambright 2005). Early analyses of African party systems highlighted such party volatility as creating a "formless" democratic arena, robbing parties of their primary function of representing cohesive sets of political ideas (Sartori 1976). When parties arise and go extinct with each election cycle, such instability lowers voter confidence in the democratic system altogether by generating additional uncertainty (Dalton and Wattenberg 2000). While this volatility is declining over time (Weghorst and Bernhard 2014), many African countries have fluid party systems in which parties lack programmatic platforms and instead appeal to voters on the basis of ethnicity or through "vague populist appeals" (van de Walle 2003).

While volatile systems may present voters with unstable choices, dominant party systems rely on patronage and rule manipulation to rob voters of choice. There are multiple ways in which Africa's electoral autocracies eliminate the possibility of opposition ascendancy, ensuring the overwhelming political dominance of a single party (e.g., Schedler 2002; Bogaards 2005; Albaugh 2011). Arriola (2013, 5) has pointed out that power becomes consolidated easily when the ruling party has access to state resources: "incumbents whose governments neither promote the public good nor respect citizen preferences are able to retain power, in part, because they do not confront . . . a viable alternative to the political status quo." The crux is that voters in a country with a "formless" party system or under a dominant party regime have few opportunities to express political ideology through elections. In many countries, when voters are dissatisfied with the status quo, voting against the incumbent simply means voting for the opposition rather than expressing a preference for a political party with a substantively different platform. Of course, the argument here is not that voters never vote or participate in politics based on ideology, identity, or other nonmaterial motivators, but that the political dynamics of African countries create a situation that is less likely to produce participation based on nonmaterial motivators and more likely to foster participation as a bid for access to resources. Indeed, the idea that voters in African democracies use local public service delivery as the primary basis for evaluating their elected officials finds support in other recent work as well.[7]

The Puzzle of Political Participation in African Democracies

This stylized account of African electoral politics highlights a fundamental problem for explaining political participation: access to state resources tends to be concentrated in elite-level patronage networks, but the promise of access to state resources—particularly through public goods provision—drives political participation. These dynamics occur within electoral contexts that present barriers to ideological or policy-driven participation, rendering elections a bid for material rewards regardless of the political sophistication of voters themselves. Bottom-up accounts of political behavior emphasize the pursuit of material benefits (sometimes on the basis of ethnic identity), but top-down accounts emphasize the concentration of state resources among the elite. Even if the dynamics of democratic politics put pressure on elites to engage in mass patronage in addition to elite-level patronage, the process of extending state resources is uneven and constrained by limited financial resources (van de Walle 2012, 119). The promise of such a reward is therefore a paltry motivator for political behavior: why would citizens mobilize, turn out, and maintain political engagement if political parties lack ideological platforms and if the material gains from electoral politics are, at best, a gamble?

The present study provides evidence that citizens' political behavior is shaped by their past experiences with government policies, particularly state service provision. These past experiences provide valuable information about the utility of participating in politics, by conveying information about state capacity and government responsiveness—the likelihood that the government has both the ability and the political will to respond to community demands. In electoral contexts marked by information asymmetry, citizens' experiences with service provision provide a tangible indicator of government investment in the community. As such, I argue that these experiences also shape citizens' degree of interest in the political realm, their adherence to the dictates of the state, and the degree to which they engage in other political behaviors, such as collective organizing.

Service provision is an essential indicator of government responsiveness in low-capacity states in particular. While access to basic services like electricity, running water, and public education is near universal in higher-capacity states, low-capacity states face challenges to service extension. Thus, both uneven extension of services and the particular experiences that individuals have with attempts at service extension are indicative of government interest in a community. Faced with government absence or abdication of its role as a service provider, communities may turn their political energies toward nonstate actors, exiting national politics altogether. In low-capacity states, extension of basic services is highly consequential: it builds not only the state but citizens as well. The following section of this chapter elaborates the theoretical underpinnings of this claim.

POLITICAL PARTICIPATION AND THE POLICY FEEDBACK APPROACH

While most approaches to political science emphasize how politics affect policy outcomes, this study's point of departure is Lowi's observation that public policies affect politics. Specifically, he notes that "the most significant political fact about government is that government coerces. Different ways of coercing provide a set of parameters, a context, within which politics takes place" (Lowi 1972, 299). This idea has been systematized further in the policy feedback literature in American politics, which posits that social policy can affect the political behavior of target populations by defining the boundaries of citizenship and educating citizens about their relationship to the state (Mettler and Soss 2004). Different types of social policy, which target specific groups within the polity, define parameters of appropriate political behavior for target groups (Schneider and Ingram 1993). When the state targets different types of policies at different groups of citizens, each group will have a different type of relationship with the state, translating to different forms of political participation (Soss 1999, 2007; Schram et al. 2009). For example, in the United States, the GI Bill, which targets veterans for services, increased political participation among that group (Mettler 2007). Similarly, seniors who rely on state benefits like Social Security and Medicaid are more likely to vote, even though their relative poverty would predict lower rates of participation (Campbell 2002). While the majority of work on policy feedback effects has occurred in the context of advanced industrial democracies, an emerging body of work examines these effects in non-Western contexts and in African politics specifically. Recent work demonstrates that Africans' experiences with public schools and health facilities increase political participation, presumably because interaction with the government through exposure to public services increased political engagement and a sense of accountability among service consumers (MacLean 2010; Bleck 2013).

Two primary pathways of policy feedback are of theoretical interest to this study: resource effects and interpretive effects. Social policies can influence both the amount of resources to which certain groups have access and that group's sense of political engagement (Campbell 2012). These pathways affect an individual's ability and desire to participate. The first pathway is material: distributive or redistributive policies that direct material goods toward certain groups may increase their capacity to participate in politics, by providing them with more time or financial resources (Pierson 1993, 598). Because income is known to be an important predictor of political participation, social policy that increases the income of a group may also increase the probability that members of the group participate in politics. Interpretive effects are psychological, altering attitudes: social policy can influence the extent to which a group feels included in the polity. At the most basic level, this proposition suggests that the targets of social policy should feel more "included" in the polity and therefore more politically engaged. However, the manner in which policy "includes" a group matters: social policy can differentiate target populations in such a way as to make them feel alienated rather than engaged (Schneider and Ingram 1993). Policy feedback research thus demonstrates that public policies can alter political participation through objective processes that influence the material goods to which citizens have access, as well as through subjective processes concerning the way citizens interpret their experiences with policies.

The majority of work in policy feedback occurs in liberally oriented and advanced industrial democracies in which the government has a pervasive presence in people's daily lives and in which the nuances of social policy have a potentially large effect on political mobilization. These studies tend to focus on the interpretive effects that emerge from universal versus meantested benefits, following the insight that "universal eligibility criteria may help incorporate beneficiaries as full members of society, bestowing dignity and respect on them. Conversely, means-tested programs may convey stigma and thus reinforce or expand beneficiaries' isolation" (Mettler and Stonecash 2008, 275). This distinction between different types of social policy on the basis of nuanced design features is ubiquitous in the policy feedback literature of advanced democracies but is less relevant for low-capacity states. The fundamental framework of this approach is analytically useful, but in a low-capacity state with a limited ability to provide basic services, the types of policies that "matter" for shaping political participation are different.

Low-capacity states struggle with the conferral of basic services but still frame the benefits of citizenship in terms of access to these services. Olivier de Sardan (2014, 400–401) has noted that Africans view public service provision as an "entitlement" of citizenship; even when the government has a limited capacity to provide these services, the public still considers the government to be ultimately responsible for this provision. Indeed, African publics continue to demand access to universal public services and express the sentiment that basic service delivery is the government's responsibility (M. Bratton 2007; MacLean 2010). The process of state-building in such low-capacity countries entails basic service extension to incorporate more citizens under the umbrella of state-run service provision (Bratton and Chang 2006). In low-capacity states, the distinction between "universal" and "means-tested" benefits may not be terribly salient, but access to services rhetorically deemed "universal" is both salient for individuals and indicative of political processes that may influence citizen engagement with the state itself.

Building States and Citizens

The policy feedback framework directs scholars' attention to the political implications of the public policies that are important for people's daily lives. In the context of low-capacity states, public service delivery is perhaps the most consequential form of public policy for the majority of citizens; access (or lack thereof) to water, electricity, schools, and health care has a dramatic capacity to shape individual lives. Service delivery is therefore a deeply important point of contact between citizens and governments in low-capacity states. In low-capacity democracies—where citizens have the opportunity to engage in meaningful political participation—access to state services may shape the experience of citizenship and therefore influence both patterns and rates of political behavior.

One might expect basic service delivery in low-capacity democracies, as in advanced industrial democracies, to influence subsequent political participation through both material and interpretive channels. First, the presence or absence of basic services has significant consequences for quality of life, influencing the time that citizens have to channel energies toward political pursuits, as well as magnifying the necessity of pursuing solutions to the lack of basic service provision. However, state service delivery provides important information in addition to its material consequences for daily life. At the most basic level, service delivery is a key indicator of state capacity. State presence through service delivery signals to voters the credibility of the promise that support of political parties will win them access to state resources. State presence is also an indicator of the degree to which the state is willing to expend resources on a community.

State presence is not simply a binary division between the presence of state services and the lack thereof. The quality and nature of the services that states extend send powerful messages to citizens about the government's likelihood of being responsive to their needs. Citizens may be tolerant of low-quality services if they believe that the government is doing the best it can under severe resource constraints, and this belief may improve citizens' sense of political efficacy and willingness to engage with political processes. Neglect, service retrenchment, or unfulfilled promises of service improvements may reduce the extent to which citizens believe in the utility of pursuing their interests through the state. Where there are reliable alternatives to the state, such as traditional authorities or nongovernmental organizations, negative experiences with service provision may trigger exit from the political system altogether.

The implication of this theoretical framework—and the argument this study develops—is that citizens' experiences with public service delivery in low-capacity states influence their political behavior. In the context of African politics, such experiences provide essential information about the possible utility of participating in politics. As such, one would expect that access to basic services and citizens' experiences with particularly salient services will shape their expectations of the government's capacity and will to be responsive to their needs.

COMPLEX CAUSALITY AND INFERENTIAL CHALLENGES IN POLICY FEEDBACK

While the policy feedback approach has become more prevalent and increasingly sophisticated in recent years, it suffers from significant inferential challenges. Because the framework generally assumes reciprocal causality between policies and political participation, it is challenging to convincingly establish causal direction. To gain causal leverage, many policy feedback studies have focused on one or a closed set of policies to determine, with greater theoretical precision, how certain design features of different types of policies may influence participation. However, a narrow focus on certain policies or specific design features does not match the theoretical scope of policy feedback, which suggests that individuals' experiences with policies broadly influence their participation. As such, policy feedback designs generally face a trade-off between causal precision and scope. This section of this chapter describes these two related problems in greater depth, introducing how my research design addresses this trade-off.

Almost by definition, policy feedback approaches face an endogeneity problem: assuming both that policies affect political participation and that political participation influences policy creation makes it difficult to establish the exogeneity of policy as a causal variable. Using the example of gender and political participation, feminist institutionalists have argued that states with more "gender-inclusive" policies foster more participation among women (Beckwith 2010). However, it is possible that the states that have more gender-inclusive policies may simply be states that were already predisposed to women's participation, due to some other underlying variable. While gender-inclusive policies coincide with a smaller gender-based gap in political participation, it is impossible to know from existing studies whether such policies caused higher women's participation or vice versa. For example, one study shows that the states that enact "maternalist" policies have a higher proportion of elected female representatives (McDonagh 2010). However, another study demonstrates that female representatives are also more likely to enact maternalist policies (K. Bratton 2005). Furthermore, we do not know why some states enacted maternalist policies while others did not—perhaps the states with maternalist policies already had a large number of politically active women. Because most models of policy feedback rest on assumptions of reciprocal causality—assuming that policies influence participation and that participation also influences which policies governments enact—it is unnecessary to assert that causality runs only one direction. However, it is essential to demonstrate the plausibility of policy having a causal effect on participation.

Another challenge the policy feedback approach presents is that of designing an instrument that can both capture the elements of public policy that theoretically influence political participation and also reflect the way people actually experience public policies—as varied, overlapping, sometimes contradictory, and more or less salient. While it is easier to estimate the causal effect of one or a few policies, such an approach invariably ignores the other policies that may also influence citizens' political participation. For example, a person might have a dramatically different experience with government services provided through a public housing authority and those provided through a food assistance program; focusing on the causal impact of only one agency would present an incomplete understanding of how that individual experienced public policy more broadly. Furthermore, different types of policies or services are salient for different people, so similar experiences may generate different political effects, as a function of policy salience.

In policy feedback designs, there is an inevitable trade-off between causal precision and the number and scope of policies that one can consider. For this study, I elected to design a survey instrument that would generate a broad and holistic measure of each individual's experiences with policies. This approach sacrifices causal specificity for a more accurate representation of respondents' policy experiences writ large. Using this approach required a way of comparing people's varied experiences across multiple policies. As such, I developed a typology of different policy experiences and used this typology to generate hypotheses about how certain types of experiences influence different categories of political participation.

However, as noted above, it is still essential to establish the plausibility that policies can affect political participation. Herein, I employ historical analysis to leverage certain features of the Zambian case to demonstrate that while public policy and political participation are correlated, it is unlikely that the correlation is solely the result of political participation influencing the way public officials choose to disperse resources. Furthermore, while the bulk of the empirical analysis in this study derives from a large-N survey, additional in-depth interviews provide mechanisms linking respondents' experiences with public policy and their subsequent political participation, providing more weight to a causal interpretation.

The following section of this chapter introduces a few key details of the Zambian case that influenced the logic of the research design employed in this study. The subsequent section elaborates the design, with an emphasis on how I dealt with the trade-offs between causal identification and a holistic account of how public service provision, writ large, influences various categories of political participation.

ZAMBIA AS A PARADIGMATIC CASE

This study treats Zambia as a paradigmatic case through which to explore the relationship between public service delivery and political participation in a developing democracy. Because Zambia has adhered to many of the political and economic trends in Africa since independence, it may be considered emblematic in many regards.[8] However, a few of its unique features make it particularly well suited to this research agenda.

Zambia (then Northern Rhodesia) was developed as a British enclave economy around profitable copper deposits in an area that became known as the Copperbelt. The colonial economy in Northern Rhodesia revolved around the urban mining industry and the rail line that transported copper, lead, zinc, and some other high-value raw materials to Southern Rhodesia and South Africa. While mining was an economic boon for the colony, it resulted in a pronounced pattern of uneven development, in which the urban areas linked to the rail line were generally well developed, whereas the rural areas were largely neglected. This pattern of urban investment and rural neglect would prove to be a persistent challenge for Zambian political and economic development alike.

In line with continental trends, Zambia won its independence, in 1964, in a largely peaceful political transition. As in many of its other colonies, the British had spent the past decade gradually increasing African political representation in the territory, yielding a nascent African political class that led the charge for independence. Independent Zambia, led by President Kenneth Kaunda and his United National Independence Party, initially had bright prospects: the lucrative copper industry had yielded a large amount of foreign exchange reserves, and Kaunda's (largely) peaceful democratic election augured well for the new republic (M. Bratton 1980, 31). Indeed, Kaunda's regime spent its early years embarking on an ambitious program of expanding basic service delivery to address the colonial legacy of uneven development that had privileged the urban industrial areas linked to the Copperbelt over the rural hinterlands (Bates 1976).

However, as chapter 2 describes in more detail, initial optimism around Zambia's political and economic future faded within the first decade of independence. Due partly to mismanagement and partly to terrible luck, Zambia was unable to diversify its economy away from dependence on copper before commodity price crashes and the oil shocks of the 1970s reverberated through African economies.[9] Several years after independence, President Kaunda began consolidating power by nationalizing lucrative industries, establishing a large network of parastatals, and ultimately, in 1972, declaring Zambia to be a one-party state. The collapse of global copper prices robbed the government of the funds to pay for such a massive state expansion, and by the 1980s, the economy crumbled under the weight of corruption, mismanagement, and depressed global commodity prices. As a result, the stark urban bias evident during the colonial period proved intractable.

Like many other African countries, Zambia had a troubled relationship with the International Monetary Fund over the course of the 1980s, committing to and then reneging on economic reforms (Rakner, van de Walle, and

Mulaisho 2001, 535). It finally achieved both economic and political liberalization in 1991, as it transitioned to multiparty democracy with the momentum of the democracy's third wave (Young 2012, 200–201; Huntington 1991). Zambia's political and economic systems have remained predominantly open since its dual transition, though its political and economic sectors continue to face problems shared by many of Africa's democracies, such as allegations of corruption, infringements on press freedom, political malfeasance, and clientelist political linkages (Resnick 2013, 201). The political realm remains ostensibly open, and citizens can voice their political preferences unimpeded by violence or intimidation, but substantive political choice remains limited. The political sphere is still dominated by a revolving door of candidates, and opposition parties have been unable to achieve any sort of coordination to counter the consolidation of power in the presidency.[10] Political parties still exhibit ethnoregional (rather than programmatic) logic, so the political system provides little opportunity for the expression of political ideology (Posner 2005; Larmer and Fraser 2007, 612; Resnick 2013, 153–56).

Chapter 2 presents a deeper exploration of the political and economic context in Zambia, but the sketch here underscores the features of Zambian development that make it a particularly good subject for this study. As has already been suggested, the political and economic history of Zambia shares key features with the histories of other African countries, making it paradigmatic in many ways (Posner and Simon 2002). It provides an excellent example of the trends that are important to this study. As in many other African democracies, the extension of state service delivery has remained problematic in Zambia, particularly in the rural areas that lie far from the developed areas known as the "line of rail." Furthermore, while Zambia's political realm is generally open and adheres to the minimum criteria for "democracy," the country's voters lack substantive choice. As a result, political participation tends to reflect ethnoregional logic and serves as a bid for access to state resources rather than an expression of ideological preference.[11] Finally, while voters may express ethnoregional preferences as a way to access state resources, the Zambian state has repeatedly demonstrated an inability (or at least an uneven ability) to deliver on those promises. Zambia thus reflects the previously mentioned trends in African polities.

At the same time, Zambia's unique political geography—a result of its colonial legacy—makes it particularly easy to identify areas that are more or less likely to experience consistent, high-quality service provision. As chapter 2 details, the dichotomy between areas on and off the rail line continues to be an excellent proxy for service provision more broadly, even accounting for partisanship and other political factors that tend to influence service delivery. This feature of Zambian political geography produces predictable variation in state capacity and service delivery across Zambia's ten provinces. Furthermore, the ethnoregional nature of political support creates predictable variation in partisan affiliation from region to region. These two features of Zambia's political geography make it possible to leverage variation in quality of service delivery while accounting for political variables that may also influence service provision. While I treat Zambia as a paradigmatic case, I am also sensitive to the ways in which it is unique. The conclusion to this book includes a multicountry generalizability probe to assess the extent to which the findings of this study are broadly applicable across African countries.

RESEARCH DESIGN

Commensurate with the two methodological concerns presented above, this study uses a two-part research design, to first establish the expectation of reciprocal causality between political participation and policy outcomes and then to systematically examine how experiences with public policy through service provision vary with different forms of political participation. The first component of the design, presented in chapter 2, employs archival data to establish that some variation in public resource distribution is exogenous to political participation. The second component of the design entails the implementation of an original survey constructed explicitly to capture respondents' experiences with service provision, to examine the relationship between such experiences and political behavior.

Historical Case Analysis and the Targeting of Public Goods

Because its conceptualization of policy experience aims to capture respondents' overarching experiences across a broad swath of policies, this study is unable to use specific features of policy design to plausibly identify the causal effect of any specific policy experience on political participation. However, the theory underlying this study relies on the reasonable expectation of reciprocal causality: that policy has an effect on participation, even while participation may influence policy outcomes. Reciprocal causality is a lower bar than causal identification; for the empirical evidence to be convincing, it is necessary only to demonstrate that the direction of causality is not exclusively from participation to policy. If political participation completely determined the distribution of public goods and services, it would be implausible to argue that the relationship between patterns of policy distribution and patterns of political participation are due at least partly to the influence of policy on participation. Such an expectation is particularly important in the context of a country like Zambia, which has a long history of patronage-based politics and allegations that governments use policy instruments to reward active supporters. It is necessary to establish that the government's distribution of resources through policy is not only a response to the political behavior of groups. In other words, it is necessary to identify an exogenous source of variation in service delivery.

To establish a reasonable expectation of reciprocal causality, I herein identify two other (related) plausible motivations for government agencies to allocate state resources in an uneven manner across the country: economic productivity and state capacity. In short, a primary motivation of government investment in programs such as service delivery is possible return on investment, which is related to the economic productivity of various regions within the country. Patterns of economic production likely influence the distribution of public resources, as one fundamental function of states is to extract revenue. Tilly's famous assertion "War makes the state, and the state makes war" hinges on the concept that the institutions of the state emerged as a way to efficiently raise and allocate revenue in a sustainable manner (Tilly 1992). Similarly, Levi's *Of Rule and Revenue* argues that the primary goal of rulers is to "maximize revenue to the state," though perhaps not as they would please (Levi 1988, 10). The primacy of extraction is prevalent in the Africanist literature as well. For example, Albaugh (2014) theorizes the centrality of revenue sources for African leaders' calculations regarding public spending, and Bates's ([1981] 2014) examination of African politics hinges definitively on economic extraction. Initial investments in economically productive areas create path dependency: investment begets growth and attracts additional investment, contributing to a persistent divide between areas of historically greater economic productivity, better infrastructure, and stronger state capacity, on the one hand, and areas that are economically undeveloped and physically remote, on the other. The resulting variation in economic productivity and state capacity may influence government service delivery in a way that is completely unrelated to political participation.

To establish the likelihood that the Zambian government allocates public resources for a combination of economic and political concerns (as opposed to political concerns alone), this study examines the creation and execution of public policy during Zambia's First Republic (1964–72).[12] Examining government documents and official publications, it assesses the government's rationale for its very explicit approach to public policy during that period, particularly through the First National Development Plan, the cornerstone of domestic policy during that time. These primary sources allow the reconstruction of the thought process behind policy creation, matching the rationale of government officials with the actual distribution of resources across different parts of the country. The historical data employed in this study enable a qualitative case analysis to evaluate the motivations underlying the pattern of resource distribution. Did the Zambian government distribute resources purely in response to existing patterns of political participation, to shore up political survival? Or was resource allocation due partly to other concerns, like economic production?

In chapter 2, I examine the spatial distribution of public goods across four different Zambian provinces with distinct economic characteristics: the Central, Southern, Luapula, and Northwestern Provinces. Because each region played a different role in the national vision of economic production, each had a dramatically different experience with public policy during the First Republic. These regions also held distinct patterns of political participation at the advent of the First Republic, allowing comparison of actual resource allocation to what one would expect if the government were allocating resources for purely political or economic reasons. Chapter 2 proceeds to explore the path-dependent economic and political development of each of these provinces into the contemporary period, establishing the expectation that service delivery will continue to vary in degree and quality across these field sites. In that chapter, I supplement the historical data with information from contemporary interviews with public officials regarding how they make their resource allocation decisions.

Quantitative Analysis of Contemporary Survey Data

This study addresses the relationship between service delivery and political behavior through an original survey of 1,500 Zambians across three provinces—Southern, Central, and Northwestern Provinces—selected based on historical variation in public policy experience, as explored in chapter 2. Establishing how respondents experience service delivery through an analysis of three services each respondent finds salient, the survey proceeds with a suite of questions regarding various dimensions of respondents' political participation. Using three measures to capture both objective and subjective dimensions of policy experience, the survey data allow analysis of the relationship between various types of policy experience and political participation, controlling for other factors known to affect participation. Using policy experience as an independent variable, this component of the study allows a more systematic evaluation of how experience with public policy corresponds with reported political participation.

Because this study seeks to understand the relative impact of material and interpretive feedback effects, the survey operationalizes "policy experience" in three ways to delineate the difference between the two types of effect. One measure is of the objective level of key public services to which respondents have access. The second measure is semisubjective, asking respondents to assess their experiences with *specific* policies that they identified as being personally important to them. The last measure is completely subjective, asking respondents to assess their *general* overall experience with government service provision. The intuition behind including all three measures in the analysis is that some forms of political behavior may be more closely related to material effects, others to interpretive effects. Chapter 3 details the logic of the policy experience typology, the operationalization of these variables, and the survey methodology.

PLAN OF THE BOOK

The overarching goal of this book is to demonstrate the importance of citizens' experiences with service delivery in shaping political participation. While this study explores the relationship between service delivery and political participation in Zambia specifically, the theoretical framework is designed to account for the relationship between services and participation in low-capacity democracies more broadly. This study uses the policy feedback framework to conceptualize this relationship, but scholars developed this framework in the very different context of advanced industrial democracies. The theoretical exposition this study undertakes involves adapting the policy feedback framework specifically to address features of low-capacity states that complicate the policy feedback narrative. The empirical work of the study is to use this adapted framework to explore the ways in which Zambians' experiences with service provision influence various forms of political behavior.

To this end, chapters 2 and 3 elaborate the case detail, theory, and methodology, while chapters 4 through 7 present and discuss the main findings.

Chapter 2 provides greater detail about the Zambian case, leveraging archival data to establish a reasonable expectation of reciprocal causality between public service provision and political participation. The chapter traces how the patterns of resource allocation persist over time in Zambia and how these spatial differences inform the contemporary site selection of the large-N survey. Chapter 3 conducts a more detailed analysis of the promise and limitations of the policy feedback framework and presents an adaptation of the framework for low-capacity democracies. As part of this adaptation, it proposes a typology of "policy experiences" and uses this typology to advance a series of hypotheses regarding the relationship between the different experiences and their likely relationship to different forms of political participation. After presenting the theory and hypotheses, chapter 3 proceeds to describe the survey design and methodology employed to test these hypotheses.

Chapters 4 through 7 present the empirical results of the survey. Each chapter focuses on a different category of political behavior, highlighting the unique relationships that policy experiences have with the different categories. Chapter 4 focuses on the relationship between service delivery and collective behavior, describing communities' reliance on collective organizing to provide services in the absence of state service delivery. It explores how collective behavior emerges to fill the gaps left by inadequate state service provision in the least-served areas and how the government uses partial service provision and advocacy of "self-help" projects to stimulate collective behavior elsewhere. Chapter 5 focuses on political engagement, demonstrating the importance of contact with state services for cultivating interest in the political realm. The evidence in this chapter suggests that any experience with state services is enough to spark political engagement, though (as chapter 6 explores) such political engagement does not automatically translate into increased political participation. Chapter 6 focuses on formal political participation, like voting and contacting officials. It provides evidence that only the most positive experiences with state services result in a higher degree of participation—though neglect can stimulate collective behavior and though all manner of experiences can trigger political interest. Chapter 7 examines some alternative and subversive political behaviors, exploring the extent to which experiences with state services drive citizens to rely on nonstate providers, evade attempts at state revenue collection, or engage in protest behavior.

Chapter 8, concluding this study, uses Afrobarometer data to examine how well the findings from Zambia generalize to other sub-Saharan countries, and it further explores the relative impact of material and nonmaterial motivators of political participation in African countries. In Zambia, as in other low-capacity African democracies, the government's ability to provide basic services is a consistent political preoccupation for citizens. However, the government's ability to expand basic services like education, health care, and infrastructure has political consequences in addition to affecting citizens' quality of life. The government's decisions about where to target resources, which services to extend or maintain, and how to allocate limited funding send powerful messages to citizens about how much the government cares about their communities. Their interpretations of their experiences with service provision influence the way they subsequently interact with the government. In Zambia, physical and political development are concurrent processes; as the government constructs infrastructure and extends services, it also constructs citizenship, shaping patterns of political participation across the country.

CHAPTER 2

The Zambian Context

Spatial Distribution of Public Services and Political Behavior

As chapter 1 described, the premise of policy feedback relies on reciprocal causality between policy and participation: public policies have an independent effect on patterns of political participation, even as existing patterns of participation dictate how governments allocate public resources. Because works on policy feedback focus on the way policies influence political behavior (rather than the reverse), inferences under this framework require the reasonable expectation that policies have an independent effect on participation. To justify using "policy experience" as an independent variable explaining political participation, it is necessary to establish that governments create public policy and allocate public resources in a way that is at least partially independent of existing patterns of participation. This chapter undertakes the task of understanding variation in resource allocation in Zambia, to determine whether it is plausible to claim that policy experience is at least partially exogenous to existing patterns of political behavior. To understand the logic driving resource allocation, this chapter examines the political and economic pressures on President Kaunda's government under the United National Independence Party (UNIP) during Zambia's First Republic, assessing the extent to which patterns of resource allocation match predictions based on political or economic exigencies.

During Zambia's First Republic, from 1964 to 1972, the political and economic pressures on the new government at times demanded contradictory policy responses. The country's pattern of economic development during the colonial period left the national economy perilously dependent on copper revenues, and unpredictable trade with regional neighbors due to raging independence struggles and civil wars rendered national self-sufficiency in food production essential. Economic development necessitated increasing investments along the already developed line of rail, which connected the mines of the Copperbelt to the capital of Lusaka and the southern export route. Industrialization occurred predominantly in towns along the line of rail, and commercial agriculture was limited almost exclusively to white farmers settled around it (Tordoff 1974, 3). Beyond the rail, the undeveloped hinterland hosted subsistence farming and dire poverty.[1] While long-term development plans emphasized the need to address uneven development, meeting immediate economic needs demanded the rapid returns on investment that were only available along the rail.

In addition to these economic concerns, President Kaunda and his ruling party faced challenges of political consolidation. While Kaunda had won a decisive UNIP victory over his African National Congress (ANC) opponent Harry Nkumbula, the ANC had won several seats in Parliament. ANC supporters loudly critiqued the new government, sometimes clashing violently with UNIP supporters. ANC supporters were concentrated primarily in Southern Province, within the line of rail, in the economically important industrial and commercial farming corridor. While the new government enjoyed support in the urban areas of Lusaka and the Copperbelt, its most ardent supporters could be found in the more remote hinterlands of Northern, Luapula, and Northwestern Provinces. The distribution of UNIP's supporters and opponents created tension between economic and political goals: economic pressures, including pressures from the (sometimes violent) opposition, demanded investment in the line-of-rail provinces, while political demands from core supporters insisted that the government direct the "fruits of independence" to the remote rural areas that had rallied behind UNIP during the independence movement.

President Kaunda's firm stance that Zambia should be a frontline state in the battle for majority rule across Southern Africa created additional constraints on resource allocation, by creating the political exigency to nationalize the economy and limiting the amount of regional trade in which the new country could feasibly engage. This chapter argues that the pattern of resource allocation during Zambia's First Republic was a response to economic exigency as much as—if not more than—political considerations. While government policy responded partly to political participation, the pattern of resource allocation during the First Republic suggests that economic necessity was an important motivator for policy design, allowing the reasonable conclusion that the government allocated public resources in ways that were at least partially independent of existing patterns of political participation.

This chapter delineates the competing hypotheses about the motivations behind national resource allocation, discusses the observable implications of each, and describes the structured case comparison this study employs to test them. Four provinces—Southern, Central, Luapula, and Northwestern, selected for political and economic variation—provide the data for case comparison. I examine resource allocation across these provinces during Zambia's First Republic, comparing observed allocation against what one would expect given the competing hypotheses. Using historical trends to establish what variation exists in the quality of service delivery, this chapter explains the purposive site selection for the contemporary survey and describes the political and economic trajectories since 1972 at each of the selected field sites. While limitations on the availability of archival documents after the mid-1970s makes it impossible to extend this comparative analysis to the contemporary period, interviews with officials in local planning and development offices confirm that similar economic and political motivations still drive resource allocation in contemporary Zambia.[2]

INDEPENDENCE, UNEVEN DEVELOPMENT, AND MOTIVATIONS FOR RESOURCE ALLOCATION, 1964–72

Northern Rhodesia gained its independence as Zambia in 1964, during an era of great optimism. While the independence struggle was emotionally and politically charged, Zambia was born with comparatively little bloodshed. Despite being comprised of 72 different tribal groups, Kenneth Kaunda and his UNIP managed to pull the country together under the nationalist slogan "One Zambia, One Nation." Kaunda ascended to the presidency with great popular support, international legal recognition, and a budget surplus. Though the economy was nearly entirely dependent on copper, rising commodity prices promised ongoing economic security and gave the new government flexibility to pursue an ambitious policy agenda for development and economic growth (M. Bratton 1980, 31). This agenda was embodied in the First National Development Plan (FNDP), the cornerstone of Zambian public policy during the First Republic.

To implement this development agenda, the government had to contend with a few key problems. Possibly the most pernicious issue was that of uneven development. Regarding Northern Rhodesia as an enclave economy, the colonial administration neglected the rural areas and treated the countryside as a labor reserve for the lucrative copper mines in the center of the colony (Bates 1974, 1976; Tordoff 1977; Beveridge and Oberschall 1979; Craig 1999). The underdeveloped rural areas posed both economic and political challenges. Achieving shared national development would require massive investments in the agricultural sector, particularly in remote regions, to help smallholder farmers cultivate beyond the subsistence level and bring their goods to market.[3] Many of UNIP's most ardent supporters during the independence struggle were from remote areas of Northern and Luapula Provinces and levied additional pressure on the government for urban-to-rural redistribution (Rasmussen 1974, 56–57; Tordoff 1974, 15). The pressures to redistribute national resources to rural areas are captured in the influential 1963 Seers Report, the result of a joint economic mission to Zambia by the Economic Commission for Africa and the Food and Agriculture Organization of the United Nations, immediately preceding the country's independence. The report cautioned, "To maintain national will, especially after the first flush of enthusiasm over Independence, is a task for political leadership, not economic advice. . . . It means that there must be visible returns to the development effort, if popular support is to be maintained."[4] This observation was particularly true in the remote regions that had been excluded from economic development during the colonial period.

The political pressure to direct government investment toward neglected rural areas existed in tension with the need to invest heavily in the most economically productive sectors of the economy, the urban centers of mining and secondary industry in the line of rail. Government officials noted that the existing dual structure of the economy—the developed, urban areas in the line of rail and the underdeveloped, rural hinterland—was ultimately unsustainable, and the FNDP emphasized the need to "redress urban/rural imbalances" (Republic of Zambia 1966, 2). Finance minister A. L. Wina noted that the impulse to concentrate national investment into the (already more economically productive) urban areas was shortsighted: "Unless we are careful we will continue this process of imbalance which we have inherited from previous governments. . . . This would be disastrous."[5] Nevertheless, given the need for economic growth to create capital to invest in rural areas, "it proved impossible to reconcile fully the concept of regional balance with that

of investment in the growth areas of the economy" (Tordoff 1974, 17–18). Ultimately, the Ministry of Finance and the national development planners had
to decide where they would yield between the economic pressures toward
concentrating investment in the line of rail and the political pressures toward
regional redistribution.

These tensions were compounded by the material constraints imposed
by Rhodesia's Unilateral Declaration of Independence (UDI) in 1965 and
the political pressures brought by increasing political factionalism over the
course of the First Republic. When Rhodesia's Ian Smith rejected Britain's call
for transition to majority rule in its remaining colonies and issued his UDI,
he created a rebel white-led regime that was hostile toward Zambia (Callaghy
1990, 289). Suddenly, Zambia's geographic position as a landlocked, resource
rich, labor-poor country became a much bigger problem: the colonial administration in Southern Africa had designed the infrastructure in its territories
to channel all things from Zambia out via the southern route, through Southern Rhodesia and South Africa (Beveridge and Oberschall 1979, 44–45). With
Southern Rhodesia claimed by a hostile white regime, Zambia was cut off
from its main supply route. In addition, the country's primary source of electricity was the hydropower plant on Lake Kariba, on the border of and shared
with Southern Rhodesia. Civil wars against the Portuguese in Mozambique
and Angola and chaos in the Republic of Congo (later Zaire) eliminated those
bordering states as possible export routes, leaving only Tanzania to the north
as a possibility for extending the country's export infrastructure (Bates and
Collier 1993, 395).

The full impact of the UDI became manifest by 1966: it caused the collapse of the tourist industry, dramatic materials shortages (particularly of oil
and construction materials), rising costs, and expensive and hurried attempts
to expand export routes to the north (Tordoff 1974, 21). These circumstances
created more intense competition for resources between geographic regions
and economic sectors, which contributed to factionalism both between and
within the parties. While Kaunda initially responded to such political threats
with "exhortation, diversionary tactics, generous patronage, and sectoral bal-
ancing," diminishing material resources and rising factional competition ultimately made such politicking ineffective, resulting in increasingly coercive
responses to political threats (Tordoff 1974, 31). The political crisis came to a
head by the end of 1971, when the declaration of the one-party state brought
an end to Zambia's initial experiment with multiparty democracy.

The end of the FNDP implementation period coincided with the advent of the Second Republic, which was characterized by political consolidation under UNIP's one-party state, ongoing nationalization of industry and the creation of a sprawling parastatal sector, and widespread corruption and economic mismanagement. However, while the Second Republic was characterized by economic and political centralization, the First Republic offers an opportunity to assess government policy-making during a period of relative political and economic openness. Given the tensions between economic and political motivations for public resource allocation during Zambia's First Republic and the candid explanations in official documents for the rationale behind the government's policy choices, resource allocation during the FNDP provides an opportunity to examine which motivations proved the most influential.

Political Motivations for Resource Allocation

Given the context described above, a number of political motivations may have influenced allocation of public resources. One likely scenario, expressed in hypothesis 1a, is that the UNIP government would target goods to reward their most ardent supporters.

H_{1a}: The Zambian government allocated public resources to reward political supporters.

This hypothesis reflects the logic of the "core supporter" model, in which political parties or government agents attract and sustain support by rewarding those who have demonstrated political loyalty (Weinstein 2011). Some critiques of the UNIP government allege that officials used state resources, such as access to credit for farm inputs, to unduly reward supporters (Gertzel 1984, 12). Indeed, material payoff was implied in the party's slogan, "It pays to belong to UNIP."[6] Such allegations of patronage politics continue to plague Zambian politics in the present: recent studies suggest that the government of the Movement for Multiparty Democracy, which held power from 1991 to 2011, directed resources toward the districts where it found the highest levels of support (Mason, Jayne, and van de Walle 2017).

It is also conceivable that the government might allocate resources to sway opposition voters (Banful 2010). The UNIP leaders' preoccupation with the creation of a single-party state from the early days of independence involved a strategy of opposition co-optation, as they considered threats to the party's dominance to be threats to the stability of the state (Gertzel 1984, 4). Thus, as

expressed in hypothesis 1b, a possible political motivation for resource allocation could be attempts to woo voters away from the opposition.

H_{1b}: The Zambian government allocated public resources to nonsupporters
to undermine political opponents.

While this charge is less frequently levied against Zambian politicians, there
is some evidence that the UNIP government preferred to co-opt potential
adversaries at the elite level, which may be indicative of a broader strategy of
co-optation (Larmer 2011). In regions where competition between UNIP and
the ANC was fierce, some observers alleged that the new government allocated more agricultural inputs toward ANC-supporting districts, presumably
to sway public opinion in their favor (Bates 1974; Johns 1979, 105).

A final possibility, expressed in hypothesis 1c, is that the Zambian government allocated resources to the most politically active areas to palliate those
who were already most likely to pursue their grievances in the political realm.

H_{1c}: The Zambian government allocated public resources to the most politically active areas.

Political analysis during the period under consideration in this study indicates that intraparty factionalism was just as large a threat to UNIP dominance as pressures from the opposition party, which suggests that the ruling
party was likely concerned with ensuring that any signs of political activity
were channeled safely into support for UNIP (Tordoff 1974, 15; Rasmussen
1974). This possible motivation for resource allocation is the most threatening to the concept of policy feedback, particularly because of the positive
relationship between access to material resources and likelihood of political
participation. Each of these three patterns of political allocation of resources
is plausible in the context of Zambia's First Republic and must therefore be
considered alongside the hypothesis regarding economic motivations for
resource allocation.

Economic Motivations for Resource Allocation

As noted above, UNIP faced an economic quandary during the First Republic. The country's short-term economic viability (especially after the UDI)
depended on rapid expansion of industry and national self-sufficiency in agricultural production. The most effective way to achieve these goals quickly

was through investment in already economically productive areas along the rail, where infrastructure was already in place to support economic growth. Therefore, a key hypothesis—hypothesis 1d, competing with the three hypotheses described above—is that the government ultimately prioritized short-term economic gains over the political impetus for long-term shared development.

H_{1d}: The Zambian government allocated public resources to the most economically productive areas, regardless of preexisting political support in those areas.

If this fourth hypothesis finds support, it is plausible that at least some element of public resource allocation is independent of existing patterns of political participation, meaning that such allocation can feasibly be used as an independent variable predicting rates of political participation. However, if any combination of the first three hypotheses appear more likely than the last hypothesis, it is not possible to claim that public resource allocation is partially independent of existing patterns of participation.

DETERMINING MOTIVATIONS FOR RESOURCE ALLOCATION

To adjudicate between the competing hypotheses described above, this chapter uses planning and reporting documents from the First and Second National Development Plans. By examining resource allocation across a diverse set of cases, it is possible to rule out the plausibility of some of the above hypotheses. However, examining outcomes provides little in the way of understanding process. Therefore, the second stage of the present analysis relies on government documents from the National Archives of Zambia and the United National Independence Party Archives, as well as newspaper articles from the *Times of Zambia*,[7] to illuminate the government's logic behind the policy design and implementation of Zambia's FNDP. These government documents—including internal memos, correspondence, and official reports—provide insight into the logic behind policy design and official decisions regarding how to target state resources.

Case Selection

Addressing the competing hypotheses requires case selection that allows for differentiation across all possible combinations: high levels of political activi-

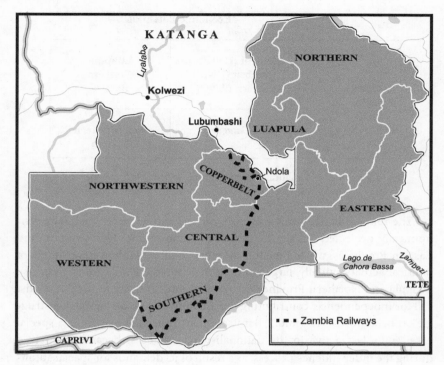

Fig. 1. Provincial Map of Zambia, ca. 1964

ty (both opposition and ruling party strongholds) versus areas with low levels of political activity, areas of high immediate economic potential versus those of low economic potential. During Zambia's First Republic, the country was divided into eight provinces (fig. 1).[8] Of these eight provinces, three fell in the line of rail and had a privileged economic position at the time of independence: Copperbelt Province, which housed the vast majority of mining operations; Central Province, which had the infrastructure connecting the mines of the Copperbelt to the capital and the southern export route and contained most of the country's secondary industry; and Southern Province, which held the southern border posts and boasted most of the country's large commercial (predominately white-run) farms. All these line-of-rail districts had high levels of political activity; Central and Copperbelt Provinces predominately held UNIP supporters, while Southern Province was an ANC stronghold. Indeed, while pockets of ANC support existed across the country, Southern Province was the only province that was dominated by ANC supporters.

		Economic Potential	
		High	Low
Level of Political Activity	High	Central (UNIP) Copperbelt (UNIP) Southern (ANC)	Luapula Northern Barotse
	Low	Null Category	Northwestern Eastern

Fig. 2. Economic and Political Activity in Zambian Provinces, ca. 1964

The remaining five provinces were off-rail and had been generally eco-nomically neglected during the period of colonial rule. Northwestern and Eastern Provinces, while generally supportive of UNIP, had lower levels of political activity initially, largely due to their remoteness (Tordoff 1974, 10). Luapula and Northern Provinces responded most actively to the nationalist call for independence, contributing great manpower to the nationalist strug-gle on behalf of UNIP (ibid.). Barotse (later Western) Province is a special case: while less active in the nationalist movement, it became politicized during the independence process, as a result of its demands for special auton-omous status (partly due to the precolonial centralized political structures in the region). While President Kaunda later reneged on the Barotse Agree-ment, the question of Barotseland's special status remains hotly politically contested. Figure 2 presents the distribution of these provinces by their eco-nomic potential and political activity.

The diversity of the eight provinces along the indicators of interest allows for case comparison to determine how various combinations of political activity and economic potential influenced resource allocation during the First Republic. I used a purposive strategy to select provinces for compari-son based on variation along the dimensions of theoretical interest identified above: political affiliation, levels of political activity, and economic potential (Gerring 2008, chap. 28). To include variation across all the available catego-ries, the analysis in this study continues with Central, Southern, Luapula, and Northwestern Provinces (bolded in fig. 2).

I ruled out Copperbelt Province because the influence of the foreign-owned mines and their service provision in the mining compounds compli-cates questions of national resource allocation. For the on-rail provinces, this leaves Central Province as an example of a politically active region (predominately) supporting UNIP, while Southern Province was a hotbed of ANC activity. For the off-rail, politically active provinces, I eliminated Barotseland because of its special relationship to the independent government, leaving Luapula and Northern Provinces, both of which demonstrated high levels of UNIP support at independence. I selected Luapula because a greater amount of information is available about that province during the period under study. In the category of low political activity off-rail, I selected Northwestern Province because its geographical proximity to Luapula Province, shared border with Congo, and similar climate make it more directly comparable.

Analytic Strategy

The first step in my analytic strategy is to determine where the government allocated resources during the First Republic. By leveraging the variation between these different provinces, it is possible to compare observed resource allocation against what each of the hypotheses would predict. Table 1 provides the allocation predictions for the competing hypotheses.

To determine whether resource allocation is "disproportionate," I examine the difference between planned and actual resource allocation. The FNDP was an exceedingly careful (albeit optimistic and ambitious) document, designed to take into account both short-term and long-term economic necessities of the country, as well as the need to counter the underdevelopment of rural areas (Tordoff and Molteno 1974). This document was not designed to allocate patronage; it was designed explicitly to counter the prevailing economic patterns of rural underdevelopment, and it was technocratic to the point that ANC leader Harry Nkumbula described it (derisively) as "purely academic and professional" (Tordoff and Molteno 1974, 275). Observers noted that the

Table 1. Competing Hypotheses and Predicted Provincial Resource Allocation

If the government allocates resources:	*Then one should observe disproportionate resource allocation in:*
To reward political supporters (H_{1a})	Central, Northwestern, and Luapula Provinces
To sway the opposition (H_{1b})	Southern Province
To politically active regions (H_{1c})	Central, Southern, and Luapula Provinces
To economically productive areas (H_{1d})	Central and Southern Provinces

FNDP policies were sound, alleging that economic problems emerged (and compounded) not due to the design of the policies but due to the government's inability to implement them (Tordoff 1974, 36). Therefore, I consider resource allocation to be "disproportionate" in the extent to which it deviates from the original plan, under the assumption that deviation implies political or economic pressures that would shift investment away from (what technocrats presumed was) optimal allocation.

The Second National Development Plan (SNDP), published in 1972, includes reports and assessments of public investment and resource allocation during the period of the FNDP. While the later document is candid about the shortcomings of the FNDP, it is possible that (for political reasons) the government overestimated its progress. However, the analysis below relies on comparison of relative expenditures in each province rather than absolute numbers. Therefore, if the government inflated its progress everywhere, it would not distort comparison of relative expenditures. The other possibility is that the government inflated the numbers for the worst-served regions, in which case this comparison would underestimate the differences between the provinces. I assume that if the numbers in the SNDP are distorted, they are most likely to diminish differences between the provinces in a way that biases this analysis against finding differences.

The use of these statistics allows me to identify little more than which provinces received more or less than they were promised. Therefore, the second step in my analytic strategy is to employ case analysis to understand the political and economic conditions in each of the four provinces and how these conditions influenced resource allocation. This analysis relies on government documents and official reports, corroborated with secondary historical accounts where possible.

RESOURCE ALLOCATION BY PROVINCE, 1964–72

As is evident in figure 3, resource allocation in general during the First National Development Plan prioritized investment in already economically productive regions. Both Southern and Central Provinces were targeted for relatively large per capita public investments. The more remote regions of Luapula and Northwestern Provinces had much smaller allocations.

Breaking down planned provincial expenditures by sector, the funding priorities become clearer. Despite the importance of national food self-

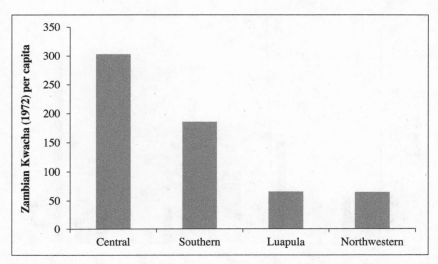

Fig. 3. Planned Per Capita FNDP Expenditure, by Province. (Data from the SNDP, Republic of Zambia, 1971.)

sufficiency, a small portion of the budget was allocated toward agriculture, though it was spread relatively evenly across the four provinces in question. Health expenditures, another small portion of the total budget, were also relatively evenly allocated. The sectoral statistics (fig. 4) demonstrate that the areas of highest priority are manufacturing, transport, and electricity/water generation. Central Province is favored in manufacturing and transport, while Southern Province had a comparatively large electricity/water allocation. The high level of "general services" reserved for Central Province again demonstrates its relatively favored position in planning, suggesting emphasis on the industrial activities that were concentrated in the line of rail in that province. The planned allocation of funds in the FNDP indicate that the government had an economic preference toward industrial development during the planning period, concentrated in Central Province and, to a lesser extent, Southern Province.

Over the course of the FNDP period (1966–72), the country's economic situation worsened, the problems of political disunity were exacerbated, and the deterioration of regional politics made it even more important for the country to have both a functioning economy and a disciplined political system. The divergence between planned and actual expenditures indicates which problems were more influential for resource allocation. Figure 5 dis-

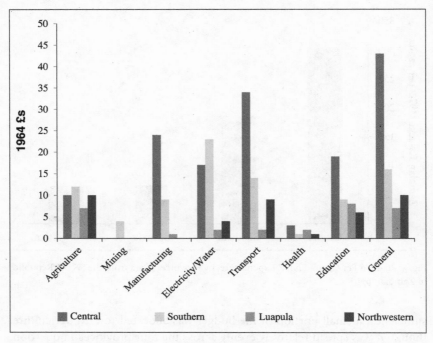

Fig. 4. Per Capita Planned Sectoral FNDP Expenditures, by Province. Currency is denoted in 1964 pounds. The Zambian government changed its currency to the kwacha in 1968, at which time it was pegged at 2:1 with the British pound. (Data from the SNDP, Republic of Zambia, 1971.)

plays the percent difference between planned and actual per capita expenditures in each province. Central Province received 57 percent more than it was promised, while Southern Province received nearly its exact allocation (just 3 percent less). Northwestern and Luapula Provinces did not fare well during the plan period: Northwestern received 31 percent less than it was promised, while Luapula received 41 percent less. The divergence between planned and actual expenditures is striking, though not terribly surprising. However, the patterns of expenditure call into question the plausibility of some of the competing hypotheses.

The most obvious hypothesis to dispense with is H_{1c}, the idea that the government would allocate resources according to higher levels of political activity. If this were true, one would expect Luapula Province, which had higher aggregate levels of political activity (and a large number of former freedom

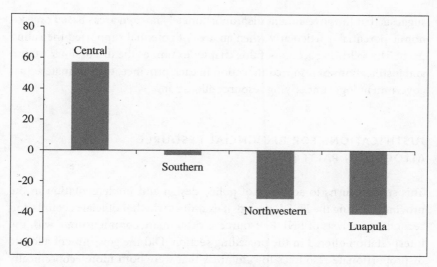

Fig. 5. Percent Difference in Planned versus Actual FNDP Expenditures, by Province. (Data from the SNDP, Republic of Zambia, 1971.)

fighters making claims on the government), to have received a greater allocation than Northwestern Province, which predominately supported UNIP but was relatively inactive. That Luapula fared worse than Northwestern in terms of overall allocation suggests that the government was not using rates of political activity to determine allocation in the provinces that were less economically productive. In addition, the pattern of resource allocation to Southern Province, an opposition stronghold, undermines H_{1b}, the notion that the government allocated resources to sway opposition voters. The amount of resources that the province received was almost exactly what it was promised and far less than Central Province (which generally supported UNIP).

This logic leaves H_{1a} (that the government disproportionately targets supporters) and H_{1d} (that the government targets areas of greater economic potential). The relatively high proportion of funds that Central Province received compared to Southern Province indicates the possibility that the UNIP government was targeting supporters over the opposition. The comparison between allocations to the on-rail versus the off-rail provinces demonstrates clearly that the government disproportionately favored economically productive areas, even though some of its most ardent supporters were in the remote hinterlands. Taken together, this pattern of allocation suggests that the government disproportionately favored areas based on economic potential, particularly when an area of potential supported the ruling party. The following section of this chapter examines the discussions around and justifications of resource allocation in each province, to illuminate actual government logic underlying resource allocation.

JUSTIFICATIONS FOR PROVINCIAL RESOURCE ALLOCATION PATTERNS

This section turns to accounts of policy design and implementation in the provinces during the FNDP period. It examines whether official accounts and secondary analysis of FNDP resource allocation are commensurate with the interpretation offered in the preceding section. Did the government allocate disproportionate resources toward areas that were both more economically productive and more actively supportive of UNIP?

Central Province

Since Central Province housed the country's capital, is situated in the line of rail, and hosted mining and industrial activities in its urban centers, it is no surprise that the FNDP directed a large amount of government investment there. In the planning document, Central Province was specifically singled out as one of the "areas of prosperity which will . . . contribute directly or indirectly to raising the prosperity of neighboring provinces" (Republic of Zambia 1966, 2). It was targeted for a large amount of agricultural inputs, "both because of its high potential and, more important, because it houses many of the central institutions required for the agricultural industry" (ibid., 135). These "central institutions" and that province's location along the rail also made it the obvious choice for the expansion of industrial activities such as iron and steel manufacturing, agricultural processing, and textile production (ibid.). Already essential to Zambia's economic development, the impact of the UDI increased the importance of Central Province's economic production. Facing shortages of building materials due to a limited ability to import anything, the extant copper industry became even more central to the province's—and the country's—economy. While the insecure borders made agricultural self-sufficiency important, this challenge also reduced the materials available for agricultural extension, such as petrol and spare parts for tractors.[9]

The material constraints brought on by the UDI can help explain why

Central Province ultimately received such a disproportionate amount of resources. One of the biggest challenges posed by resource constraints during the UDI was road construction; the government was much better able to serve areas that already had infrastructure, and additional infrastructure development was concentrated in areas where the highest returns on investment were expected (Tordoff and Molteno 1974, 277). Resource distribution within Central Province was a microcosm of this national problem. Larger towns there faced few problems gaining access to the financing and materials to complete their projects, as areas with existing roads won road extension projects, and these road extensions brought additional construction. The areas that struggled to receive access to promised funds were those that started with less road access.[10] While the rural areas in Central Province still received some goods and services through the FNDP, the amount received diminished with distance from the rail, reflecting the broader pattern in the country.[11] Although the rural areas of Central Province undoubtedly fared better than more remote provinces, most rural reports from Central Province reported insufficient access to resources.[12] Government-issue tractors were sent for harvests too early or too late and frequently broke down,[13] and farming loans issued by the Credit Organization of Zambia (COZ) were directed only to the places that already had "markets and roads."[14]

The preceding observations regarding subprovincial resource allocation suggest that the government's underlying motivations for resource distribution were economic. However, political motivations probably influenced the distribution of some goods, particularly in the agricultural sector. Multiple reports from the time allege that local civil servants distributed rural loans through the COZ as a form of patronage to reward UNIP supporters (Tordoff and Molteno 1974, 282; Johns 1979). In Mumbwa District, where ANC support remained strong throughout the First Republic and where political violence was a regular problem, the local government struggled to attract resources.[15] However, it is difficult to tell if the lack of resources in this area was due to opposition support or geographical remoteness. One civil servant in Mumbwa District lamented, "It is a plain fact that without good roads and a pontoon connecting these two areas with the line of the rail we cannot expect any development in these areas."[16]

In sum, it appears that both economic and political considerations contributed to Central Province's disproportionate share of resources during the First Republic. However, most reports suggest that political considerations were most pronounced in the provision of agricultural loans and other forms of agricultural support, which comprised a relatively small amount of the total budget (see fig. 4). Most of the investment in Central Province appears to be related to its economic advantages, its geographical advantage as a centrally located province with relatively extensive infrastructural development at the time of the FNDP (and the UDI), and its ready access to markets.

Southern Province

Like Central Province, Southern Province held an advantageous position at the beginning of the FNDP period because of its location in the line of rail. However, two key differences exist. First, while Central Province held a comparative advantage in the development of secondary industry, Southern Province's advantage fell predominately in commercial agriculture. It also had important hydroelectric potential, housing both the Zambian side of the Kariba Dam and potentially productive portions of the Zambezi River. These priorities are reflected in the two sectors in which Southern Province's allocation was larger than Central Province's: agriculture and electricity/water provision (see fig. 4). The second key difference is that Southern Province was an ANC stronghold throughout the First Republic and until opposition parties were banned in 1971, constituting a strong threat to UNIP's political dominance in the region (Tordoff 1979, 8; Gertzel 1984, 9).

The economic importance of Southern Province is evident from its prominent role in the FNDP. Because of a combination of fertile soil and access to markets through the line of rail, Southern Province was home to the few white farmers who decided to settle in Zambia at independence, creating large commercial farms on the most productive land. By the 1930s, most of the African population had been forcibly removed from the fertile crown land in the line of rail and resettled into overcrowded native reserves further away from any infrastructure (Vickery 1986, 204–8). After independence, development planning in Southern Province focused on resettling African farmers back onto more fertile land; setting up large state-run farming schemes; encouraging cooperatives, agricultural extension, and farm mechanization; and promoting the growth of food crops to preserve the province as "the granary of Zambia."[17] This ambitious plan included the resettlement of 5,000 families from the overpopulated African reserves to 250 "emergent commercial farms" on state land (Republic of Zambia 1966, 157).

This focus on resettlement of farmers in the rural areas was matched with a second set of development goals concerning Livingstone: developing it as a major tourist center and constructing dams at the third and fifth gorges near

Victoria Falls, to create additional hydroelectric schemes. Most of the industrial investments were for secondary manufacturing and agricultural processing, such as the creation of a fertilizer factory and a sugar mill at Mazabuka (Republic of Zambia 1966, 158). Furthermore, due to the country's growing need for electricity and irrigation, Southern Province's allocation included provisions for multiple schemes concerning hydroelectricity and water supply in the commercial agricultural areas along the rail (Ibid.).

Once it became clear that the Rhodesian UDI was not going to be resolved quickly, Southern Province became essential for both food and energy security. Because Zambia was a net importer of food at independence and because the country's overland trade routes were compromised by the UDI to the south and civil wars to the south, north, and west, Southern Province's potential to close the gap in food production gained grave national importance. In addition, Zambia drew its electricity from the Kariba Dam, which had been a joint project with Southern Rhodesia during the years when the two countries belonged to the short-lived Central African Federation. The electricity scheme was on the Rhodesian side of the border, and given frosty relations with Ian Smith's regime, Zambia's access to electricity suddenly became uncomfortably tenuous (Beveridge and Oberschall 1979, 43).

That Southern Province received almost exactly the resource allocation it had been promised suggests that its economic importance outweighed political considerations regarding ANC dominance in the area. While some civil servants complained that the ANC interfered with FNDP projects,[18] Southern Province's good record of project implementation suggests that these complaints were probably not serious (Tordoff and Molteno 1974, 280–81). Furthermore, while agricultural disbursements through the COZ are the most common target for those alleging clientelism and patronage, that Southern Province was the largest beneficiary of this program indicates that politics was unlikely to be the only consideration in the distribution of agricultural projects (Johns 1979, 105).

Government reports and internal memos from Southern Province regarding implementation of the FNDP tend to focus on administrative bottlenecks as the biggest challenge (aside from material shortages),[19] which is commensurate with Tordoff and Molteno's (1974) assessment of the primary obstacles to implementing the FNDP. The challenges to project implementation highlighted in government documents are generally apolitical, referencing the same challenges associated with the UDI and inefficient bureaucracy that were endemic at the time. Nothing in these documents suggests that the region suffered a bias in resource allocation as a result of the ANC. Internal party documents were preoccupied with the challenges of having to contend with the ANC.[20] However, these memos and circulars focused on the challenges of swaying voters away from the ANC and on the perennial problem of interparty violence rather than on threats to the implementation of government policy. The balance of the evidence suggests that Southern Province received a proportional allocation of resources because of its extant infrastructure (in the line of rail) and economic potential. That it did not receive a disproportionate amount like Central Province might be due partly to the nature of its economic potential (agricultural rather than industrial). Alternatively, its lack of UNIP supporters may explain why it received comparatively less than Central Province, though this is unlikely; as mentioned above, agricultural spending was the most common vehicle for patronage, and given the large amount of agricultural credit issued in Southern Province, it is unlikely that the difference between Southern and Central Provinces came from uneven amounts of patronage.

Northwestern and Luapula Provinces

Given their similar profiles and experiences throughout the course of the FNDP, it is useful to examine Northwestern and Luapula Provinces in concert. At independence, both provinces were remote and economically underdeveloped. In 1964, Northwestern Province had no paved roads, no commercial agriculture, and no notable industry. Having served for years as a labor reserve for the mines in Copperbelt and Central Provinces, Northwestern Province had such a low rate of subsistence agriculture that it was still importing staple foods. The economic development of Northwestern Province constituted a long-term economic goal rather than a short-term necessity; it was part of the broader goal to narrow the economic gap between the line of rail and the hinterland and to create a rural base for shared development. The first steps toward this long-term vision were to eliminate dependency on food imports, extend the national infrastructure to make the province more accessible, and increase access to education and health care. The FNDP stipulated, "First priority will be given to achieving self-sufficiency in maize and to encouraging the production of ground nuts. . . . Settlement schemes will be undertaken to aggregate sparse population under co-operative forms of settlement" (Republic of Zambia 1966, 207). Unlike Southern and Central Provinces, which were integral to UNIP's national plans, Northwestern's role in the FNDP was simply to gain self-sufficiency.

Luapula Province also served as a labor reserve for the mines of the Copperbelt. It was more densely populated than Northwestern Province, and its economy revolved around the local fishing industry in addition to migrant labor. Despite an earlier period of economic productivity, the region experienced a steep economic decline in the 1950s and was one of most economically disadvantaged provinces at the time of independence (Macola 2006, 47; Baylies 1984, 163). As in Northwestern Province, the government's goals for Luapula Province during the FNDP were modest and focused on reviving the fishing and forestry industries in the region (Baylies 1984, 179).

The primary difference between the two provinces at the time of the FNDP was their relative levels of political activity. Residents of Luapula Province had been particularly active during the independence movement, producing many freedom fighters and party activists (Rasmussen 1974, 56; Baylies 1984, 163–64). While Northwestern Province was generally supportive of UNIP, it was late to receive the nationalist message and generally demonstrated lower levels of political activity (Tordoff 1974, 9). Because the participants in the independence struggle—particularly the freedom fighters and rural cadres—exerted substantial pressure on the government to distribute patronage in the form of credit, access to government projects, and civil service jobs, one would expect UNIP to have directed more resources toward Luapula than toward Northwestern Province (Dresang and Young 1979, 73). However, those two provinces received approximately the same amount of consideration in FNDP planning, and Luapula Province received proportionately less.

Actual allocation of resources was disappointing for both Northwestern and Luapula Provinces. The economic projects in both provinces were of low national priority, and the constraints on resources caused by the UDI exacerbated the shortages in these relatively remote areas. In particular, the diversion of road-building materials to the more economically productive parts of the country made Northwestern almost entirely unable to build any all-weather roads, rendering most of the province completely inaccessible during the annual rainy season, from December to May. This state of affairs stymied all other development plans in the region. A civil servant's tour report at the end of the 1965 Transitional Development Plan in Mwinilunga illustrates the depth of the problem.

In Mwinilunga we have twelve projects under the Transitional Development Plan. Of these, unfortunately only three are under way, i.e. the Mwinilunga main hospital, the Mwinilunga secondary school, the Mwinilunga police station. These three will be completed on schedule, but it must also be noted that . . . there is some slackening, due to transport difficulties in the construction of certain education projects. . . . Government Policy is in serious jeopardy in this province.[21]

Similarly, Luapula Province was left with a large number of uncompleted projects (Baylies 1984, 179). Luapulans found this particularly insulting, as they presumed that their high levels of activity in the independence struggle would yield fruits through fast economic development and high levels of government investment after independence (Macola 2006). That these two remote provinces had such similar experiences despite such different levels of political activity suggests that government resource allocation was influenced more by economic viability than by extant political support.

Evidence from Zambia's First Republic indicates that resource allocation was likely influenced by a combination of economic and political motivations. Economically productive regions received the lion's share of public resource allocations in the FNDP planning document, but only Central Province—both economically productive and a UNIP stronghold—received a disproportionate amount of resources. Most important for the claim of reciprocal causality between policy and participation, the evidence undermines the claim that the government simply directed resources toward the most politically active areas. Such an observation would have been particularly devastating to the policy feedback argument. Due to limitations on document availability, it is not possible to extend this archival analysis to the contemporary period. However, the next section of this chapter proceeds to discuss political and economic path dependence in the Zambian case, as well as evidence from interviews with civil servants working in local development offices, which indicate that a similar logic continues to dictate the allocation of public resources in Zambia.

POLITICAL-ECONOMIC PATH DEPENDENCE AND CONTEMPORARY ZAMBIA

Zambia has changed in many ways since the 1970s, yet some important historical trends persist. While having returned to multiparty democracy, the political system still exhibits centralized consolidation of power in the presidency. Despite two decades of austerity in the style of the International Monetary

Fund (IMF) and explicit attempts to diversify the economy, Zambia's GDP still rises and falls with copper prices, and concerns about copper windfalls and the responsibilities of foreign countries (particularly China) still loom large in the public debate. While some improvements have been made in the way of infrastructure and electrification, the country is still divided into areas "on the rail" and "off the rail," the former with far better access to government services, the latter still remote and poorly served.

The increased political openness in Zambia provides an opportunity to examine political participation in the country during a period when individual participation perhaps feels more meaningful. At the same time, the continuities in regional economic and political development allow careful comparison between different parts of the country that continue to have very different experiences with service provision. In this section of this chapter, after tracing Zambia's political and economic trajectories since the First Republic, I briefly explore ongoing imbalances in resource allocation to the sites selected for the contemporary survey (explored further in chapter 3).

Zambian Political History

Zambia was constitutionally a multiparty democracy during the period of its First Republic (1964–72), but despite the legal context of political openness, President Kaunda and UNIP party leaders made no secret of their preference for a one-party state. After eight years of increasing political consolidation and rhetoric about the dangers of party competition, President Kaunda officially banned all other parties, realizing that preference. The country remained a "participatory democracy," but ballot choice was limited to UNIP candidates, and all political associational life was registered and incorporated into UNIP. Where opposition existed, it was concentrated within the trade unions, which together remained a strong interest group (even after mandatory affiliation to a central union body), due to the economy's heavy dependence on copper production (Rakner 2001, 513–14; Larmer 2006). The Zambia Congress of Trade Unions (ZCTU) accounted for about 70 percent of formally employed workers in 1991, lending the organization strong bargaining power vis-à-vis the government (Rakner 2001, 514). UNIP politics during this period was characterized by increasing levels of corruption, particularly regarding the management of the myriad nationalized industries. Union leadership became increasingly political over the course of the 1980s, and disagreements with UNIP's policies ultimately spawned the first viable opposition party in 20 years, the Movement for

Multiparty Democracy (MMD), led by ZCTU chairman-general Frederick Chiluba (Larmer 2006). Responding to widespread urban discontent with UNIP policies—particularly its on-again, off-again approach to structural adjustment—the MMD was initially a pressure group organized around the reinstatement of multiparty democracy (Larmer and Fraser 2007, 615). The movement culminated in a referendum that overwhelmingly demonstrated the desire for a multiparty system, and UNIP acquiesced with elections in 1991. The MMD won this contest with a decisive margin and ushered in a new era of multiparty democracy in Zambia.

While the 1991 transition occurred in an atmosphere of celebration, the fruits of the multiparty system were disappointing.[22] Larmer and Fraser note that there was "an almost total lack of substantive political choice" and that each party was "backed by different regional supporters" and offered "different styles of leadership, but with essentially similar policies" (Larmer and Fraser 2007, 620). In addition to the lack of programmatic policy options, the initial political openness marking the transition quickly disintegrated into a familiar landscape of corruption, electoral rigging, and centralization of power in the presidency (Burnell 2001, 240). MMD support diminished after the first few years, and the next elections, in 1996, are widely recognized to have been manipulated in the MMD's favor (Rakner 2001, 508; Rakner, van de Walle, and Mulaisho 2001, 659). Suspicions about the MMD's waning commitment to political liberalization were confirmed in 2001, when Chiluba attempted to secure an unconstitutional third presidential term. While a popular backlash halted Chiluba's bid, the lack of a viable alternative resulted in the MMD's Levy Mwanawasa ascending to the presidency (Resnick 2013, 67). Mwanawasa's tenure marked the beginning of a brief period of renewed faith in MMD leadership: he launched an anticorruption campaign, presided over the beginnings of an economic recovery, and was reelected in what were generally considered to be free and fair elections in 2006 (Resnick 2013, 68). Mwanawasa suffered a stroke and died in office in 2008, and his successor, Rupiah Banda, proved much less successful at coalescing support around the MMD.

In 2011, the MMD's 20-year period in office came to an end with the election of Michael Sata of the Patriotic Front (PF). Sata had campaigned since 2006 on a populist platform, characterized by appeals to the urban labor force, criticism of foreign (particularly Chinese) companies draining revenue from the country, and the need to increase the copper windfalls remaining in Zambia (Larmer and Fraser 2007, 627). His populist mobilization of the urban poor was successful largely because many urban Zambians blamed the MMD's policies of economic liberalization (discussed below) for increasing urban poverty (Rakner 2001, 213–14). While Sata's ability to mobilize the urban poor across ethnic lines is evidence that Zambian politics cannot be defined as a purely ethnic phenomenon, the support from his "ethnoregional heartland" in the Bemba-speaking areas of Copperbelt, Luapula, and Northern Provinces highlights the ongoing importance of ethnoregional electoral dynamics (Cheeseman and Hinfelaar 2009, 53). The elections from the mid-2000s to the present have a strong regional flavor and a distinct urban/rural divide: the urban poor have been mobilized along populist lines, contributing increasing levels of support to the PF over the elections in 2006 and 2008, until Sata's victory in 2011 (Resnick 2013, 146). Meanwhile, the MMD maintained rural support partly by reintroducing rural subsidies and partly by (allegedly) buying votes in rural areas (ibid., 213–14).

While the transition of power from the MMD to the PF in 2011 was peaceful, marking the first alternation of political parties since the reinstatement of multiparty democracy 20 years earlier and thereby qualifying Zambia as a "consolidated" democracy (Rakner 2001, 200), Sata's tenure became plagued by allegations of corruption, attempts to stifle the press and civil society organizations, tampering with the judiciary, and increasing centralization of power in the presidency.[23] Sata died in office in October 2014, leaving no clear successor.[24] By-elections took place in early 2015, and the PF's Edgar Lungu (minister of defense under Sata) won a narrow victory against opposition candidate Hakainde Hichilema in a hotly contested election.[25] This standoff was repeated during the regular tripartite elections in August 2016, in which Lungu narrowly eked out a contested victory over Hichilema. While international observers indicated that the election appeared to be free and fair, Hichilema's United Party for National Development (UPND) alleged that the Electoral Commission of Zambia was biased toward the PF.[26] The UPND pursued the matter in Zambia's High Court, but the case was dismissed.

Generally speaking, while Zambia has undergone a process of political liberalization over the past 25 years, significant problems remain in its democratic system. While elections are, for the most part, free and fair, the incumbent parties have a troubling tendency toward corruption, silencing of opposition voices, and centralization of power (Rakner 2001, 201). Nevertheless, as Larmer and Fraser (2007, 613–14) describe, while Zambia's democracy remains "partial, 'disciplined,' and intolerant of dissent," the country's "democratic culture—in the form of public expression of popular social attitudes towards political, economic and social change—is, at least in urban areas, healthily undisciplined." Indeed, despite problems with elite expression of political opposition, the general public is willing and able to voice political opinions, misgivings, and disappointments. Unfortunately, as the optimism surrounding Sata's initial election transformed into disappointment, more Zambians are questioning whether the alternation of political parties will produce better social or economic outcomes.

Zambian Economic History

Like Zambia's political system, its economic system has undergone substantial liberalization since 1972, though its underlying structure has remained the same since independence. Starting with the Mulungushi Accords in 1968, President Kaunda began to nationalize major sectors of the economy, beginning with the mines. Over the next several years, this nationalization project continued in conjunction with the establishment of parastatal industries across most sectors of the economy. In the late 1960s, the expansion of state-owned enterprise largely comprised the takeover of expatriate or foreign-owned businesses, including manufacturing, brewing, transport, and retail (Craig 1999, 26). By 1970, 61.2 percent of industrial output took place through government-run programs (Baylies and Szeftel 1982, 191). Initially, in the boom years of the late 1960s, the state-owned enterprise performed well compared to the (often foreign) privately owned companies with no commitment to developing the domestic economy of the new country (Craig 1999, 34). However, by the mid-1970s, declining copper prices, global recession, and increased corruption in state-owned enterprise (under the auspices of the one-party state) contributed to major economic decline.

For the first ten years of nationhood, Zambia's economy, fueled by high global copper prices, expanded steadily, and the UNIP government invested heavily in social programs and infrastructure. This boom period ended in 1974, with a global crash of copper prices, a sudden increase in oil prices, and declining performance among state-owned industries. By some estimates, per capita growth between 1975 and 1990 decreased by 30 percent (Rakner, van de Walle, and Mulaisho 2001, 521–22). While the government engaged in some austerity agreements with the IMF during the late 1970s and 1980s, it failed to commit fully to these reforms, and the reforms failed to address underlying problems in Zambia's economy, specifically the wasteful public sector, inefficient agricultural production, and ongoing dependence on copper as the mainstay of the economy (Rakner 2001, 516–17). Parastatal industries became a mechanism for distributing patronage, and government revenues declined precipitously (Baylies and Szeftel 1982, 191). While President Kaunda made several attempts to implement structural adjustment reforms recommended by the IMF, these reforms caused severe economic hardship in urban areas, and the subsequent "bread riots" convinced Kaunda to abandon the reforms (Rakner, van de Walle, and Mulaisho 2001, 535).

The MMD's ascendance to power in 1991 marked a dramatic change in economic policy. President Chiluba managed to attract large amounts of debt relief and foreign aid to assist in stabilizing the economy, by promising widespread economic liberalization (Rakner 2001, 518). His approach included the privatization of 250 parastatals, cuts to tariffs, withdrawal of food and agricultural subsidies, and removal of exchange controls (Larmer and Fraser 2007, 616). However, despite rhetorical commitment to structural adjustment, partial implementation of adjustment policies and political manipulation of major financial institutions contributed to further contraction of the already weak economy. As Larmer and Fraser (2007, 616) explain, these reforms led to "the collapse of manufacturing, a significant contraction of the economy, soaring unemployment, and a severe pension crisis. Once privatized, companies established to provide essential goods in a closed economy were typically unable to compete against multinational corporations. . . . Formal sector employment fell by 24 percent between 1992 and 2004." Ending currency controls caused rapid inflation, while austerity reduced funds available for public spending, resulting in an increase in unemployment and poverty across the country, particularly in urban areas (Resnick 2013, 63). At the same time as the MMD government was aggressively pursuing privatization, it became apparent that the agricultural sector—the majority of which was made up of smallholder farmers—could not survive without state intervention, so the government reintroduced agricultural credit, followed by subsidized agricultural inputs (Mason, Jayne, and Mofya-Mukuka 2013). Even though the MMD found its initial support in urban unions, many perceived its policy over the course of the 1990s and 2000s as biased toward the rural areas, leaving the urban poor to contend with the consequences of economic liberalization while continuing to support the rural population through government subsidies and patronage (Rakner 2001, 202).

The Zambian economy has made a modest recovery since the mid-2000s. During his tenure, Mwanawasa created a friendlier investment climate, resulting in reduced inflation and positive economic growth (Resnick 2013, 68). However, the recovery has largely been driven by the increase in global copper prices, making the copper industry profitable for the first time since the 1970s (Larmer and Fraser 2007, 618). This economic expansion has dramatically slowed with the decline of copper prices since 2013, resulting in a dramatic weakening of the Zambian kwacha relative to the US dollar. Zambia still relies excessively on copper revenues; agricultural output and tourism have grown only modestly in recent years, and domestic industry and manufacturing still account for only a small portion of national GDP. As of 2011, metals comprised nearly 80 percent of Zambia's exports, and nearly all its exports are raw or intermediate goods; only 8 percent of total exports can be categorized as "consumer" or "capital" products.[27] Concerns still exist about the influence of foreign-owned enterprises, particularly the role of Chinese companies importing their own labor and remitting profits from the domestic economy.[28] Despite Sata's populist campaign rhetoric, the PF's economic policy has still erred on the side of attracting foreign investment, though recent discussions about increasing the windfall tax for foreign mining companies suggests ongoing ambivalence about the extent of economic liberalism and the role of the state in developing the industrial economy.

In sum, while Zambia has undergone ostensible economic and political liberalization since the 1970s, it maintains striking continuity in both political and economic trends. Politically, while Zambia has a multiparty democracy with reasonably free elections, ongoing concerns about centralization of power in the presidency and the difficulty of elite expression of opposition mar the political landscape. Nevertheless, public expression of political attitudes remains robust. Economically, partial adjustment has not addressed the underlying structural problems in the Zambian economy. While the mining sector has performed well in the past decade, buoying the national economy, it is hypersensitive to volatile global copper prices. Economic development remains concentrated in mining areas and in the capital, and despite ongoing government transfers to the agricultural sector, rural poverty has remained unchanged, hovering at about 80 percent (Burke, Jayne, and Sitko 2012). Zambia's political economy thus continues to yield very different circumstances across different regions and economic sectors.

Public Resource Allocation in Contemporary Zambia

Considering the continuity in Zambia's political economy, one would expect motivations for resource allocation during the First Republic to remain relevant in the contemporary period. As mentioned above, limitations on the availability of archival documents preclude extending the document-based analysis to the present. The historical data indicate that the government distributed resources in response to economic imperatives but disproportionately favored areas of core support. Interviews with local government officials and some secondary research suggest that the patterns described above persist.

Decisions about resource allocation occur at two points: the national government and the local government. While the national ministries of education, transportation, agriculture, and other areas make decisions about how to allocate resources across different provinces, additional funds are reserved through the Constituency Development Fund (CDF) and allocated through local government offices. The general sense among the population is that national resources are concentrated in areas that support the ruling party. One outgoing ward councilor noted that the government appears to favor Lusaka and the Copperbelt and invests in urban areas over rural ones.[29] While observational and anecdotal, this assessment of national service provision finds support in some analyses of distribution of subsidized seeds and fertilizer to farmers during the previous MMD administration. One study indicated that famers living in areas that supported the MMD received, on average, greater amounts of agricultural inputs (Mason, Jayne, and van de Walle 2017). However, this resource distribution was also influenced by proximity to urban areas and paved roads and by the amount of acreage a farmer owned, so access and economic productivity played a role in decision-making. Because the PF draws its greatest support from economically productive urban areas, it is difficult to distinguish between economic and political motivations for resource allocation at the national level. Subprovincial variation in resource allocation can illuminate some of these broader patterns.

Interviews with local government officials responsible for implementing projects funded by the CDF provide additional support for the idea that resource allocation is a function of both economic and political exigency. Nearly all interview subjects highlighted the importance of extant economic productivity in areas targeted for projects. One official stated that the two most important criteria her office used to allocate projects were a project's visibility to voters and its revenue-generating potential.[30] Both these factors result in rural areas being neglected in favor of urban areas, where council projects are both more visible and more likely to draw in money. Another civil servant reported deciding how to allocate scarce resources by prioritizing "critical points," including markets, town centers, and areas tourists might frequent. He gave the example that the local government prioritizes solid waste removal in areas where trash buildup would stall businesses or be visible to tourists.[31] Another civil servant simply said that the planning officers "do not see beyond the central business district" when it comes to allocating funds, presumably because of the potential for tax revenue.[32]

While all the interviewed local government officials agreed that economic potential was an important factor in allocating local funds, they disagreed about the impact of political pressures. One insisted that the council makes its decisions in a strictly technocratic manner, based on needs assessments and cost-benefit analyses.[33] Some officials who noted that they faced intense political pressure disagreed on the source. One, noting that whatever local representative is "most provocative" will get the most projects funded specified that members of the ruling party are those that "push the hardest." That civil servant elaborated that representatives from opposition parties receive fewer projects, because the council does not want to be seen as "supporting the opposition."[34] Another planning official reported that PF councilors want favors as part of the ruling party and make such statements as "I know so-and-so" and "If you do not do this, you will not be sitting in this chair tomorrow."[35] One planning official who confirmed that the councilors can put pressure on planners by threatening to recommend their demotions stated that the most powerful party was not necessarily the national ruling party but, rather, the one with the majority on the local council. In his case, that was the UPND, the primary opposition party, not the PF.[36]

These accounts lend support to the idea that the government continues to allocate resources on the basis of a combination of economic and political considerations. Those political considerations seem to be a function of constituency party affiliation rather than overall rate of constituency participation. Consistent with the idea that resource allocation is at least partially independent from existing rates of political participation in different areas, these accounts do not rule out the policy feedback approach. In addition, the contemporary and historical data provide clear expectations of expected variation in service provision, allowing purposive site selection for the large-N survey.

CONTEMPORARY PROVINCIAL VARIATION

The historical exploration in this chapter provides a logic for site selection for the contemporary survey, explored further in chapter 3. Given the political and economic developments and consistencies in Zambia since the early 1970s, I selected field sites for variation across key dimensions that one would expect to influence respondents' experiences with service provision. My first consideration was to include regions with varying levels of service provision, to ensure variation across material feedback effects. Based on the above analysis, the key division was between on-rail and off-rail regions: all off-rail provinces received similarly low levels of material support, regardless of their political circumstances, while on-rail provinces received relatively more, particularly in the case of Central Province, which was both on-rail and a stronghold of the ruling party. The field sites for the survey reflect three different anticipated levels of service provision: Central Province, as an on-rail province that supported the ruling party during the 2011 elections, should have the highest levels of service provision; Southern Province, as an on-rail province and opposition stronghold, should have a moderate level of service provision; and Northwestern Province, as an off-rail province, should have the lowest levels of service provision.[37]

Preliminary examination of some services supports the expectation that variation in provision persists in the contemporary period, though not precisely as predicted. Figure 6 illustrates public service provision as reported by various Zambian government ministries, standardized by the number of agricultural households (for 2006 agriculture expenditures), territorial area (for road works), and population (education and health).[38] The same pattern obtains for all spending indicators (aside from health): Southern Province receives the lion's share of all resources (standardized by population and size), followed by Central Province, which is trailed by Northwestern Province. Health is the only category that breaks the pattern, due to Southern Province's low expenditure in this area. The Provincial Development Index (PDI) is constructed by the Zambian government based on measures of life expectancy, education, and average household income. According to the Sixth National Development Plan, "Southern and Central were just above the average index at 0.43 and 0.41, respectively," while Northwestern scored below average, at 0.35 (Republic of Zambia 2011, 185–86).

These data indicate that compared to what was initially anticipated, Central Province has received less, and Southern Province has received more. As chapter 3 explores in more detail, this shift may be explained by Central Province's reversal of economic fortune over the past two decades. The continuing positive performance of Southern Province, the ongoing resource distribution to Central Province despite its relative decline, and the lack of resources

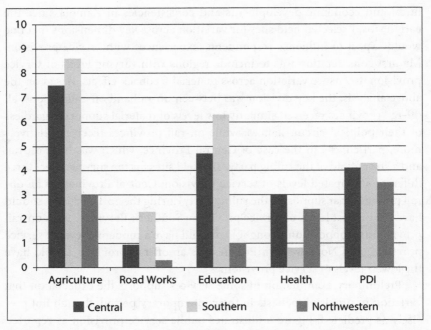

Fig. 6. Comparative Service Delivery by Province, 2006–9. Agricultural spending measured in 100,000 (2006) kwacha per agricultural household. Roads in number of kilometers "rehabilitated or graded" in 2009 (from NDP-6) per square km (×1,000). Education in number of basic schools and teacher houses built from 2006–9 (NDP-6), by 2010 population (×100,000). Health in number of rural health centers and health posts built 2006–9 (NDP-6), by 2010 population (×100,000). PDI is the Provincial Development Index, an index of life expectancy, household income, and education, multiplied by 10. (Data from the Sixth National Development Plan, Republic of Zambia, 2011; agricultural data from Govereh et al. 2009, 34.)

directed toward Northwestern Province indicate the ongoing importance of the line of rail in dictating national resource distribution. As noted above, the development of the line of rail had an enormous impact on patterns of industrialization, economic development, and government presence from the colonial period through Zambia's economic development as an independent nation. However, the relatively large amount of resources allocated toward Southern Province differs from initial expectations: as an opposition stronghold, one would expect Southern Province to receive less in the way of government spending, especially considering the received wisdom that the government targets resources toward supporters. At least as far as planning is concerned, it appears that economic concerns trump political ones for resource allocation.

This variation in the expected quality of service delivery informs purposive selection of field sites for this study. Chapter 3 describes this selection and methodology in greater detail and elaborates the framework of policy feedback, detailing how I adapt it to make it more applicable to low-capacity states like Zambia. As described in chapter 1, this adaptation involves the development of a typology of policy experiences, allowing the systematic categorization of respondents' experiences with the variation in service delivery elaborated above.

CHAPTER 3

How Policy Shapes Participation
A Theoretical Framework

The claim that citizens' experiences with public policy influence their political participation is intuitive on the surface but theoretically complex and empirically challenging to demonstrate. The theoretical challenge emerges from determining precisely how a policy might influence political participation, particularly since different policies are salient for different people and since the same policy may affect two people in radically different ways. Furthermore, because policy feedback assumes a degree of reciprocal causality between policies and participation, causal identification is a perpetual difficulty. To overcome these challenges, many policy feedback works focus on a specific policy or set of policies and make narrower inferences. This approach has yielded an increasingly sophisticated body of work, but the overwhelming majority have used data from liberal advanced industrial democracies with capacious welfare programs. While these studies have advanced scholarly understanding of policy feedback in high-capacity democracies like the United States and Great Britain, their findings are less relevant for low-capacity democracies.

In this chapter, I discuss the current limitations of the policy feedback framework for low-capacity democracies. Considering these challenges, I propose an adaptation of this framework to improve its relevance for low-capacity democracies like Zambia. While the fundamental insights of policy feedback are still useful, I argue that one must tailor the application of the theory to account for different features in a low-capacity context. To this end, I propose a typology for understanding the way that people in low-capacity states experience service provision. I use this typology to generate a set of hypotheses regarding the relationship between different policy experiences and various categories of political participation. This chapter subsequently proceeds to describe the survey design and methodology I employed to test these hypotheses, along with the use of qualitative interview-based data to allow better understanding of the processes at play.

CHALLENGES AND LIMITATIONS OF THE POLICY FEEDBACK FRAMEWORK

Through material and interpretive pathways, social policy can affect political participation in both the amount and the type of resources it directs at certain groups. These resources may affect the ability of different groups in the population to attain education, workforce experience, and income (all important material predictors of participation), and they may also influence relative levels of political engagement. The number of scholars using policy feedback approaches has expanded in recent years, and policy feedback studies have grown increasingly sophisticated, yet two related problems persist. First, because of the nature of policy feedback as a theoretical framework, it is challenging to establish causal direction. To address this issue, many policy feedback studies have focused on one policy or a closed set of policies, to determine with greater theoretical precision how certain design features of different types of policies may influence participation. The second problem is a consequence of this precision, which has resulted in the creation of a series of studies that are oriented around design features of policies in advanced industrial democracies and are less relevant for low-capacity democracies. Chapter 2 addressed the issue of complex causality. In the present chapter, I focus on the second challenge.

Approaches to Inferential Challenges in Policy Feedback

In existing literature, there are two broad strategies to addressing the problem of causal inference in policy feedback: focusing on the effects of one specific policy or identifying certain design features of a group of policies that may generate the political effect of interest. The first approach characterized earlier scholarly work on policy feedback. Using case-specific knowledge, researchers have been able to convincingly isolate the effects of a single policy on recipients. For example, Bruch, Ferree, and Soss (2010) examined the different rates of political participation for recipients of Temporary Assistance to Needy Families (TANF), a welfare program in the United States. Although

TANF is a national program, it is implemented by states, and each state has latitude in establishing the specific rules of implementation, which vary in the degree to which they are punitive. By conducting a state comparison of TANF recipients, who are similar across other observable characteristics, the researchers convincingly demonstrated that different ways of implementing the program create distinct effects on political participation: state bureaucratic agencies that are more punitive diminish the level of political participation for TANF recipients as compared to states that are less punitive.

Methodological approaches like the one described above provide compelling evidence of the precise causal effect of specific program experiences. However, research designs that single out the effects of one policy are unable to capture the way that people actually experience government policy. People experience multiple government policies, some more salient than others. They may have similar experiences with each policy they encounter, or they may have dramatically different experiences with different bureaucratic agencies, different sectors, or different levels of government. The experiences (with one or a few policies) that studies with a narrow policy focus test do not match the scale of the theoretical underpinnings of policy feedback—that experiences with public policy condition citizens' relationships to their state, influencing their level of political participation. Some works have attempted to overcome this problem: Mettler (2011) surveyed Americans about their experiences with a broad array of American policies; Bruch, Ferree, and Soss (2010) included several policies with which the poor are likely to have experience; and other macrolevel studies have sought to characterize the overall nature of government policy (Holzner 2010).

To make convincing theoretical claims about how broader constellations of government policies influence political participation, other scholars have sought to identify which design features of various policies are responsible for producing particular political effects. As most of this literature emerged in the United States and other advanced industrial democracies, many of these studies focus on different forms of welfare provision, interrogating the difference between means-tested and universal benefits. By shifting focus from one particular policy to a design feature that might help categorize a whole slate of social policies, researchers were able to compare the political effects of similar programs based on eligibility criteria, following the insight that "universal eligibility criteria may help incorporate beneficiaries as full members of society, bestowing dignity and respect on them. Conversely, means-tested programs may convey stigma and thus reinforce or expand beneficiaries' isolation" (Mettler and Stonecash 2008, 275). Following this premise, a large body of work has convincingly demonstrated the distinction between, on the one hand, universal or contributory programs that can increase political engagement and participation and, on the other, means-tested programs that depress participation (particularly when they have paternalistic or punitive design features).[1] The challenge with this work is that while such a distinction is relevant and theoretically important for social policy in advanced industrial democracies, it has little resonance in low-capacity democracies. In poor countries where governments face barriers to even basic service provision, the distinction between means-tested and universal benefits hardly captures the most salient features of public policy in people's lived experiences.

Policy Feedback in Low-Capacity Democracies

The few studies that apply the policy feedback framework to developing democracies provide evidence that policies do, in fact, "feed back" in countries with a generally low capacity to provide basic services. However, these studies also indicate that the current framework for policy feedback must be tailored to analyze policy configurations in a context of "limited statehood" (Krasner and Risse 2014). While studies in advanced industrial democracies differentiate between various policies based on nuanced design features, studies in low-capacity states tend to focus on the distinction between those who do and do not receive basic state services. For example, both MacLean (2010) and Bleck (2013) found that those who had direct experiences with public schools and health clinics in African countries had a higher likelihood of political participation. Even though these services are generally low in quality, contact with the state through basic provision was enough to stimulate greater political participation. Another study in Brazil, a state that has a much greater capacity for service delivery than the countries included in MacLean's and Bleck's studies, indicates that design features like means testing do not necessarily have a stigmatizing effect outside advanced industrial democracies (Hunter and Sugiyama 2014). Rather, the means-tested conditional poverty reduction program Bolsa Familia improved recipients' sense of empowerment and political inclusion.

These studies suggest that state capacity is an important variable mediating how policies "feed back." When a state lacks the capacity or revenue for universal service provision, citizens are likely to be concerned less about paternalistic design features and more with whether they receive basic services at all (Hern 2017). Other researchers have argued that for low-capacity states, the act of extending services is a form of state-building. This act therefore has the potential to incorporate citizens into the polity through sustained contact with state services (Bratton and Chang 2006). In low-capacity states, the method and process of extending basic services has the potential to influence citizens' relationship to their state. Citizens' experiences with service provision are therefore likely to be more salient (and more likely to influence political participation) than nuanced design features.

The presence or absence of the state through service provision is likely to have both material and interpretive implications for citizens. The lack of state services indicates a level of material deprivation that may influence political participation; additionally, the absence of the state may signal to residents that their well-being is not a government priority, which may decrease residents' expectation of the utility of political participation. Among those who do have contact with state services, the quality of these services may also produce both material and interpretive effects. Dysfunctional or low-quality state services are unlikely to be much of a material improvement over outright neglect; however, such services likely send a very different message to recipients than neglect would. Scholarship has demonstrated that satisfaction with services in developing countries is only weakly related to objective measures of service quality and is more closely related to perceptions of how hard the government is trying (Sacks 2011; McLoughlin 2015). Michael Bratton's (2007) analysis of Afrobarometer data demonstrated that though Africans are quick to point out the shortcomings of basic services, they are also surprisingly tolerant of these inadequacies. Reported satisfaction with government services was not related to survey respondents' reports of the quality of the services but, rather, determined by their assessments of how responsive civil servants were to their needs. Such analyses of the relationship between service provision and attitudes toward the government in low-capacity states indicate the importance of "procedural justice," the sense that government policies are fundamentally fair, even if they do not produce the most ideal outcome (Sunshine and Tyler 2003).

ADAPTING THE THEORY: POLICY FEEDBACK IN LOW-CAPACITY DEMOCRACIES

The policy feedback framework needs to be adapted to capture the elements of public policy that are most salient for citizens of low-capacity states. Based on the empirical literature discussed above, the theoretical framework I advance here reflects a shift in focus from welfare policies to basic service provision. It presents a novel analytical framework for understanding the likely interpretive effects these services yield.

In low-capacity states, basic service delivery is far more likely to be salient than the broader category of welfare policies that policy feedback studies in advanced industrial democracies examine. Simply put, many states are not capacious enough to pursue a broad-based, coherent set of welfare policies. In states that are unable to achieve universal provisioning of basic services, both the government and the citizenry are more likely to be concerned with the extension of such basic services. In the African context, the public continues to demand and expect the state to extend basic services such as health care and education, even where the state has limited ability to achieve their provision (M. Bratton 2007; MacLean 2010; Olivier de Sardan 2014). Access to basic services is therefore likely to be the most salient form of government contact for many residents of low-capacity states. At the most fundamental material level, access to basic services like water, electricity, health care, and education has an important impact on quality of life and may influence the extent to which people have the time and capability to participate in the political process. In addition, as mentioned above, citizens' assessments of how sincerely the government tries to extend services likely influences the interpretive effects that these services may precipitate.

Citizens of low-capacity states understand that their governments lack the ability to execute perfect service provision. With limited resources, a combination of capacity and political will determines which communities gain access to what degree of service provision. As the studies by Michael Bratton (2007) and McLoughlin (2015) indicate, citizens evaluate government attempts at service provision subjectively. In some cases, the degree to which citizens believe that the government is trying to be responsive or to meet their needs is more important than the quality of the services. It is therefore not enough to measure service delivery and estimate its effect on political participation; it is also necessary to understand citizens' subjective assessment of the services that are important to them and of the government's attempts at service extension overall. To this end, an appropriate application of policy feedback requires determining which types of experiences with service delivery are likely to generate different political effects—in other words, how different interpretations of government attempts at service delivery are likely to influence recipients' perceptions of the political realm and understandings of the utility of political participation. To consider the political effects of a broad swath of services, I develop a typology of policy experiences that can theoretically apply to any number of services that an individual deems salient.

A Typology of Policy Experiences

As described above, one conceptual problem faced by many policy feedback works is the tendency to focus on the specific effects of one or a few policies. Such focus does not reflect the way individuals actually experience policy. Each person encounters a suite of policies, with varying levels of salience, all of which may or may not influence that person's perception of the government and his or her subsequent political participation. Of course, considering the entire array of policies to which governments expose individuals is even more causally complex, particularly since the same individual might have dramatically different experiences with various policies. Returning to the example of American welfare policy discussed earlier, one individual might have a negative experience with TANF but a positive experience with the public school system or public works department. To understand how the balance of peoples' policy experiences influences their relationship to the government and their proclivity for political participation, it is necessary to theorize how and why different policies affect people in different ways. In advanced industrial democracies, as discussed above, scholars have categorized policy based on their eligibility criteria or visibility (Mettler and Stonecash 2008; Mettler 2011). In the context of low-capacity democracies, I suggest that two dimensions of service provision, one objective and one subjective, are of theoretical importance. These dimensions are the degree to which services actually confer material resources to a group and the degree to which people feel that those services reflect awareness of their needs.

The first dimension—conferral of material resources—is largely objective: policies may be inclusionary or exclusionary. An inclusionary experience with service provision is one in which an individual or community actually receives tangible, material goods from the government through a process of service delivery. Alternatively, individuals or communities may be excluded from basic services. In a low-capacity state characterized by "brown spots," where the government has limited ability to achieve its goals, service provision is unlikely to be universal (O'Donnell 1993). Exclusion from services may be a simple function of state capacity: communities in more remote regions—further from capital cities, ports, and infrastructure—are less likely to experience broad-based service provision. Alternatively, inclusion or exclusion from basic services may be political: access to services may be a function of partisanship, access to patronage networks, or ethnicity.

Regardless of the source of variation, inclusion or exclusion from basic services has the possibility of influencing political participation through either material or interpretive pathways. Whether or not individuals or groups have access to basic services is indicative of their material prosperity. Those lacking basic services must find ways to compensate for their absence; those who receive basic services may be motivated to ensure their continuity. Inclusion or exclusion may also generate political effects through interpretive pathways: being targeted for service delivery, regardless of the quality, may make recipients feel that the government is at least attempting to meet their needs, that there is some sense of procedural justice in service provision; exclusion from services may make citizens feel that the government does not particularly care about their well-being and would be unlikely to respond to their needs. In this sense, being excluded from basic service provision undermines the sense of procedural justice that the included population may experience.

Simply distinguishing between inclusion and exclusion is insufficient for understanding how experience with service delivery might feed back into political participation. As the studies mentioned above made clear, citizens' subjective perceptions of how responsive the government was—regardless of the quality of the service in question—has a substantial impact on their attitudes toward the government. For those included in service delivery, it is useful to think about this dimension in terms of "responsiveness," the extent to which government service provision actually addresses the community's expressed needs in a way that is constructive and responsive. For those excluded from service delivery, the equivalent would be "intentionality," the extent to which the government purposefully (or incidentally) excluded a person or community from services. In neutral terminology, this concept is the degree to which individuals perceive government policy toward them to be aware of their needs. In this context, "awareness" is an experience enhancer: it amplifies the positive experiences associated with inclusion as well as the negative experiences associated with exclusion. Together, the objective and subjective dimensions of service delivery comprise four broad policy experiences, illustrated in figure 7, where the policy characteristics are in bold, the policy experience types are in standard text in the center of the figure, and the interpretive dimension of the policy characteristics are italicized at the figure's bottom and right.

		Inclusionary	Exclusionary	
Policy reflects awareness of group needs?	Yes	Empowering	Burdensome	*Visible*
	No	Marginalizing	Neglectful	*Invisible*
		Engaged	*Unengaged*	

Fig. 7. Policy Experience Typology and Interpretive Dimensions

In the typology, each policy characteristic has an associated theorized interpretive dimension. Based on the interpretive logic of policy feedback, I expect those exposed to inclusionary policies to experience a higher level of engagement in the political system, whereas the excluded should feel less engaged. Policies that reflect awareness of group needs make recipients feel visible, while policies reflecting lack of awareness make people feel invisible. I theorize that people who fall into each policy experience category will develop a different relationship to the government and political sphere as a function of their experience.

Recipients of service delivery may subjectively assess whether the services reflect awareness of their needs. Aware inclusionary policies generate empowering experiences: recipients enjoy access to services that they perceive as being responsive to their needs, reflecting procedural justice. Theoretically, one would expect citizens in this category to be the most engaged, to feel visible to the government, and to have a greater degree of efficacy derived from positive experiences with service provision. Alternatively, inclusionary policies that lack awareness generate marginalizing experiences. Citizens in this category have access to basic services but feel that these services do not actually address their needs. They may feel that government agencies lack responsiveness, that service delivery is rote rather than reflective of a system that adequately takes stock of their needs and takes measures to address them. Citizens with these experiences are still likely to be engaged in the political sphere as a function of being included in service delivery, but they are less likely to feel particularly visible or efficacious.

Applied to those excluded from basic services, awareness magnifies the negativity of the experience. Aware exclusionary policies generate a burdensome experience. People in this category experience their exclusion as intentional, a deliberate action undertaken by the government to bar them from accessing specific services. Those who fall into this category are likely to feel highly visible to the government but have no reason to believe that the government is interested in responding to their needs. Quite the opposite, they may feel that the government deliberately undermines their ability to meet their needs. Finally, exclusionary policies lacking awareness generate a neglectful experience. People subjected to these policies feel that their exclusion from services is due to thoughtlessness or perhaps lack of state capacity, rather than intention. They experience their exclusion as evidence that the government does not particularly care about their needs and has made little or no effort to extend services to them. Those in this category are likely to feel invisible and unengaged and have little reason to believe that they might influence the political process.

While the subjective dimension of this typology introduces a level of complexity in measuring these experiences, these subjective assessments are closely related to actual experiences with government service provision. For example, a common agricultural service that the government provides in African countries (including Zambia) is provision of subsidized seeds and fertilizer to farmers at the beginning of the planting season, often as a loan to be repaid during the harvest. In the Zambian case, farmers must be part of a registered cooperative and have acreage of a certain size to be eligible for such inputs (Mason, Jayne, and van de Walle 2017). For farmers who receive these inputs in a timely manner, the result is likely to be an empowering experience: this program is very popular, and farmers who receive subsidized seeds and fertilizer can substantially increase the size of their harvest. However, the agency responsible for distributing these inputs is generally slow and inefficient; while some farmers may receive their inputs far enough before the planting season to be useful, unlucky cooperatives may only receive such inputs after the optimal planting window has closed, resulting in a marginalizing experience that is both disheartening and economically detrimental. Farmers with acreage slightly too small to qualify for cooperative membership may feel burdened by their intentional exclusion from this program, particularly if they must compete with neighbors who are able to benefit. Farmers in more remote rural outposts, beyond the target area that government agencies might reasonably reach, may not even be part of the cooperative network and therefore may be unintentionally excluded from this program (Hern 2015).

This typology provides a tool for comparing individuals' experiences across a broad array of government services. Different services will be salient to different people (as a function of their needs) and for different reasons (as a function of their experience). Individuals may have dramatically different experiences across various salient services—some empowering, some marginalizing, some neglectful—all of which contribute to their relationship to the government and the extent to which they pursue their interests through politics. With this tool, it is possible to understand how different types of experiences influence different forms of political participation. The following section of this chapter asserts a series of hypotheses regarding how various policy experiences will influence four different forms of political participation: collective behavior, political engagement, formal participation, and alternative forms of political behavior. These hypotheses are specific to low-capacity states, like Zambia, in which there is a salient distinction between parts of the population that have access to basic services and those who do not.

HYPOTHESIZING THE EFFECTS OF SERVICE DELIVERY ON PARTICIPATION

This study examines four categories of participation: collective behavior, political engagement, formal political participation, and alternative or subversive political acts. The study treats each form of participation separately, in its own chapter, based on the assumption that each type of political behavior reflects a different set of motivations and should therefore be theorized separately. The following subsections of this chapter provide a preliminary rationale for the hypotheses that this study tests, each of which is explored in greater depth in its dedicated chapter.

Collective Behavior

The first dimension of political participation that this study examines is collective behavior, especially in the form of civic associationism, the likelihood that members of a community gather together to solve problems, make local improvements, or achieve collective goals. This dimension is distinct from formal political participation in that it relies on local social capital and organization as the first step for achieving change, rather than on elected officials or formal political channels. Civic associationism is an important indicator of social capital, which is widely believed to improve civil society and promote positive outcomes in democratic governance.[2] However, government institutions and policies themselves can foster or undermine civic behavior (Brehm and Rahn 1997; Tarrow 1996; Skocpol, Ganz, and Munson 2000). In the context of low-capacity governments, previous studies have demonstrated that communities engage in collective behavior to meet basic needs the government cannot meet (M. Bratton 2006; MacLean 2010; Cammett and MacLean 2014).

Based on existing studies and the logic of the policy experience typology, several types of policy experience may increase the likelihood of collective behavior. Drawing from studies in advanced industrial democracies, one might expect collective behavior to be more likely when the government promotes engagement through inclusive policies. But drawing from studies in low-capacity states, collective behavior may be more likely in a context of material deprivation. If the government is unwilling or unable to meet basic needs, communities may be compelled to provide basic services for themselves. These possibilities reflect anticipated differences in the two pathways of policy feedback: inclusive policies may stimulate collective behavior through interpretive pathways, or lack of access to services may necessitate collective behavior through material pathways. Chapter 4 examines the plausibility of these two competing (but not mutually exclusive) possibilities, expressed in hypotheses 2a and 2b.

H_{2a}: Collective behavior is more likely for individuals with lower objective access to government services.

H_{2b}: Collective behavior is more likely for individuals with inclusive policy experiences.

Political Engagement

Political engagement, the second form of political behavior that this study examines, is generally conceptualized as level of political interest, including willingness to talk about politics or answer survey questions that are politically oriented, and sometimes as political knowledge. Like collective behavior, political engagement is one of the most consistently important predictors of formal political participation (Verba, Schlozman, and Brady 1995; Burns, Schlozman, and Verba 2000; Bowler, Donovan, and Hanneman 2003). Because political engagement is a measure of an attitude, a general orientation toward the political realm, I expect the link between policy experience and political engagement to run primarily through interpretive pathways. Furthermore, I expect a wide array of policy experiences to stimulate political engagement, with one important caveat: expressing interest in politics is not the same as believing one has recourse through political channels.

Deducing from the policy experience typology, there are several ways that policy experience might promote political engagement. First, I would expect recipients of policies along the inclusionary dimension to be more politically engaged. As described above, my typological theorizing includes the idea that those who are subject to inclusive policy types should have the psychological sense that the government is attempting to meet their needs, even if the government is not ultimately successful at doing so. I assume that political engagement should increase with the sense that the government is open or responsive, a sense that should be more prevalent for those subject to inclusive policies (Reingold and Harrell 2010). However, I would also expect a greater degree of political engagement for those subject to policies reflecting an "awareness" of community or individual needs. The typology suggests that these recipients should feel highly visible. The sense that the government "sees" you should make individuals more attuned to politics, whether out of interest in capturing more resources (in the case of those experiences empowering policies) or out of fear or anger (in the case of those experiencing burdensome policies). This expectation is expressed in hypothesis 3.

H_3: Political engagement will be higher for those experiencing policies that are inclusive or reflect awareness.

The implication of this hypothesis is that all policy experiences, save neglect, should generate higher levels of political engagement. However, while exposure to government policies may increase engagement, I do not expect that all these experiences would necessarily translate into formal political participation.

Formal Political Participation

Formal political participation includes activities such as voting, party affiliation, and contacting officials. While most studies about political participation consider collective behavior, political engagement, and formal political participation to be linked closely, political participation has a uniquely negative cost-benefit structure: political participation generally entails some sort of cost (related to time, material resources, or both) and has a remote, intangible benefit. Thus, policy experiences must be exceptional to generate formal political participation. I expect that policies will precipitate this form of participation only when they are inclusionary and reflect awareness of need.

By typological definition, recipients of inclusionary policies are more likely to feel that the government has at least a nominal interest in them, and they should feel more engaged with politics. But inclusion on any terms is not enough to precipitate political participation; those subject to marginalizing policies (inclusive, but lacking awareness of individuals' needs) are likely to have less political efficacy, as a function of the sense that the government does not really understand what they need. Furthermore, those subject to exclusionary policies have no reason to believe that the government is interested in their needs. If citizens feel that the government is using policy to actively exclude them or that the government does not care enough about them to even consider their needs through policy, they would have no reason to believe that participation in "politics as usual" will have much benefit. Therefore, as expressed in hypothesis 4a, I expect that only empowering policies will increase recipients' formal political participation.

> H_{4a}: Formal political participation is more likely for those with empowering policy experiences or assessments.

While I expect empowering experiences to have a direct impact on political participation, other policy experiences may indirectly influence formal participation, through their relationship with either collective behavior or political engagement. Because both collective behavior and political engagement have been shown to be positively related to participation, these variables may mediate the relationship between policies and participation. First, as expressed in hypothesis 4b, if low levels of service provision encourage collective behavior (H_{2a}), such collective behavior may, in turn, generate political participation.

> H_{4b}: Mediated by collective behavior, lower levels of objective service provision will be associated with higher rates of political participation.

Similarly, as expressed in hypothesis 4c, if political engagement is higher for all forms of policy experience except for neglect, it may confound the relationship between policy and participation.

H_{4c}: Mediated by political engagement, marginalizing or burdensome policy experiences or assessments will increase political participation.

Chapter 6 explores this hypothesis and the other hypotheses in this section.

Alternative or Subversive Political Acts

The topic of alternative or subversive political acts includes the issues of reliance on nonstate actors, negative attitudes toward tax compliance, and protest behavior. Beginning with the issue of reliance on nonstate actors, I conceptualize NGOs and traditional authorities as nonstate service providers that provide possible alternatives to the state. If survey respondents view state and nonstate service providers as distinct, one would expect greater reliance on nonstate providers when needs are not being met through the government. These relationships may work through either material or interpretive pathways, when respondents do not have access to the services they need or do not believe the government is likely to be responsive to their needs. According to the typology, respondents experiencing policies along either the exclusionary or "unaware" policy dimensions would belong to this group. Those "not getting what they need" from the government (to varying degrees) include those with marginalizing, neglectful, or burdensome experiences. The expectations expressed in hypothesis 5a apply to this group.

H_{5a}: Reliance on chiefs or NGOs for service provision is more likely when respondents have less access to services or interpret government services as exclusionary or unaware.

Regarding attitudes toward revenue collection, one would expect, according to the logic of the "fiscal contract," that people would hold noncompliant attitudes about revenue collection when they have been excluded from the benefits thereof. The typology provides a clear expectation that those who would fall into this category are those who are materially excluded from state service provision. In the typology, this group includes those who have been neglected or burdened by their experience with public services. While those who experience marginalizing policies are also unlikely to be satisfied with service provision, their inclusionary experience should make them feel as though they have a stake in the government's continuing ability to collect revenue, which may lead to a greater sense of civic duty than for those who experience exclusionary policies (Lago-Penas and Lago-Penas 2010). Hypothesis 5b expresses this expectation.

H_{5b}: Evasion of taxes or customs duties is more likely when respondents have exclusionary interpretations of service delivery.

Regarding protest behavior, I expect a different dynamic. I conceptualize protest as a way to make claims on the government (rather than as a revolutionary behavior or an ideology-driven social movement). While protest is a dramatic form of political behavior, departing from "politics as usual," it is also a costly activity with an uncertain payoff structure. Therefore, I expect people to be more likely to undertake protest behavior when they have reason to believe that the government would listen to what they have to say. Based on the typology, this expectation is more likely for those with inclusionary policy experiences and especially for those who have empowering experiences. These experiences generate engagement and possibly also the sense of visibility. As expressed in hypothesis 5c, people who experience inclusionary policy may be more likely to feel that they have something to gain through protest behavior.

H_{5c}: Protest is more likely for those who have inclusionary interpretations of service delivery.

Chapter 7 takes up this hypothesis and the other hypotheses in this section, with their associated arguments.

SURVEY DESIGN

To examine how varied experiences with public policy (through service delivery) correspond with forms of political participation, I undertook a survey of 1,500 people across three Zambian provinces. As a later section of this chapter describes, site selection was purposive to ensure variation in the level of service provision. The survey is not nationally representative but, rather, represents a portion of the Zambian population with variation across the key explanatory variable, policy experience. The primary goals of the survey were to ascertain respondents' overall experience with government policy through service provision and to assess their level of political participation. This section of this chapter describes the operationalization of the independent variables (public policy experience) and the various ways of measuring the dependent variables (forms of political participation).

Independent Variables

Many policy feedback studies have focused on a single policy or closed set of policies to understand how a specific interaction with a government body affects political participation. The goal of this study, however, is to uncover how people understand their relationship with the government broadly, through multiple policies and citizen-state interactions. Therefore, the survey was designed to uncover the balance of respondents' experiences with the government through service provision. Because this study seeks to understand the relative impact of material and interpretive feedback effects, the survey operationalizes "policy experience" in three ways to delineate the difference between those effects.

The first measure captures the objective level of key public services to which respondents have access. The second measure is semi-subjective, asking respondents to assess their experiences with specific policies that they identified as being personally important to them. The last measure is completely subjective, asking respondents to assess their general overall experience with government service provision. The intuition behind including all three measures in the analysis is that some forms of political behavior may be more closely related to material effects, others to interpretive effects. The following subsections detail the operationalization of each measure.

Material Effects and the Objective Provision of Services

The first measure reflects the presence of basic government services. At each of the 65 field sites, I recorded whether each of the following services was present and accessible to respondents: a secondary school, access to a main (paved) road, a functioning health clinic (rather than an empty building), and a police post. I selected these four services for two reasons: first, there was real variation in their presence, particularly in rural areas; second, the presence of these services is an indicator of government presence more generally. In the sample, 73 percent of respondents had access to a secondary school, 71 percent to a "main road," 78 percent to a functioning clinic, and 50 percent to a police post. Urban areas generally had all four services present, while more variation occurred across peri-urban and rural areas.

Remote rural areas with easy access to a paved road were far more likely to have access to other government services, such as farm input delivery or visits from agricultural extension officers. While nearly every field site had a primary school, access to secondary schools was less common and a better indicator of "remoteness" from government presence. Similarly, nearly every site had a clinic building, but the worst-served areas were unlikely to have any nurses or clinic staff. Finally, the presence or absence of a police post serves as a crude indicator of the government's coercive powers. Based on the presence or absence of these four services, the count variable "government projects" runs from 0 to 4.

Interpretive Effects and Reported Project Experience

Understanding respondents' overall experience with government policy and service provision is potentially unwieldy, given the broad array of government policies and projects that each respondent encounters. Attempting to ascertain respondents' experience with a list of all major government policies and projects is not feasible, but it is also not necessary; from a theoretical standpoint, all respondent interactions with the government are not equal. Only the most salient policies and projects are likely to influence respondents' perception of the government and therefore affect their political behavior. However, which projects are "salient" is unavoidably different for different people and from region to region. It was therefore essential to design a survey instrument that was sufficiently flexible but not so open-ended as to overwhelm respondents.

To generate such an instrument, I used a funnel approach to narrow down respondents' answers from broad policy areas to specific important policies. At the beginning of each survey, the respondent was presented with a list of seven "issue areas," with several examples of each: agriculture, education, water and electricity, health, transport, public safety, and "something else." Respondents were asked to select up to three issue areas and, within those areas, services, projects, or policies that were important to them (they also had the option of saying that no government policies or projects were important to them). While this strategy could theoretically produce hundreds of answers, respondents consistently reported similar policies: for "agriculture," subsidized seeds and fertilizer; for "education," quality of or access to public schools; for "health," access to staff or supplies at local clinics; for "water/electricity," boreholes (rural) and load shedding (urban); for "transport," "road construction or maintenance"; and for "public safety," access to a police post. While significant variation in access to specific services was evident, the majority of responses clustered around these salient examples. A few respondents spoke about broader policy issues like fiscal policy and women's rights, but such responses were few and far between; the overwhelming majority of respondents were more concerned with service provision.

Once respondents had identified a specific service, project, or policy, they were asked to describe their experience with it. Commensurate with the typology, their qualitative responses were categorized using the coding scheme described in table 2. In the operationalization of the concept, each respondent received a score from 0 to 3 on each of these policy experiences, indicating the number of projects each respondent listed that corresponded to that "type" of experience. This strategy generates four experience variables that, when included together in regression analysis, capture the respondent's total reported experience. For example, a respondent describing two marginalizing projects and one burdensome project would have the following variable specification: empowering = 0; marginalizing = 2; neglectful = 0; burdensome = 1. Including all measures together allows the analysis to take stock of the effect of higher scores along one dimension while controlling for other possible experiences.

Subjective Assessment of Government Services

The final assessment of respondents' overall experience with government services is completely subjective, in that, unlike the previous indicator, it is not anchored to a description of an actual policy experience. This measure comes from a question at the very end of the survey (after respondents had been primed by talking about their experiences), asking respondents explicitly what they think about government service provision. Their answers were coded into the four categories presented in table 3, again categories based on the policy experience typology. Five percent of the sample stated that they

Table 2. Project Experience Categories

If respondent spoke about the service:	It was coded as:	Frequency (Rate)
Positively	Empowering	465 (11%)
As though it did not meet their needs	Marginalizing	1,936 (47%)
As something they did not receive / have access to	Neglectful	1,651 (40%)
As something that makes their life more difficult	Burdensome	104 (2.5%)

could not assess government services because they never thought about such services. The four categories in table 3 correspond to a categorical variable indicating whether a respondent expressed the corresponding point of view. In the regression analysis, "neglect" is the base category, so the coefficients can be understood as the marginal effect of a respondent's reported experience as compared to those who think the government ignores them.

These three independent variables allow a careful analysis of how political participation varies according to three different measures of policy experience: objective measures of government presence, actual description of salient policies, and the subjective interpretation of respondents' overall experiences with the government. As will become apparent in the analyses in subsequent chapters of this study, these three ways of operationalizing "policy experience" hold different levels of importance for predicting different forms of political participation.

Dependent Variables

The dependent variables in this study concern various forms of political participation. The precise specification of each form of participation will be examined more fully in subsequent chapters. This section provides only a brief overview of the how I operationalized the different forms.

The first form of political behavior that this study examines is collective behavior. It includes the respondent's proclivity to participate in various forms of community organizing, including attendance at community meetings, joining together with neighbors to solve local problems, and group membership. Political engagement, the second form of participation studied, includes respondents' proclivities to talk about politics, express interest in politics, and follow the news. The third form, formal participation, includes a

Table 3. Subjective Government Assessment Categories

If respondent spoke about government services as though:	*It was coded as:*	**Frequency (Rate)**
The government usually tries to help	Empowering	349 (23%)
The government might try but does not understand the people's needs	Marginalizing	524 (35%)
The government ignores the people	Neglectful	449 (30%)
The government makes things harder for people	Burdensome	105 (7%)

broad swath of formal behaviors, including contacting politicians (local and national), support for political parties, and prospective voting. The fourth form, alternative/subversive forms of political behavior, includes behaviors that undermine the authority of the national government. The first set of questions on the fourth form assesses the likelihood that respondents turn to nonstate agents (NGOs or traditional authorities) for services. The second set determines respondents' attitudes toward taxation and customs. The third set examines protest behavior as an exceptional form of political voice.

Each of the following chapters is organized around one group of these dependent variables. Because both collective behavior and political engagement are predictors of political participation (in addition to being political behaviors in their own right), they appear as independent variables in chapter 7 (which examines formal political participation), to ensure that the relationship between various policy experiences and formal participation is not epiphenomenal. For example, if an empowering policy experience is associated with higher levels of political engagement and political participation, it is important to ensure that the relationship between the policy experience and participation is not mediated by the relationship between the policy experience and engagement.

Control Variables

A standard series of control variables is included in each of the regression analyses. To control for other factors known to influence political participation, the demographic controls include sex, age, level of education, religiosity (measured as frequency of church attendance),[3] tribe,[4] marital status, and number of children.[5] Income is an important predictor of political participation, but as self-reporting of income in African countries is notoriously unreliable, several other proxies were used, including urban/rural residence, formal versus informal employment, and unemployment.[6] I included a variable indicating whether the respondent worked as a civil servant (as civil servants are not supposed to express any political attitudes). The variable "on-rail" is included due to the expectation that government presence may influence the extent to which respondents actively think about and interact with the political sphere.

Some additional controls help to correct for biases inherent in the structure of the survey and its execution. Fixed effects are included to control for unobservable differences across the three provinces, and the standard errors are clustered by ward (urban) or village (rural), the unit of stratification.[7] In addition, fixed effects for the 12 survey enumerators are included to account for biases caused by interviewer effects.[8] Full coding information regarding all the variables in the analysis is available in this book's appendix.

SITE SELECTION

As described in chapter 2, the primary consideration for my purposive site selection was to include variation in the quality and rate of service provision. Based on the logic explored in that chapter, this expectation led me to select Southern, Central, and Northwestern Provinces as regions with different expected rates of service provision. The second consideration behind my selection was to ensure variation in the proximity to urban areas. The urban/rural divide remains highly salient; former president Sata's populist platform was built around supporting the urban poor, in stark contrast to the MMD's emphasis on the rural population (though the efficacy of each set of policies was unremarkable). This rhetorical shift may be accompanied by policy changes that alter the nature of the policies that those in urban and rural areas experience. To ensure variation, I stratified the survey sample to include 50 percent rural and 50 percent urban populations in each province. The following sections discuss the contemporary context of each field site, demonstrating that the political-economic realities of the districts selected within each province portend different public policy experiences for respondents across (and within) each province. These field sites—Solwezi District in Northwestern Province, Kabwe District in Central Province, and Kazungula/ Livingstone Districts in Southern Province—are demarcated by black diamonds in figure 8.

Southern Province: Livingstone and Kazungula Districts

Of the three provinces examined in this study, Southern Province has maintained the most consistent place in the national political economy since the 1960s. In the line of rail and along a major southern import/export route, some parts of Southern Province have received significant infrastructural development, especially the urban centers that house commercial activity related to these trade routes. The border town of Livingstone, along the shores of the Zambezi River and near Victoria Falls, is the country's major tourist destination. Towns along the road south from Lusaka to the border posts with Botswana (in Kazungula District) and Zimbabwe (in Livingstone Dis-

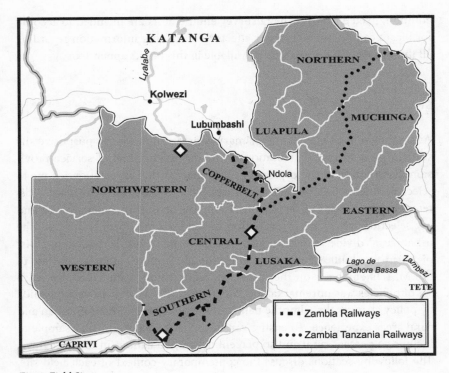

Fig. 8. Field Sites

trict) accommodate a large volume of traffic. The roads are comparatively well maintained, transport to the capital is regular and easy to access, and government presence (in terms of service provision) is relatively high. In Livingstone, infrastructure was greatly improved in preparation for hosting the World Tourism Organization's major international conference in August 2013. Similar to assessments of the region's potential in the FNDP, Zambia's Sixth National Development Plan (NDP-6) notes that Southern Province has a comparative advantage across multiple sectors: agriculture, energy generation, mineral deposits, and tourism (Republic of Zambia 2011, 201).

However, many residents of Southern Province live beyond the reach of the main road and the rail. While there are some major commercial farming enterprises in Southern Province, most rural residents are engaged in small-scale or subsistence farming. Villages close to the main trade routes have a comparatively easy time getting their products to market, but those in more remote areas face persistent marketing problems. The NDP-6 notes that decline in agricultural productivity is the primary challenge that the province faces, due to poor infrastructure, which becomes problematic farther away from the main road north to Lusaka (Republic of Zambia 2011, 201). These problems are compounded during the rainy season, when the roads to more remote rural areas become impassable.

Experience with government presence and service provision is starkly different based on proximity to the main road, the border posts, and the tourist destination of Livingstone. The two districts selected for the survey—Livingstone and Kazungula—include both groups. Livingstone is an entirely urban district that reaps the benefits of being on the rail. Kazungula, which surrounds urban Livingstone, is predominately rural and has variable access to the amenities of the rail. Some of Kazungula's rural villages are remote, while its peri-urban wards near Livingstone have much better access to government services.

Central Province: Kabwe District

Since the economic boom period of the 1960s, Central Province has experienced a reversal of fortune, specifically in its Kabwe District. During Zambia's First Republic, Central Province held the capital of Lusaka, the north–south rail infrastructure connecting the northern Copperbelt to southern export routes, and productive lead and zinc mines in Kabwe (formerly known as Broken Hill). In 1976, Lusaka and the surrounding productive agricultural area became its own province, separating from Central Province. Kabwe became Central Province's new capital and remained both economically and politically active through the 1980s, providing strong support for the emerging MMD (Larmer 2006). However, most of Kabwe's mines were decommissioned by the 1990s, and secondary industrial activity also declined. While Kabwe District still holds the advantage of being on-rail and hosting large-scale commercial agriculture, it is no longer an industrial powerhouse. This new reality is reflected in the NDP-6's goals for Central Province, which emphasize its "potential as a transport hub" and "huge agricultural potential," rather than possibilities for revitalizing its industry (Republic of Zambia 2011, 187–88).

Nevertheless, Kabwe District maintains some of the advantages of being well connected to Lusaka and holding urban infrastructure (even if it is not as well maintained as it once was). The local economy is bolstered by the nearby national army service camp, a major prison, a prominent teaching college, and a large nursing school. While the urban area lacks road maintenance, most urban residents have reasonable access to services like education and health care, and proximity to the capital makes it easy to access most urban amenities. The residents in the rural areas around Kabwe are engaged in both subsistence and commercial agriculture; while most farm their own plots, many also work as contract laborers on nearby commercial farms. Some of the rural areas in Kabwe District are difficult to reach—particularly in the rainy season—but they are comparatively well integrated into the national infrastructure. Located in the country's maize belt, Central Province receives a large allocation of public agricultural expenditures (Govereh et al. 2009). While service provision is not what it was during Kabwe's economic peak, government presence is still strong, and the region is closely integrated into Zambia's core economy.

Northwestern Province: Solwezi District

The final field site of this study is Solwezi District in Northwestern Province. Historically speaking, Northwestern Province has always been a remote, neglected region. While the reach of the state extended to the neighboring (economically important) Copperbelt Province, initial prospecting for minerals and metals in Northwestern Province was not fruitful, so neither the colonial nor the independent governments had much interest in it. As such, the province has a long history of expressing a sense of disconnect and neglect. This relationship began to change in 2005, with the reopening of Kansanshi Mine in Solwezi. Massive discoveries of copper reserves in the formerly defunct mine launched a series of production expansions, including the establishment of the Kansanshi Golf Estate, a gated community that houses thousands of (mostly expatriate) mine employees and features a golf club. The NDP-6 notes that while the province is still largely agricultural, it "has been earmarked for the development of one Multi-Facility Economic Zone to promote value addition. The opening up of mining ventures in the Province requires more investments in infrastructure, including energy, to accommodate the expected increase of economic activities" (Republic of Zambia 2011, 199). At the time of the fieldwork for the present study, these investments had not yet materialized, but the region was potentially on the brink of major economic expansion.

The NDP-6 also notes a lack of the human capital required to maintain the new industrial activity in Solwezi. The reopening of the mine has spawned a massive population increase, as skilled and semiskilled Copperbelt workers have migrated to rapidly expanding settlements in the outlying areas of the town of Solwezi. The government has planned infrastructural improvements, but at the time of the fieldwork for the present study, in January and February 2014, government investment in infrastructure and services had not kept up with population expansion. In the urban areas, the roads were dismal, there were not nearly enough schools or health facilities to cater to the population, and import traffic was so slow that retail stores could not keep enough inventory on the shelves to serve the growing population. While First Quantum, the company running Kansanshi Mine, had invested in some social services in the area, the population's general impression was that neither the government nor the mine was doing nearly enough to provide basic services to the population.

In rural areas, little (if anything) had changed since the reopening of the mine. The rural areas of Solwezi District are remote, located far away from the poorly maintained main road. Nearly all of the district's rural residents are subsistence farmers, and most report a total lack of government provision of agricultural resources. Rural villages have a difficult time maintaining schools and health clinics, because government-appointed teachers and nurses are reluctant to keep posts in such remote areas. While popular sentiment in the urban areas of Solwezi runs toward frustration with the government's lack of service provision, those in rural areas have low expectations, as their experience has always been one of remoteness and government neglect.

In Southern Province, urban and peri-urban wards sampled near the town of Livingstone and the Kazungula border post have reaped the benefits of being on-rail, while the more remote rural areas in Kazungula District are beyond easy reach of the main road (which runs alongside the rail). In the 500-person sample covering the Livingstone and Kazungula areas, 350 of the respondents were urban or peri-urban, with access to the benefits of the rail, while 150 of the rural respondents were so remote as to be off-rail, despite their relative proximity to commercial areas. In Central Province, both the urban and rural areas of Kabwe District are on-rail. The line of rail and the major north–south road run through the urban center, and the rural areas are reasonably well integrated economically, through the large amount of commercial agriculture in the area. All 500 respondents from Kabwe District are on-rail, which may explain its ongoing ability to attract government funding despite its economic decline.

In contrast, both the urban and rural areas of Solwezi are well beyond the line of rail. Even after the reopening of Kansanshi Mine, the urban center of

Solwezi is poorly connected to the national infrastructure (the straight, flat road connecting Solwezi to the mines of the Copperbelt is so riddled with potholes that driving faster than about 30 miles per hour becomes exceedingly dangerous). The rural areas of Solwezi are well beyond the reach of the rail; therefore, this study's 500 respondents from Solwezi District are off-rail. The district's unfortunate geographical location may explain its relatively low levels of public funding, despite its potential for an economic renaissance. In total, this study's sample of 1,500 people is split between 850 on-rail and 650 off-rail.

DATA COLLECTION AND METHODOLOGY

This survey was executed using a random walk strategy, stratified by sex and local government ward. In each district, I obtained a map of local government ward boundaries and stratified the provincial sample based on the number of constituencies in urban and rural areas. The sample covers as many constituencies as safety and travel time allowed. A small number of urban constituencies were excluded due to safety concerns, and rural constituencies that required driving farther than two and a half hours from the town center were ruled out to ensure completion of enumeration by sunset. All other constituencies were included in the sample. At each constituency, each enumerator started at a different, randomly selected spot and sampled every seventh household in an area.[9] Enumerators were instructed to achieve a gender balance by the end of the day and to skip households if a respondent of the necessary sex was not present. Following this strategy, the survey had an overall response rate of 83 percent (82 percent in Southern Province, 84 percent in Central Province, and 83 percent in Northwestern Province).[10] Most of the "nonresponse" category was due to households in which nobody (or nobody of the correct sex) was home; very few individuals elected not to take the survey when asked (particularly in rural areas).

Because it was not feasible to work from a list of residents or to return to houses to sample absent residents, some bias is inherent in this sampling strategy. In urban areas, those formally employed in office-type jobs are less likely to be part of the sample. However, because of the low level of this type of formal employment, it is unlikely to introduce too much bias into the sample. Many of those who are formally employed work irregular hours and are often home at random hours during the day. In fact, 23 percent of the sample reported formal employment, compared to 11 percent of the total 2010 population in Zambia (Republic of Zambia 2010). In rural areas, women were more likely to be out of the household during a portion of the survey, because of the planting season (women tend to perform most of the planting). We adjusted for this likelihood by scheduling part of the enumeration during the period when women typically return from the fields to prepare lunch.

Because of the apparent randomness with which people were home during the day, there does not appear to be too much of a bias in the sample. Unemployed youth are overrepresented, while middle-aged working people are underrepresented. However, there is no reason to believe that the link between policy experience and participation differs due to age. Because this study is not attempting to extrapolate from the sample to the total population of Zambia, controlling for demographic traits should be sufficient to account for sampling biases.

In addition to the survey data, my research assistants and I recorded 172 in-depth interviews with respondents from Livingstone, Kazungula, and Kabwe in July 2016. These interviews provide important qualitative data to facilitate the interpretation of the quantitative data. Like the survey, these interviews were performed using a random walk strategy. Interviews with respondents who did not speak English were performed with the help of interpreters.

The survey and interview data form the empirical basis of the following four chapters. The survey allows regression analysis to identify trends in the data, while the interviews provide context, nuance, and narrative essential for interpreting those trends. Each of the following four chapters uses this data to examine one of the four forms of political behavior of interest in this study: collective behavior, political engagement, formal participation, and alternative or subversive behaviors.

CHAPTER 4

Filling the Gaps the State Left
Service Delivery and Collective Behavior

Sitting at a lodge in Lusaka, a Zambian colleague described how the ruling PF had made dramatic improvements to the roads within Lusaka town but left the roads in the peri-urban outskirts disastrous.[1] The latter roads, made of dirt and gravel, wear easily and become bumpy and uneven during the rainy season. Sometimes, he said, instead of waiting for the government to repair the roads, members of the community would come together to patch it up. When I asked how they organized such projects themselves, he responded that their local community chairman—elected through a community organization within the neighborhood—would go around to publicize the project and recruit people to come and help. Mostly, he explained, people would volunteer their labor to patch parts of the road that had become impassable.

This example is one of many community-based projects described to me. Particularly in the rural, peri-urban, and poorly served urban areas, survey and interview respondents had numerous examples of community members coming together to solve local problems. Most of these examples, like the one recounted above, had to do with communities organizing to compensate for inadequate service provision from the state. These accounts illuminate the conditions under which collective organizing is most likely to occur in the Zambian case. In many instances, respondents described collective organizing as a direct result of inadequate service provision. These observations highlight an interesting puzzle: political scientists tend to treat high rates of collective behavior as indicative of a society with inclusive and responsive political institutions, yet examples of collective organizing in the Zambian context often appeared precisely when the government had failed to provide basic services for communities.

Collective behavior is of interest to those studying political participation because it is so closely linked to other forms of political behavior and is sometimes indicative of the broader political context. Communities that are able to organize themselves effectively can secure better political outcomes. Political scientists often treat collective behavior as a measurable indicator of other underlying characteristics, including social capital, civic skills, and civic engagement (Putnam 1993; Verba, Schlozman, and Brady 1995). These characteristics help individuals and communities to engage more effectively with political systems: social capital enables communities to overcome problems of collective action and achieve optimal outcomes despite the myriad difficulties of organizing (Ostrom 1990); individuals can apply the civic skills that they learn through group organizing to participation in the formal political sphere; and joiners may develop higher levels of civic engagement by virtue of being involved regularly with the broader community (Brady, Verba, and Schlozman 1995).

Because of these links, examining collective behavior is essential to understanding broader patterns of political participation. A growing body of literature considers the ways in which public policy may influence an individual's or a community's proclivity to engage in collective behavior. However, this literature highlights different trends when considering high-capacity versus low-capacity states. In high-capacity democracies, researchers tend to consider how inclusionary policies can promote collective organizing, either by intentionally promoting civic organization or by creating interest-group behavior around desirable goods. In low-capacity countries, observers have noted that collective behavior often emerges to fill the gaps left by the state, rather than in response to inclusive policies (e.g., MacLean 2010). These two descriptions of the ways in which government policy might stimulate collective behavior are not mutually exclusive, but they suggest that two different, possibly countervailing processes may be at play.

In this chapter, I examine both government neglect and inclusionary policy experiences as possible sources of collective behavior. I argue that the divergence in the literature on the subject results from different assumptions about what drives collective behavior—either the material or the interpretive effects of policies. In short, studies of high-capacity democracies have tended to focus on the interpretive effect of inclusionary policies on participation, demonstrating how various forms of inclusion promote collective organizing, whereas studies in low-capacity states tend to examine how the material effects of inadequate service provision necessitate collective organizing, in order for communities to meet basic needs. In this chapter, I explore both possibilities, to determine whether collective behavior in Zambia has a stronger relationship to material or interpretive channels of policy feedback.

The evidence presented in this chapter supports an argument including both channels: that government service provision in Zambia promotes collective behavior both through material neglect and through empowering interpretations of government service provision. The survey results establish correlations between these variables, while the qualitative analysis of interview data and the structured comparison of some of the different field sites provide additional evidence regarding the circumstances under which collective organizing is more likely. In the Zambian case, respondents consistently describe collective behavior as a way either to replace government service provision in the absence of the state or to complete self-help projects where the government provided some assistance. These descriptions portray collective behavior as instrumental and related to material needs, rather than as a method for pursuing superfluous goods or leisure. As this chapter concludes, such community organization is not an indication that the absence of the state should be celebrated. Despite the high level of collective behavior in neglected areas, communities are almost never able to achieve the same degree of service provision that the state theoretically could.

COLLECTIVE BEHAVIOR IN LESS-DEVELOPED DEMOCRACIES

Political scientists have long considered collective behavior to be an important indicator of social capital, which is widely believed to improve the quality of civil society and promote positive outcomes in democratic governance. It is common to measure social capital through the presence of various collective behaviors, including civic or social groups, neighborhood organizing, or spontaneous self-help collectives (Putnam 1995, 67). In general terms, collective behavior is the process through which individuals organize into groups to further the interests of their members (Olson 1965). Because the process of collective organizing requires overcoming problems of collective action, scholars of Western democracies have argued that it improves the quality of democratic institutions, by bolstering citizens' civic skills and enabling them to participate effectively in politics (Putnam 1993; Verba, Schlozman, and Brady 1995). While communities exhibiting more collective behavior may be more politically efficacious, there is also evidence that policies themselves can stimulate or undermine collective organizing. As noted above, the literature on this issue tends to be divided among those examining high-capacity and low-capacity democracies.

In high-capacity democracies, there is evidence that inclusive public policy can generate both collective behavior and political efficacy, by cultivating civic skills (Tarrow 1996; Brehm and Rahn 1997; Pierson 2000; Skocpol, Ganz, and Munson 2000). The balance of the evidence suggests that when states can generally provide for the basic needs of their citizens, collective organizing emerges in response to inclusive policies: positive experiences with government policies generate a greater level of political efficacy, leading citizens to lobby for a greater share of resources, defend an existing share of resources, or organize in the pursuit of postmaterial concerns. In some cases, this behavior emerges specifically because the government enacted policies actively promoting or encouraging citizen engagement (Skocpol, Ganz, and Munson 2000; Tarrow 1996). In other cases, this collective organizing emerged organically as a way to defend entitlements or other policies beneficial to a group (Campbell 2002; Mettler 2007). While some caution that collective organizing is not always cause for celebration, most of the evidence from high-capacity democracies suggests that collective behavior is the result of policies that actively include citizens in the public arena.[2]

In the African context, however, associational activity exists alongside institutions that Africans generally regard as nonresponsive and exclusionary. Afrobarometer data has confirmed that "associational life is alive and well in Africa, and high by world standards" (Bratton, Mattes, and Gyimah-Boadi 2005, 251; see also Englebert 2000, 63). Such behavior does not always correspond with political participation or engagement with the democratic system (Bratton and Logan 2006).[3] Some observers have suggested that while civic behavior in the Western context developed with clear links to the political realm, civic behavior in African countries exists in a "primordial public" without a direct relationship to the political sphere (Ekeh 1975; Hutchful 1996). The simultaneous existence of collective behavior and unresponsive institutions suggests a different dynamic than has been described in the context of advanced industrial democracies: despite the frequent and regularly documented pursuit of collective goals, African associational life has had limited impact on the political sphere (Bratton, Mattes, and Gyimah-Boadi 2005, 251).

Studies of collective behavior in Africa and in other developing countries suggest that this divergence is not due to "African exceptionalism" but is instead related to the context of low-capacity states with a limited ability to meet the needs of their citizens. In a study of Yemen, Wedeen emphasized that civic behavior emerged in spaces where the state lacks control, suggesting that "civic engagement" is not "an instrumental good leading to formal democratic institutions" but "the very activity of energetic political participation in its own right" (2009, 100). Berman's examination of Egypt indicates that associational behavior in a weakly institutionalized state emerges "as a reflection and a cause of local states' declining effectiveness and legitimacy" (2003, 259). In broader studies of Africa, Maclean (in Cammett and MacLean 2014, 157) has noted that informal collective behavior emerges "to address unmet social needs," Bratton, Mattes, and Gyimah-Boadi (2005, 251) proposed that Africans create their own civic institutions "when faced with falling economies and failing states," Bodea and LeBas (2016) observed that community associations construct "substitutes" in the absence of state provision, and van de Walle (2003, 2) noted that associational activity fills "the vacuum left by state retrenchment" after structural adjustment. These studies indicate that collective behavior emerges not only in response to inclusive policies but also as a way to compensate for ineffective service provision by the state. In this context, government neglect, rather than inclusion, produces collective behavior.

When government capacity is so low as to preclude basic service provision, exclusion from services often means exclusion from basic necessities such as health care or schooling. The material consequence thereof is that communities must find another way to provide such basic goods. In this context, collective behavior arises in response to "depressingly low expectations" regarding state provision of basic services, and it may not automatically generate political efficacy (Cammett and MacLean 2014, 208). The excluded have the option of going without, organizing to provide for themselves, or approaching nonstate service providers. These strategies are not mutually exclusive, but given the inability to rely on the government, exclusion from basic services in countries with low government capacity, such as Zambia, may increase collective behavior, as expressed in hypothesis 2a.

H_{2a}: Collective behavior is more likely for individuals with lower objective access to government services.

However, there is little reason to expect that being in a low-capacity democracy would eliminate the link between inclusionary policies and collective organizing. While material neglect may make organizing necessary, those citizens experiencing inclusionary policies may still be encouraged to engage in collective organizing, as appears to be the case in high-capacity democracies. This possibility leads to the expectation, expressed in hypothesis 2b, that those citizens may be more likely to participate in collective behavior.

H_{2b}: Collective behavior is more likely for individuals with inclusive policy experiences.

In a low-capacity state, "inclusionary" experiences—either marginalization or empowerment—indicate the interpretation that the government is at least trying to help through service provision. In this context, such service provision may lead to collective behavior through two mechanisms. First, receipt of high-quality goods and a belief in government responsiveness may generate interest-group behavior to protect those goods. Second, the government may use a collaborative approach to service provision to explicitly promote collective behavior. A political strategy of many African governments has been to encourage "self-help," where the government provides some resources while the community provides time and labor to produce basic services (Kelsall 2011, 15). In an analysis of Zambia, Baldwin (2015, 73) estimates that 23 percent of rural citizens provided their labor to such co-produced projects, while another 7 percent provided cash. These projects tend to be highly visible, as the members of the community must interact with government representatives to negotiate the terms of the project and coordinate provision of materials and labor.

This chapter analyzes this study's survey data to determine the plausibility of the two hypotheses just presented. Qualitative evidence from interviews provides additional evidence about the mechanisms driving the correlations in the survey data. A structured comparison of several field sites provides some additional causal leverage for understanding the conditions under which collective behavior is most likely in Zambia.

MEASURING AND ASSESSING COLLECTIVE BEHAVIOR IN ZAMBIA

The survey used in this study includes three questions to measure the respondents' proclivity for collective behavior and community organization: attending community meetings, joining together with neighbors to solve problems, and group membership. The distribution of each variable is in table 4. "Community meeting" is a binary variable that takes the value of 0 if the respondent reported never attending community meetings, 1 if he or she reported attending these meetings sometimes, usually, or always. "Join to solve problems" is an ordinal variable measuring the frequency with which respondents state that they organize with their neighbors to help solve community problems.[4] "Group membership" is a binary variable that takes a value of 0 if the respondent is not a member of a voluntary association, 1 if she or he is.[5] These indicators were selected to represent an array of forms of collective organizing, capturing different dimensions of collective behavior.

In addition to the indicators for specific behaviors, the analysis includes a "collective behavior index," an additive index of the other three variables.[6] Ranging from 0 to 3, this index indicates the number of collective behaviors in which each respondent reported participating. The average inter-item covariance of these three variables is quite low (0.10), an indication that engaging in one behavior does not predict the others. Therefore, this index is included due to the expectations that respondents' precise form of collective behavior may vary according to necessity and social context and that there may be a substantive difference between those who never participate, those who report one instance of collective behavior, and those who report multiple forms of

Table 4. Distribution of Dependent Variables Measuring Collective Behavior

Variable	Distribution
Attend community meetings	51.46% report some attendance
Join together with others to solve local problems	Never: 31.3% Rarely: 3.7% Sometimes: 11.6% Frequently: 53.2%
Group member	41.6% are members
Collective Behavior Index	None: 25% One: 19% Two: 27% Three: 30%

collective behavior. The models include the suite of control variables and are specified as described in chapter 3.

The data from the survey respondents allow a quantitative analysis of the relationship between their experiences with service provision and various forms of collective behavior. To interpret the patterns emerging from the quantitative data, the chapter turns to descriptions of various forms of collective organizing undertaken by interview respondents, analyzing the way they themselves conceptualize the relationship between their actions and government policy. A structured comparison of field sites provides additional evidence of the conditions under which collective behavior in Zambia is most likely. While imperfect, the qualitative data allow both an exploration of the mechanisms at play and a check against reverse causality.

Table 5 displays the result of logistic and ordinal logistic regressions (depending on whether the outcome variable was binary or ordinal, as described above). The results are expressed as odds ratios to facilitate interpretation, meaning that coefficients less than 1 indicate a negative relationship, while coefficients greater than 1 indicate a positive relationship. In table 5, coefficients for primary explanatory variables that achieved statistical significance are boxed. The results indicate a relationship between forms of collective behavior and two of the variables for service delivery: collective behavior is less likely among those respondents who have better access to government projects, and it is more likely for those who hold an empowering assessment of the government's attempts at service delivery.

Specifically, for each additional government project in their enumeration area, respondents are 27 percent less likely to join together to solve a problem, 51 percent less likely to report attending community meetings, and 27 percent less likely to engage in each additional activity listed in the index. Such results indicate a substantively large and consistent relationship between lower levels of service provision and a higher degree of collective organizing. Interestingly, however, collective behavior is also more likely for those who believe the government is trying to help them by providing services: those holding this belief are 63 percent more likely to join together to solve a problem and 36 percent more likely to participate in an additional form of collective behavior, compared to those who believe the government ignores them (the base category for the subjective assessments of government services).

These results appear contradictory: collective behavior is most likely not only for those with less objective access to resources but also for those with a more positive subjective impression that the government is trying to

Table 5. Public Service Delivery and Collective Behavior

	Group Member	Join to Solve Problems	Community Meetings	Collective Behavior Index
Objective Measure				
Government Projects	0.88	0.79**	0.66**	0.77**
	(0.06)	(0.06)	(0.05)	(0.05)
Semi-subjective Measures				
Project Experience: Empowering	1.03	1.09	1.19	1.10
	(0.15)	(0.18)	(0.19)	(0.12)
Project Experience: Marginalizing	0.97	1.12	1.11	1.01
	(0.12)	(0.15)	(0.15)	(0.09)
Project Experience: Neglectful	1.01	1.17	0.98	1.08
	(0.12)	(0.17)	(0.14)	(0.10)
Project Experience: Burdensome	1.11	1.03	0.94	1.06
	(0.26)	(0.29)	(0.24)	(0.22)
Subjective Measures				
Assessment: Empowering	1.21	1.63*	1.39	1.36*
	(0.21)	(0.32)	(0.27)	(0.20)
Assessment: Marginalizing	1.19	1.38	0.93	1.26
	(0.18)	(0.24)	(0.15)	(0.17)
Assessment: Burdensome	1.17	0.72	0.88	0.87
	(0.32)	(0.22)	(0.22)	(0.20)
Northwestern	0.68	1.21	2.63*	1.05
	(0.30)	(0.65)	(1.22)	(0.42)
Southern	0.88	1.79	14.06**	3.04**
	(0.27)	(0.64)	(4.80)	(0.77)
On-Rail	0.79	1.18	4.74**	1.37
	(0.22)	(0.38)	(1.46)	(0.32)
Urban	0.90	0.27**	0.80	0.50**
	(0.16)	(0.05)	(0.16)	(0.07)
Male	1.23	1.06	1.11	1.22
	(0.15)	(0.15)	(0.14)	(0.13)
Age	1.37**	1.50**	1.24*	1.37**
	(0.11)	(0.14)	(0.11)	(0.10)
Education	1.07*	1.01	0.99	1.03*
	(0.03)	(0.02)	(0.02)	(0.01)
Religiosity	1.09	1.08	1.26**	1.15
	(0.11)	(0.15)	(0.07)	(0.12)

Table 5.—*Continued*

	Group Member	Join to Solve Problems	Community Meetings	Collective Behavior Index
Children	1.09**	1.10**	1.05	1.10**
	(0.03)	(0.03)	(0.03)	(0.03)
Married	1.03	2.09**	1.41*	1.43**
	(0.14)	(0.32)	(0.22)	(0.18)
Formal Employment	0.89	0.91	0.84	0.86
	(0.17)	(0.19)	(0.17)	(0.15)
Unemployed	0.93	0.60**	0.67*	0.72*
	(0.15)	(0.10)	(0.11)	(0.09)
Civil Servant	1.00	0.87	1.78*	1.30
	(0.28)	(0.28)	(0.51)	(0.35)
N	1,478	1,489	1,488	1,475
F	4.26	7.40	11.25	13.31
Pr > F	0.00	0.00	0.00	0.00

help them. However contradictory, this pattern supports both of this study's hypotheses describing the relationship between service provision and collective behavior: collective behavior may arise out of the material necessity brought on by lack of government services; it might also be promoted by inclusionary interpretations of government policy. In the context of a country like Zambia, where the government actively promotes collective behavior through partial service provision and the advocacy of "self-help" projects, the latter result may be a product of the government "trying to help" through partial provision.

One additional note concerns those most likely to engage in collective behavior generally: the preceding results indicate that collective behavior is more common among older cohorts, the married, and those with more children. These demographic features indicate that such organizing is more common for those who are more established in the community and later in their life course. These results are consistent with the patterns that emerged in the interview data, in which younger respondents expressed much less agency than their older counterparts in terms of their ability to engage in any kind of community organizing. Also notable is that rural dwellers are more likely to engage in some forms of collective behavior. This finding is similar to results of other studies, which attribute higher levels of collective behavior in rural areas to the presence of denser social networks and more face-to-face inter-actions between neighbors.

The theoretical exposition above leads to the expectation that collective behavior should be more likely under either or both of two circumstances: when the lack of government service provision necessitates community orga-nizing to provide basic goods and when people hold empowering interpreta-tions of government service provision. The quantitative results are consistent with both expectations, but qualitative analysis is necessary in order to pro-vide additional support, particularly to address two issues. First, the relation-ship between lower levels of service provision and a higher degree of collec-tive behavior is consistent and substantive, but more information is necessary to rule out reverse causation—that the government directs fewer resources at areas able to provide for themselves through collective organizing. Second, the relationship between the empowering assessment of government services and collective behavior is less consistent and requires more unpacking. I the-orized two mechanisms: empowering assessments may be associated with interest-group behavior around protecting an existing share of resources, or the relationship may be due to highly visible government-sponsored self-help projects and the respondent's belief that such projects are indicative of the government trying to help his or her community.

To determine whether this interpretation of the data finds support, the following sections of this chapter pair case analysis of three field sites, which exemplify each of the characteristics described above, with evidence from in-depth interviews that illuminate the mechanisms driving quantitative results. Due to the overlap of the urban/rural divide with degree of service provision, the case analysis that follows focuses on rural and peri-urban communities, to remove the possibility that urban residence ultimately drives the different outcomes regarding collective behavior. The three sites have much in com-mon: each is rural or peri-urban and is dependent on small-scale agriculture and petty trading, and residents from each report that the government has promised more basic services than it has delivered. However, there is varia-tion in actual provision of services, both historically and currently.

New Israel, in the remote, off-rail Northwestern Province, has been his-torically neglected and is largely excluded from basic services. Sikaunzwe, adjacent to an export route in Southern Province, is served slightly better (by virtue of being on a transit corridor) and benefits from government contri-butions to "self-help" programs. Waya, in Central Province, lies in the line of rail, in an area that has historically had much better service provision. Of the four indicator services I measured (paved road, secondary school, staffed health clinic, and police post), New Israel has none, Sikaunzwe has a paved road and a clinic, and Waya has all but a police post, putting Waya above the survey sample average of 2.7, while New Israel and Sikaunzwe fall below the average. These wards also differ in the percent of the sample reporting "empowering" assessments of government service provision. In New Israel and Waya, respectively, only 12 percent and 16 percent reported empowering assessments. In Sikaunzwe, however, 32 percent of respondents reported empowering assessments—the only one of these sites to exceed the sample average of 23 percent.

These cases also vary on the outcome variable: of three collective behaviors (attending community meetings, joining with neighbors to solve problems, and belonging to a group), the average resident of New Israel reported participating in 2.3, the average resident of Sikaunzwe in 2.8, and the average resident of Waya in 0.6. By these metrics, residents of New Israel and Sikaunzwe are well above the sample average of 1.7, while Waya is well below.[7] These comparative descriptive statistics are displayed in table 6. Using these three exemplary cases, the following sections of this chapter examine the logic underlying the quantitative results. A comparison of New Israel and Waya highlights how low rates of service provision generate collective behavior. A comparison of New Israel and Sikaunzwe illuminates how self-help projects can both create empowering assessments and boost collective behavior, despite a low rate of service provision.

COLLECTIVE BEHAVIOR IN THE ABSENCE OF THE STATE

New Israel, a remote rural community outside of Solwezi, exemplifies the first pattern in the data: community organizing in response to a dearth of

Table 6. Comparative Descriptive Statistics for Exemplary Cases

Ward	# of Services	% of Assessments "Empowering"	Mean of Collective Behavior Index
Sample Average	2.7	23	1.7
New Israel	0	12	2.3
Sikaunzwe	2	32	2.8
Waya	3	16	0.6

government services. In Solwezi, a small city in Zambia's Northwestern Province, the local economy recently changed dramatically, with the reopening of a major copper mine just outside of town. Prior to the mine's reopening, Solwezi was well off the beaten path of the rail and had a sluggish economy. The massive expansion of mining operations brought a flurry of economic activity to the town of Solwezi, but the government has struggled to expand basic service provision to meet the demands of the booming urban population. Outside the small urban area, the rural villages of Solwezi District were still dominated by subsistence farming, and small farmers struggled to bring any surplus to market, due to crumbling or nonexistent infrastructure.

New Israel is one of the worst-served villages in rural Solwezi. The village was relocated in 2006 by First Quantum Minerals, to make way for expanding mining. As part of the relocation, the mine and the government promised basic amenities: a graded road, a primary school, a clinic, and houses. These services were supposed to be provided by the mine and maintained by the government, but during the time of this study's fieldwork eight years later, they were in abysmal condition. The road to New Israel was only passable for vehicles with four-wheel drive, both the primary school and the clinic had been built but never staffed, and residents complained that the "mine houses" were low quality.

To compensate for the lack of service provision, the residents of New Israel organized to provide the most basic of these services themselves. For example, four volunteers ran classes out of the school building that the mine had erected, though few of the villagers could afford to pay school fees and though only one of the teachers (the acting headmaster) had a high school diploma. Additionally, the village headman organized monthly travel to a national army service camp to negotiate for medical supplies, which were distributed collectively through the otherwise empty health clinic. New Israel's higher-than-average rates of collective behavior were clearly related to its exclusion from basic services and to the need to produce them some other way.

While New Israel is an illustrative community-level example of such organizing emerging from fewer government projects, numerous interview respondents described similar behavior. Of 172 interview respondents, 79 (46 percent) were able to describe in detail some form of collective behavior. Of these respondents, 33 described collective action they had undertaken explicitly to compensate for the lack of government service provision. These descriptions spanned all manner of projects, from building schools and markets to addressing community health, collecting garbage, and repairing communal water pumps. By far the most common activities reported had to do with mending or maintaining roads and constructing various structures for local schools.

In Zambia, poor road quality is a ubiquitous problem. In urban areas with paved roads, the pavement is often full of potholes and crumbling along the edges. While major roads and highways are retarred periodically (particularly in advance of national elections), smaller feeder roads going through urban neighborhoods are rarely maintained. In peri-urban and rural areas, most roads are covered with gravel or simply graded rather than paved and require regular maintenance (particularly during the rainy season) so that they are passable at all. Inadequate government maintenance of roads is a near-universal complaint.

Maintenance of paved and unpaved roads requires different resources. While most would agree that paved roads are preferable to the graded or graveled variety, they are expensive to maintain and require equipment and materials inaccessible to the average person. Nevertheless, people living in areas with poorly maintained paved roads still described some community attempts to make up for the government's lack of maintenance: community members contribute money toward renting machinery for repairs[8] and sometimes mobilize community labor to patch crumbling pavement.[9] Particularly with paved roads, however, there is a high cost associated with community maintenance. Respondents expressed their preference that the government should perform the work instead, because "they would actually do a better job."[10] One respondent described an attempt to build a small bridge connecting two roads when the existing infrastructure was washed away during the rainy season. While the community was successful in organizing the labor to perform the project, they were unable to procure proper materials, and their makeshift bridge washed away with the next rain. They remained without a bridge until the government was finally able to put one in place.[11]

Road maintenance is easier to organize and more effective for communities with graveled or graded roads. In these cases, respondents reported organizing labor to repair holes emerging in gravel roads,[12] gathering stones to fill "waterlogged" areas of dirt roads in the rainy season,[13] and clearing away trees and grass that threaten to encroach on dirt roads.[14] Respondents understood these actions as a specific response to lack of government performance. One rural respondent commented, "You can see that the government is not helping. . . . We take our tools, we cut the trees, we do what we can to maintain them. . . . Yeah, this side, *we* work on it."[15]

The other arena in which respondents commonly reported collective behavior replacing state provision was in the construction of various structures related to public schools. In particular, respondents reported collective efforts to build toilet blocks,[16] houses for teachers,[17] and classrooms.[18] In most of these situations, respondents report soliciting the parents of schoolchildren for a small amount of money, using the money to buy basic materials, and then organizing volunteer labor to build the structures. Because many communities regularly burn their own bricks and build their own structures, these types of projects are easier to complete without government help than larger-scale projects like road maintenance. However, respondents still report challenges, particularly around financial constraints for building materials. Referring to initiatives to build teachers' houses and toilet blocks, one respondent said, "It's not going very well. . . . The people who live in this area don't have a lot of money. . . . Sometimes they come together, then they build some toilets for the school. They cannot do enough. They don't have that support, so they can't do it themselves."[19] Nevertheless, the dearth of government projects in many areas makes such organizing necessary, even if the resulting community projects are underfunded and low in quality. One respondent stated, "We can't just depend on the government for all the services we need. . . . As a community, we can still come together and figure things out."[20]

These accounts provide additional context for understanding why reports of collective organizing are more likely for respondents with less access to government services. The way these respondents described their experiences, collective organizing emerges explicitly in response to a lack of material provision. In areas where the government is less able (or less willing) to invest in basic service provision, community members must organize themselves to produce basic services, or they simply go without them. New Israel is an example of this type of behavior at the community level, but similar dynamics were evident across individual reports of collective organizing. However, it is insufficient to examine only cases with low service provision and a high degree of collective behavior; the corollary of this argument is that collective behavior is less likely in areas with better service provision, because residents there do not face the same necessity. The following section turns to Waya, a peri-urban ward with more services but low levels of collective behavior, to examine the plausibility of this corollary.

ATTITUDES TOWARD COLLECTIVE BEHAVIOR
IN WELL-SERVED AREAS

In better-served areas, does the presence of basic services diminish the need for collective behavior? In the Zambian context, untangling the potential effects of higher levels of service provision from urban residence can be a challenge, as urbanites both have better access to services and are less likely to engage in collective behavior than their rural counterparts. However, peri-urban wards can provide a useful snapshot into areas that combine a rural atmosphere with better access to government amenities. Waya, a ward on the rural perimeter of Kabwe, provides an example of such a place.

At the time of survey administration, Waya had recently become better integrated into the peri-urban townships through a road extension project running adjacent to the village, which granted access to a functioning health clinic and a secondary school. Despite being served better overall, the residents of Waya were by no means content. They complained that the government had not yet delivered on its promises of extending the electrical grid, the piped water system, or roads into the village. Disappointment is evident in the survey respondents' surprisingly low rate of empowering subjective assessments: only 16 percent of residents believed the government was trying to help them, even though those in Waya were able to access many basic services with relative ease (as compared to more remote rural areas) due to the road extension. Despite their frustrations regarding service upgrades, there was little evidence that the community was engaging in collective organizing to address it. One of the best-served rural areas I visited, Waya evidenced one of the lowest rates of collective behavior.

In areas with better service provision, respondent descriptions of their lack of collective organizing is telling of the mechanism driving the behavior: in Waya, one respondent who denied engaging in collective organizing—or even seeing others organize—stated, "They depend on the government, and they think the government can provide everything."[21] This observation was corroborated by another respondent who said, "We don't have money for that. . . . The government does." In other areas with higher levels of service provision—areas near town centers or peri-urban villages that are served better than more remote locales—respondents observe government service provision, believe the government can and should provide services, and question how they could possibly provide services for themselves. While respondents in poorly served areas were brimming with examples of collective ventures to fill gaps in service provision, respondents in better-served areas expressed disbelief that they could do anything: "How can we provide for ourselves if the government doesn't provide?" one respondent scoffed.[22] "If the government can't, no—the people can't," another stated.[23] In general, when asked whether or not the community ever organized to help produce basic services, respondents in better-served areas simply made such statements as "The government produces all of those things."[24]

While the most common explanations for the lack of organization in better-served areas were lack of money and absence of leadership in the community,[25] one respondent expressed a deeper logic separating the better-served areas from the worst-served ones: need. In the worst-served areas, respondents organized to produce basic necessities that would be absent otherwise. In better-served areas, while problems still existed, these problems were less likely to threaten respondents' ability to perform basic tasks in daily life. Generally, respondents in these areas complained about the quality of services rather than their availability. This logic reflects in one interview with a respondent in a poor urban compound in Kabwe.

INTERVIEWER: Do you ever get together with other people in your community to solve problems or provide services together?
RESPONDENT: If we had a bad enough problem, maybe.
INTERVIEWER: So you haven't seen this happen yet?
RESPONDENT: No, not yet. There hasn't been a need yet.[26]

Residents in New Israel were engaging in collective organizing to fill the gaps left by the state, while residents in Waya, which has a higher level of government service provision, did not undertake the same degree of organization. Residents in New Israel explained their organizing explicitly as a way to compensate for the absence of the state, while respondents in Waya expressed surprise at the idea that the community would organize to provide services, as that was the government's role. These cases, alongside the logic that other interview subjects described, lend support to the mechanism linking lower levels of service provision and higher rates of collective behavior. In the absence of the state, communities organize because they have little other choice.

EMPOWERING POLICIES AND COLLECTIVE BEHAVIOR PROMOTED BY THE STATE

The comparison of New Israel and Waya illustrates the logic underlying the first hypothesis, but since neither of these communities reported inclusionary policy experiences, their activities and perceptions cannot illuminate the mechanisms underlying the second hypothesis: that collective behavior is more likely for those who have such experiences. The survey provided some support for this hypothesis, illustrating that respondents with empowering policy assessments were more likely to "join together with others to solve problems" and to have higher scores on the index, even after controlling for objective levels of service provision. I suggested two possible mechanisms: (1) interest-group behavior to defend a share of government resources or (2) highly visible self-help projects that illustrate government responsiveness to community demands yet require collective organizing on the part of the community. The qualitative data yields little evidence of the former explanation but numerous examples of the latter. At the community level, Sikaunzwe is an example of a place where self-help projects generate both empowering assessments and collective behavior. Based on the number of indicator services in Sikaunzwe (two), one would expect residents there to report less collective behavior than those in New Israel (which has no indicator services), yet residents of Sikaunzwe report more collective behavior. Despite having fewer indicator projects than Waya, residents in Sikaunzwe, are more likely to have empowering assessments of government provision. Sikaunzwe's experience with self-help projects may explain this pattern.

Sikaunzwe, a rural ward of Kazungula District in Southern Province, is poorly served, but there is more evidence of government intervention there than in New Israel, especially through self-help projects. For example, at the time of data collection, a project was underway to build a new primary school. One of the builders explained that the community had been asking for an additional school for years, due to overcrowding. The government had finally agreed to provide the building materials. The builder interviewed was a local volunteer, part of an all-volunteer crew that had taken it upon themselves to construct the school with the government-provided building materials. In this case, the villagers' collective behavior was directly linked to the government's incapacity to provide basic services, but with a key difference from the New Israel case: while residents of New Israel had been excluded from basic service provision, the government stimulated collective behavior in Sikaunzwe by providing some materials and advocating self-help.

Many other field sites evidenced similar activities as those I observed in Sikaunzwe, though collective organizing promoted by the state was less common in the interview sample than collective organizing to replace the state. In total, 12 interview respondents discussed self-help projects that had been organized by the government with partial provision. These initiatives were particularly common around construction of school structures and community health initiatives. Several respondents discussed projects in which the government would donate some supplies, while the community would donate labor and other materials (particularly locally made bricks).[27] In some cases, respondents reported contributing money to help support government-run projects;[28] in other cases, the government provided money while the community was expected to contribute labor and materials.[29] Other coproduced projects included clinic extensions and education efforts to stop the spread of infectious diseases, such as malaria, tuberculosis, and HIV.[30]

While such projects certainly promote collective organizing, respondents often expressed the preference that the government had completed the project itself, due to problems eliciting high-quality labor and sufficient community contributions. A school-building project in a peri-urban area of Kabwe encountered a number of problems. As one respondent described the idea of this self-help project, "The community provides upfront materials like burnt bricks, building sand, the roofer sand, things like that, and the government must provide the cement, the iron sheets, window frames, and so on."[31] However, several respondents indicated that this project was not going very well. One respondent, acknowledging that residents "are supposed to participate," reported, "On voluntary work, we have low quality."[32] Another respondent stated that the government was "very reluctant" to provide everything promised.[33]

While imperfect, these types of experiences may help explain the relationship between empowering subjective assessments of government services provision and higher rates of collective behavior. In these areas, respondents were well aware that the government was doing at least something to address the problems of service provision in the area. The government's promotion of self-help projects makes respondents in these areas more likely to think that the government is "trying to help," even if they would have ultimately preferred services provided entirely by the government. However, the nature of these self-help projects is that they explicitly rely on contributions from the community that require some form of collective organizing. Therefore, these types of projects demonstrate how government policies themselves can cultivate both an empowering assessment of services and collective organizing.

CONCLUSION

Evidence from this chapter supports both the hypotheses put forth in it. First, collective behavior is more likely for those who have less objective access to service provision. Second, some forms of collective behavior are more likely for those who hold empowering subjective assessments of government attempts at service provision. These results indicate that service provision in a low-capacity country like Zambia can influence behavior through multiple pathways. Through a material pathway, there is a strong link between lower rates of service provision and a greater proclivity for collective behavior. The qualitative case analysis and interview data support the interpretation that people living under conditions of inadequate service provision are more likely to organize, because they need to be able to provide for themselves. Considering the inverse, the qualitative analysis illuminated how lower levels of collective behavior in well-served areas are directly related to the expectation that the government should provide services and that the community would be unable to replace such services. Through an interpretive pathway, collective behavior is also more likely among respondents who believe that the government is trying to help them through service provision. This result is closer to what one would expect given previous findings in advanced industrial democracies, where policies generate a sense of inclusion and political efficacy that increases the likelihood of organizing. While a similar process may also occur in the context of Zambia, the qualitative data indicates that government-sponsored self-help projects account for at least part of the connection between inclusionary policy and collective organizing.

There are several ways of interpreting these results. Examining only the data supporting hypothesis 2a and its corollary, that collective behavior is more likely among respondents with less access to government services and is less likely among those in well-served areas, one might conclude that the government simply dampens the impulse for collective behavior. If collective behavior is understood as a generally positive social feature, it would be reasonable to suggest that government intervention undermines these desirable group dynamics and that people would perhaps be better off in the absence of the state. In particular, advocates of limited government may understand these findings to be evidence that communities work together better when the government is less involved. Referring to India, Krishna has argued, "Citizens' capacities for mutually beneficial collective action can be enhanced through purposive action. The state can retreat gracefully in this manner" (2002, 3). Indeed, some might suggest that the retreat of the state is the best possible option, particularly when the state has problems with quality of governance.

At least in the case of Zambia, however, the state does not "retreat gracefully"; rather, it leaves a gap that communities do their best to fill. Despite their best efforts, volunteer teachers without training are a poor replacement for trained educators, a community clinic cannot run without medication, and farming cooperatives cannot grow as large a surplus without promised agricultural inputs from the government. While the communities described in this chapter explained their collective organizing as an answer to inadequate government service provision, they also acknowledged that they did not have the capacity to provide for themselves the same quality of goods that the government should be able to provide. As Joseph noted, when the state atrophies, "community groups cannot operate a national health and education system" (1999, 68). Many respondents expressed frustrated desires that the government would come to provide services, since the government's capacity to achieve quality provision is theoretically much greater than the capacity of communities. However, despite respondents' general dissatisfaction with this state of affairs, it is possible that there are still positive spillover effects into the realm of political participation, if collective behavior in this context generates civic skills in the same way it has been shown to do elsewhere. This possibility is taken up in chapter 6.

Another interpretation of these results would focus on the data supporting hypothesis 2b, showing how certain inclusionary policies that the government pursued also boosted collective behavior. The qualitative data indicated that this relationship exists partly because the government intentionally promoted collective organizing through partial service provision and advocacy of self-help projects. Under these circumstances, collective organizing is not only necessary but also indicative of the government targeting a particular community for service improvements. Particularly if collective behavior generates civic skills that spill over in the political realm, this configuration represents the best of both worlds: inclusion in the government's service provision agenda alongside policies that promote collective organizing.

Most respondents agreed that the best possible situation would be if the government were simply able to engage in universal service provision. In a country with a limited capacity to provide basic services, particularly outside urban areas, the government's approach to service provision has a discernible impact on collective behavior. Collective organizing plays an important role in a community's ability to produce basic services, but it may also influence the extent to which communities can channel their political energies effectively into formal politics. Because of the expectation that collective organizing generates social capital that influences political participation, chapter 6 examines these spillover effects by including collective behavior as an independent variable predicting political participation.

CHAPTER 5

Piquing Interest
Policy Experience and Political Engagement

Like collective behavior, political engagement is consistently one of the most important predictors of political participation. In addition to being an important predictor, it is an interesting outcome in its own right; democratic governance depends not only on participation but on citizens' willingness to express an interest in the political system. A functional democracy requires an engaged populace. The quality of democracy in a country is surely compromised if citizens lack interest in the political realm, neglect to talk about political issues, or fail to follow current affairs. Scholarship in high-capacity democracies has indicated that public policy has great potential to influence political engagement. When citizens connect their experiences with policy to the political realm, such experiences may pique or dampen their interest in public affairs. In low-capacity countries in particular, service delivery is the most visible form of public policy and can serve as an indicator of whether the government is responsive to the needs of its constituents. Yet there is no clear formula for creating an engaged populace; many types of policy experience might lead to a greater degree of political engagement. On the one hand, positive experiences may create satisfaction with government performance and greater psychological investment in the political system. On the other hand, being frustrated with government performance may make people agitated, ready to mobilize around the need to change their circumstances. In a low-capacity democracy like Zambia, any kind of experience with service delivery—save outright neglect—might generate a greater degree of political engagement. However, one might not expect that engagement emerging from such varied experiences would operate the same way or have the same political consequences.

Though both collective behavior and political engagement tend to be closely associated with other forms of political participation, they operate through different mechanisms, and their relationship with policy experiences differs as well. Chapter 4 demonstrated that collective behavior was most closely related to an objective lack of services, consistent with a material effect of public services (or the lack thereof). While there was a link between empowering assessments of services and collective behavior, this link was less consistent and appeared to be related to the specific nature of self-help projects. However, as political engagement is a psychological state rather than an action, it is more likely to be subject to interpretive policy effects. Unlike collective behavior (or the other response variables discussed in this book), political engagement entails no action or costly activities; it is simply a measure of the extent to which people express an interest or psychological investment in politics. While material factors certainly influence the extent to which people allocate mental and emotional energy to politics, it is likely that substantial variation in political engagement is the result of individuals' subjective interpretations of their experiences with the government. Indeed, the results in this chapter demonstrate a close relationship between subjective measures of policy experience and political engagement, but no relationship at all with objective measures.

Furthermore, the results presented here differ from what one might expect in the context of a high-capacity democracy. Numerous policy feedback studies of the American context have found that policies influence political interest and efficacy in a straightforward manner: positive experiences increase engagement; negative experiences decrease it (e.g., Campbell 2002; Soss 1999). However, the extent to which citizens connect public policy to the political realm is likely to be influenced by expectations of what the government can do, as well as actual government presence. In developing democracies like Zambia, public expectations about what the government can reasonably accomplish vis-à-vis service provision are lower than they are in democracies with more advanced economies. As a result, citizens may have a dramatically different interpretation of the services they encounter than would a person in a high-capacity democracy.

Based on these observations, this chapter presents evidence that encounters in Zambia with any form of services should increase political engagement relative to experiences of neglect. This argument hinges on the intuition that any level of contact with government projects in a developing country like Zambia should increase the extent to which individuals are interested in politics, regardless of whether they translate such interest into action. This argument reflects expectations about the Zambian polity that differ from the context of a higher-capacity democracy. If policy influences political engagement through interpretive (rather than material) pathways, one would expect the relationship between policy and engagement to vary across different political contexts. In the Zambian context, expectations about what the government can reasonably provide are low, which influences the way that people interpret their experiences with policy.

This chapter proceeds to discuss the existing scholarship on political engagement and its relationship to public policy, with particular attention to the way this link might manifest in low-capacity democracies like Zambia. The theory elaborated here leads to the hypothesis that any contact with government-provided services in a low-capacity democracy should increase political engagement. I test the plausibility of this hypothesis quantitatively with survey data, then turn to qualitative interview data to examine the mechanisms through which different types of policy experience lead to political engagement. The chapter concludes by considering the implications of these results, especially with regard to the possible links between political engagement and subsequent political participation.

POLITICAL ENGAGEMENT IN LESS-DEVELOPED DEMOCRACIES

There is little scholarly consensus on what "political engagement" actually means and how best to measure it. Scholars sometimes measure political engagement through expressed interest in political activities, political knowledge, or (inversely) the number of times that respondents answer "don't know" to politically oriented survey questions. Its relationship to political participation is also convoluted. Researchers treat political engagement sometimes as a cause of other behaviors (Burns, Schlozman, and Verba 2000; Verba, Schlozman, and Brady 1995) and sometimes as a by-product of political participation (Bowler, Donovan, and Hanneman 2003). Despite this conceptual confusion, most literature treats political engagement as particularly important for explaining gaps in political participation that persist after controlling for other individual-level traits. As a theoretical concept, it appears most often with regard to gendered gaps in political participation, particularly in the United States. For example, such gaps that persist (statistically) in the United States after controlling for education, income, employment, and other standard individual-level traits finally disappear after including political engagement variables like "political interest" (Burns, Schlozman, and Verba 2000). Following the best practices of existing research, I here conceptualize political engagement to be a combination of interest in politics, proclivity to talk about politics, and an interest in following current affairs.[1]

While political engagement is one of the most consistently important predictors of formal political participation, engagement and participation share many of the same individual-level predictors, making it difficult to isolate engagement as its own independent (or dependent) variable. If the same slew of usual suspects—income, education, sex—predict both political participation and political engagement, the latter is not particularly meaningful as an explanatory variable or especially interesting as a response variable. However, I argue that the broader context of public policy influences political engagement beyond what demographic characteristics might predict. If context (particularly the context of basic service delivery) can influence political engagement and if such engagement can precipitate political participation under the right circumstances, it is essential to understand how contextual variables may influence political engagement.

The literature that examines political engagement directly treats it as a function of either political resources (Bowler, Donovan, and Hanneman 2003) or psychological disposition (Atkeson and Rapoport 2003). The "political resource" explanation emphasizes the same resources that predict political participation (education, income, employment, and other standard predictors) and is therefore not especially relevant to this study. These resource explanations tend to focus on material resources, such as the way increased income might provide individuals with more opportunities for political involvement. Researchers approaching political engagement in this manner tend to conflate political engagement and political participation. Furthermore, these standard resource models have performed very poorly in predicting political behavior in African countries, where income and employment are largely unrelated to political interest or participation (Bratton, Mattes, and Gyimah-Boadi 2005). Accordingly, one might not expect material effects of service delivery to have much of an independent relationship to political engagement as a dependent variable in a low-capacity context.

The psychological approach to political engagement considers that some members of a polity may feel systematically alienated from politics, resulting in low levels of engagement in the political system. For example, political interest is lower for racial minorities and women in the American context, even after controlling for education and wealth (Verba, Schlozman, and Brady 1995, 349). Rather than assuming something inherent about levels of political interest of the poor, the less educated, racial minorities, and women, it is useful to understand how structural characteristics of the polity may dampen the level of interest of these groups: the political system may erect barriers to entry for the poor or less educated, racial minorities may feel alienated from the government because of racial patterns in policing, and women may be less interested because the upper echelons of politics continue to be dominated by men. Many studies look to factors like descriptive representation to understand why marginalized or minority groups are less politically engaged, suggesting that their inability to find candidates or elected officials who "look like" them creates a psychological barrier to political participation (Atkeson and Carrillo 2007; Wolbrecht and Campbell 2007). One interpretation of this work is that certain groups become politically marginalized when they feel that the government is not open or responsive to them (Reingold and Harrell 2010).

Such findings suggest that public policies or other structural characteristics of a political system may influence political attitudes in a way that is distinct from material effects. This approach to understanding the structural determinants of political engagement is commensurate with studies from the United States that highlight lower levels of participation among groups that are subject to stigmatizing public welfare programs, despite the fact that these programs presumably improve their material circumstances and should, based on political resource explanations, increase political engagement and/or political participation (Bruch, Ferree, and Soss 2010). Therefore, one would expect those who have had positive experiences with public policy to have higher levels of political engagement, presumably due to the sense of being included in, rather than alienated from, the public arena.

This expectation, drawn from studies in high-capacity democracies, presupposes that individuals will regard empowering policies positively and marginalizing, neglectful, or burdensome policies negatively. However, such a presupposition may not translate directly to low-capacity democracies. In particular, it rests on the assumption that a high-capacity government plays an active role in deciding which benefits to confer onto which groups: the implementation of empowering policies is an intentional action meant to appease certain groups; marginalizing policies may be stigmatizing or miss the mark in a way that suggests the government cares little about certain groups; neglectful policies may indicate explicit exclusion; finally, burdensome policies may denote active repression (Schneider and Ingram 1993).

One cannot make the same assumption of a low-capacity government. While empowering policy experiences are still likely to be pleasing to the groups that receive them, people might not necessarily interpret their experiences with the degree of intentionality described above. Those receiving marginalizing policies may intuit that the government simply lacks the resources to accommodate their needs more carefully; those subject to neglect may understand that they are simply beyond the reach of government projects; those experiencing burdensome policies may attribute the policy to the myriad hardships associated with financial austerity or crises of development. Indeed, these differences are reflected in the way that scholars study policy feedback in high-capacity and low-capacity countries: studies examine the nature of programs in high-capacity countries to understand the extent to which they are stigmatizing or inclusionary, empowering or paternalistic (e.g., Soss 1999, 2007; Bruch, Ferree, and Soss 2010). In studies of low-capacity countries, scholars tend to focus more simply on whether certain services exist at all (MacLean 2010; Bleck 2013; Hern 2017).

Considering the way the low-capacity context influences respondents' interpretations of their policy experiences, it stands to reason that people may have a more generous interpretation of what the government is trying to accomplish given highly constrained resources. In a low-capacity state like Zambia, residents are well aware that the government is limited in what it can realistically accomplish. There are two major implications of this reality. First, the category of comparison is likely to be different between a low-capacity democracy and a high-capacity one. In a high-capacity democracy, one might compare the receipt of subpar services (such as an underfunded, understaffed school) to the ideal of well-functioning services (a well-funded school with an abundance of qualified personnel). In a low-capacity democracy like Zambia, one might compare an underfunded, understaffed school against the alternative of having no access to a school at all. Shifting the baseline comparison category has enormous implications for the way that people interpret their experiences with policy. In a high-capacity democracy, such an underfunded school may be an indication of relative deprivation, while in a low-capacity democracy, it may be an indicator of relative privilege—even if the objective rate of service delivery is still subpar.

The second implication related to the relative capacity of a country has to do with citizens' perceptions of the intentionality of policy. In a high-capacity democracy, citizens are likely to interpret the policies directed at them as being the product of intentional decisions made by policymakers (whether or not this assumption is accurate). As a result, receipt of subpar or marginalizing services may indicate an intentional slight on the part of policymakers. In a low-capacity democracy, real resource constraints may reduce perceptions of intentionality. It is perfectly plausible that an area has been marginalized with regard to service provision due to resource constraints rather than intention. This perception of intentionality may shape respondents interpretations of what a certain level of service provision means for them politically. While citizens in a high-capacity country may interpret the receipt of subpar services to be a consequence of political will, citizens in a low-capacity country may interpret the receipt of such services as a combination of political will and governmental capacity.

Returning to the policy experience typology with these contextual details in mind, I expect there to be a wide range of experiences that might encourage political engagement. First, I would expect policy experiences falling along the inclusionary dimension—empowerment and marginalization—to generate more political engagement. As elaborated in chapter 3, those who have experiences along the inclusionary dimension of the typology should feel more engaged because of the psychological sense that the government is at least making attempts to meet their needs. These attempts may fall short, particularly in the case of marginalizing experiences. However, as described above, even an underwhelming experience with public service provision is an indication of government effort and is likely better than the alternative (no service provision). I also expect that policy experiences along the "awareness" dimension would precipitate a higher degree of political engagement. The typology defines this dimension as the sense that the government is aware of the respondent's needs and either makes explicit attempts to meet those needs (empowering) or explicit attempts to undermine them (burdensome). Either way, respondents along this dimension should feel highly visible to the government, a condition that is likely to result in a greater degree of political engagement—whether it generates appreciation or ire.

According to this logic, this chapter proceeds to test hypothesis 3.

H_3: Political engagement will be higher for those experiencing policies that are inclusive or reflect awareness.

This hypothesis encompasses the logic above, predicting a greater degree of engagement for those with empowering, marginalizing, or burdensome experiences. Indeed, it suggests that the only group with depressed engagement should be those who feel neglected—both excluded from government provision and with no sense that the government is aware of their needs. This hypothesis predicts that a broad range of policy experiences will result in a higher level of political engagement, but I also anticipate that political engagement might manifest differently across these different groups. Therefore, this chapter proceeds to use survey data to test the hypothesis, then turns to qualitative data to examine how those in different policy experience categories explain their political engagement.

MEASURING AND ASSESSING POLITICAL ENGAGEMENT IN ZAMBIA

To assess the relationship between various experiences with service delivery and political engagement, this chapter analyzes survey questions concerning measures of political engagement, all of which are binary variables. The variable "talk about politics" takes the value of 1 if the respondent reports ever talking about politics, 0 if the respondent states that he or she never talks about politics. The variable "interest in politics" takes the value of 1 if the respondent reports being at all interested in politics, 0 if the respondent reports lack of interest in politics. Finally, the variable "follow news" takes a value of 1 if the respondent reports attempts to gain access to the news via newspapers, radio, or television, 0 otherwise.[2] The "political engagement index" is an additive index of the other three variables, ranging from 0 to 3. The index allows analysis of the degree of political engagement reported, based on the assumption that respondents who are more engaged would report more activities. Table 7 reports the distribution of each variable. The modeling strategy and the control variables are the same as described in chapter 4.

Table 8 displays the results of logistic and ordinal logistic regressions, expressed as odds ratios for ease of interpretation. These results demonstrate that the relationship between government policy and political engagement is confined to the more interpretive dimensions of policy experience: there is no relationship between the objective measure of government projects in an area and respondents' political engagement, across any of the indicators. However, there is a relationship between the likelihood of political engagement and the semi-subjective measures of "policy experience" (description of service provision anchored to a specific policy identified by the respondent) as well as the fully subjective assessments of government policy (reflecting respondents overall impressions, but not connected to a specific policy). The trend in the data is that political engagement is consistently higher for those who describe empowering or marginalizing experiences or assessments and sometimes higher for those reporting burdensome experiences or assessments.

Table 7. Distribution of Dependent Variables Measuring Political Engagement

Variable	Distribution
Talk about Politics	49.3% report talking about politics at least rarely
Interest in Politics	40.7% report at least some interest in politics
Follow News	75.3% report attempts to access news
Political Engagement Index	None: 14.3%
	One: 34%
	Two: 24%
	Three: 28%

Table 8. Government Service Provision and Political Engagement

	Interest in Politics	Talk about Politics	Follow News	Political Engagement Index
Objective Measure				
Government Projects	1.01	1.00	1.00	1.01
	(0.07)	(0.07)	(0.08)	(0.06)
Semi-subjective Measures				
Project Experience:	1.41*	1.37*	0.99	1.33*
Empowering	(0.21)	(0.21)	(0.21)	(0.17)
Project Experience:	1.41**	1.39*	0.85	1.26*
Marginalizing	(0.18)	(0.19)	(0.15)	(0.13)
Project Experience:	1.27	1.28	0.87	1.17
Neglectful	(0.17)	(0.18)	(0.16)	(0.12)
Project Experience:	1.69*	1.53	0.71	1.32
Burdensome	(0.42)	(0.38)	(0.24)	(0.26)

Table 8.—*Continued*

	Interest in Politics	Talk about Politics	Follow News	Political Engagement Index
Subjective Measures				
Assessment: Empowering	1.27	1.54*	0.96	1.37*
	(0.22)	(0.27)	(0.20)	(0.20)
Assessment: Marginalizing	1.45*	1.64**	1.60*	1.64**
	(0.22)	(0.26)	(0.31)	(0.21)
Assessment: Burdensome	1.22	1.92**	1.20	1.49
	(0.30)	(0.48)	(0.34)	(0.33)
Northwestern	1.55	2.29	0.63	1.72
	(0.68)	(1.06)	(0.37)	(0.74)
Southern	0.90	1.31	1.65	1.14
	(0.26)	(0.38)	(0.66)	(0.30)
On-Rail	1.51	1.64	1.79	1.80*
	(0.43)	(0.50)	(0.61)	(0.45)
Urban	0.69*	0.77	3.51**	1.06
	(0.13)	(0.15)	(0.81)	(0.17)
Male	1.83**	1.79**	2.35**	2.12**
	(0.22)	(0.23)	(0.37)	(0.22)
Age	1.01	0.93	0.85	0.92
	(0.08)	(0.08)	(0.08)	(0.06)
Education	1.11*	1.22**	1.44**	1.23**
	(0.04)	(0.05)	(0.08)	(0.04)
Religiosity	1.00	0.93	1.23**	1.02
	(0.06)	(0.05)	(0.09)	(0.02)
Children	1.02	0.98	1.01	1.00
	(0.02)	(0.02)	(0.03)	(0.02)
Married	0.86	1.16	1.37	1.10
	(0.12)	(0.16)	(0.24)	(0.13)
Formal Employment	1.00	0.82	0.87	0.88
	(0.18)	(0.16)	(0.24)	(0.14)
Unemployed	0.80	0.64**	0.64*	0.68**
	(0.12)	(0.11)	(0.13)	(0.09)
Civil Servant	0.45**	0.56	0.59	0.46**
	(0.14)	(0.18)	(0.25)	(0.12)
N	1,489	1,489	1,477	1,489
F	4.13	5.50	5.78	8.15
Pr > F	0.00	0.00	0.00	0.00

The relationship between the semi-subjective measures of policy experience and political engagement is substantively large. The semi-subjective measures—reflecting respondents' subjective descriptions of actual policies they had experienced—evidence a straightforward pattern: empowering and marginalizing experiences are consistently associated with a greater degree of interest in politics and proclivity to talk about politics. Empowering policy experiences are associated with increases of 41 and 37 percent, respectively, in respondents' proclivity to talk about and express interest in politics, and the relationship for marginalizing experiences attains a similar magnitude. These respondents score higher on the index as well, and additional empowering or marginalizing experiences are associated with increases of 33 and 26 percent, respectively, in the likelihood of an additional form of political engagement. Expressed another way, likelihood of reporting political interest was 38 percent among those reporting no empowering policy experiences and 56 percent among those who reported three empowering experiences. The relationship between empowering or marginalizing policy experiences and various forms of political engagement is not only statistically significant but substantively large. Burdensome policy experiences were associated with an increase of 69 percent in the likelihood that the respondent reported political interest. While this particular coefficient is large, burdensome experiences were less consistent in predicting political engagement across the other indicators.

The fully subjective assessments of government policy predict political participation in a similar pattern. They capture respondents' overall feelings about government service provision, not anchored by a description of a particular policy. The coefficients for the three subjective assessments reflect a comparison to neglect, which operates as the base category for this categorical indicator. While both marginalizing and empowering assessments are related to various forms of political engagement, marginalizing assessments have the most consistently significant relationship. As compared to the base category of neglect, reporting a marginalizing assessment of government services increases the likelihood of interest in politics, talking about politics, and interest in the news by 45, 64, and 60 percent, respectively. Marginalizing assessments also predict an increase of 64 percent in the likelihood of reporting one additional form of engagement. Empowering assessments are only significantly related to talking about politics and the index, and the magnitudes of these relationships are smaller, at 54 and 37 percent, respectively. Again, burdensome assessments are associated only with one outcome variable, talking about politics, though they nearly double the likelihood thereof (as compared to neglect).

The survey results demonstrate a clear pattern: those with any form of contact with government services, aside from neglect, are far more likely to express political engagement. The null results for objective measures of government projects indicates that this relationship operates primarily through interpretive pathways: respondents' interpretations of their experiences with government service provision (rather than the simple presence or absence of services) have the strongest relationship to their degree of political engagement. These survey questions say nothing, however, about the form this political engagement might take. Furthermore, the results were most consistent for those with marginalizing experiences or assessments, a bit less consistent for empowering experiences or assessments, and least consistent for burdensome experiences or assessments. Beyond the question of consistency, it would be surprising if political engagement emerging from empowering experiences appeared the same as engagement emerging from marginalizing or burdensome experiences. In the following section of this chapter, I use qualitative data to analyze the form that political engagement takes for respondents reporting different types of experiences with government service provision.

PARSING SOURCES OF POLITICAL ENGAGEMENT

This section of this chapter addresses the question of how political engagement manifests in response to such different types of policy experience. Specifically, how does political engagement emerging from empowering experiences differ from engagement arising from marginalization? Does engagement manifest differently for those who feel marginalized versus those who feel burdened? Finally, if political engagement for the marginalized and burdened emerges from a sense of frustration or anger, why would the frustration or anger emerging from neglect not foment political engagement? Using qualitative interview data, I analyze the reasoning that respondents provide for their political engagement (or lack thereof). Of the 172 subjects who sat for in-depth interviews, 65 were able to articulate why they were (or were not) engaged in politics. This analysis illuminates the mechanisms driving the results in the quantitative data.

Empowerment, Efficacy, and Engagement

Commensurate with the survey findings, most of the interview subjects who reported an empowering experience with government service provision also reported being engaged in politics. These subjects are those who reported their experiences with services as being inclusive as well as reflecting awareness of their needs, making their experiences uniquely positive. Some subjects connected this engagement directly to service provision. One man stated the reason that he was interested in politics: "because I have seen that the government is the only actor that can help deliver services for the people."[3] Similarly, others noted the importance of communicating with the government to ensure that the same level of "development" continues.[4] These respondents demonstrated a classic interest-group reaction to government services, evoking the idea that they needed to defend the share of resources they had acquired and to ensure that it continued through active participation in politics. As chapter 6 demonstrates, this type of justification for political interest reflects a high degree of political efficacy and translates directly into forms of political participation like voting and contacting officials.

Others gave much more vague responses evoking their "right" or "duty" to pay attention to what goes on in politics. These subjects spoke in terms that evoke a classic "social contract" idea of citizen-state relations. For example, one man said that he wanted to make sure that leaders are "doing the right thing" to help the Zambian people.[5] Another man said that he talks about politics with others so that he can know when the government is doing well, in order to "tell the government to continue."[6] A few more subjects stated that being informed about politics was essential for communicating their preferences to the government, offering such explanations as "We are deciding for our future" and "The more I know, the better I can make them do what I think."[7] For those subjects who both described empowering experiences with government services and explained their interest in politics, the pattern that emerged was a general sense of efficacy. Regardless of whether or not the respondents tied their engagement directly to service provision, they all described their interest in politics as related to the idea that their voices mattered in determining democratic outcomes, so that it was either in their interest or simply their duty to pay attention to current affairs, show interest, and talk about (and to) government officials. These interviews highlight precisely how experiences with policies that both are inclusionary and demonstrate awareness of needs can create a populace that is engaged and feels efficacious.

Marginalization and Ambivalent Engagement

While those who reported empowering experiences all struck a similar chord in explaining their political engagement, those who reported marginalizing experiences had far more diverse explanations—not all positive. These respondents reported policy experiences that were inclusive but that showed a lack of awareness about their needs. The policies they described were insufficient or somehow missed the mark, creating an experience that indicated the government cared enough to direct resources toward them but not enough to ensure that their needs were met. Like the group of interview subjects with empowering experiences, the majority of the group with marginalizing experiences reported some degree of engagement with politics. However, their responses covered much more thematic ground. Most of these subjects explained that their interest in politics was due to their desire for "change," but the tone of the explanations varied from hope to frustration to anger. Like the "empowered" group, some in the marginalized group also discussed their interest in politics in neutral terms that evidenced the idea of a social contract or responsibility.

Many subjects who reported marginalizing experiences with service provision stated that their interest in politics was because of a belief that interest could bring "development" and "change."[8] While these respondents indicated dissatisfaction with the current state of service provision and development, they also expressed an either neutral or positive attitude about their ability to effect change by engaging in the political process. One said, "I want the ruler to be more available so we can get help from the government"; another said, "We are behind. . . . For me, I am very much interested because I need to see development."[9] While they were certainly dissatisfied with the current state of government services and "development," these subjects were hopeful that the government might be able to address their problems by allocating more resources toward them.

Other subjects reporting marginalization expressed more frustration and disappointment fueling their interest. One stated that his interest was due to "too much suffering"; another explained that while the government had built schools, there was still a huge problem with unemployment, "so, it pains, —it pains."[10] These subjects focused their ire on the government itself, as opposed to the circumstances. One woman explained that she talks about politics because "people in positions of power seem unqualified."[11] Another stated that "the people in power are not doing anything, so we have to speak for ourselves."[12] Often, such an attitude coincided with the desire to change those in power. One subject described that he would like to "change the people in the government," while another explained, "I am just tired of this government."[13] Despite their frustration, however, these subjects still evidenced hope that things might be different under another government.

Like those who reported empowering policy experiences, a subset of interview subjects with marginalizing experiences discussed their political engagement in neutral terms, evoking the idea of a social contract or democratic duty. One said she had to "know if things are good or bad" so she could know whether or not to support the government.[14] Another simply said that politics is "something that affects us," explaining "at least being abreast with everything, that's being up to date so that certain issues we are not blind to."[15] Others spoke about paying attention so that they could make good decisions at the polls.[16] One commented, "It is my civic right. . . . Without me, no one can elect a leader to represent me."[17] Despite feeling frustrated about their experiences with the government through service provision, these respondents still focused on the importance of official political channels through which they could pursue their interests. Indeed, some interview subjects in this category appeared more interested by virtue of their frustration.

These responses are commensurate with the typological predictions regarding how marginalization may influence political engagement. The policies experienced by marginalized people are inclusionary but do not reflect awareness of their needs. By virtue of experiencing inclusion, citizens feel that the government is willing and able to direct resources toward them. However, the inadequacy of these resources in the past generates frustration, disappointment, and sometimes anger, all of which fuel a form of political engagement that is distinct from the form seen among those who had empowering experiences. Indeed, this political energy is oriented around the possibilities for change rather than the possibilities for continuation.

Burdensome Experiences and Engagement

The survey's final predictor of political engagement was having had a burdensome policy experience. Respondents with this predictor had a uniquely negative experience with policy: they perceive themselves as excluded from service delivery despite the government's awareness of their needs. This experience was much less common in the sample and did not come up frequently enough in the in-depth interviews to analyze patterns in the connection between burdensome experiences and engagement. However, the experience of one survey respondent is indicative of the mechanisms that might drive this relationship. A student surveyed in an urban constituency of Solwezi illustrates how a burdensome interpretation may spark interest. He complained that targeted load shedding (regular cuts to the electricity supply) and water disruptions were damaging his family's business, actively making their life more difficult. He reported the highest levels of interest in politics and frequency of talking about politics, because he was angry about the government's mismanagement of Solwezi's urban development.[18] This type of attitude was particularly prevalent among unemployed youth, either those who had recently graduated and were unable to find work, or those who were still in school and knew they would have trouble gaining employment when they finished. Some of these respondents energetically channeled their anger into support for opposition parties, while others seemed already disillusioned with the political system. It is easy to see why burdensome experiences would trigger anger and possibly foment political engagement. However, this relationship is less consistent in the quantitative data, and the qualitative data show no identifiable patterns that would help determine whether political engagement emerging from this type of experience might result in productive engagement with politics.

Neglect and Apathy

Finally, the corollary to the above findings is that neglect is associated with lower levels of political engagement. People in this category perceive being excluded from services as a result of lack of awareness of their needs, thinking that the government simply does not understand or recognize their demands. One might expect neglect to trigger the same kind of frustration, disappointment, and anger as marginalization, leading respondents in this category to have an interest in making demands on the government. However, the data do not support this idea. The results described above indicate that the other subjective assessment categories' positive relationship with political engagement is made explicit in comparison with neglect, which serves as the base category for that set of indicators. The quantitative evidence suggests that neglect operates differently from marginalization in its relationship to political engagement, and the qualitative data support this distinction.

While respondents reporting empowering or marginalizing experiences expressed some degree of efficacy and desire to pursue their needs through formal political channels (even if that meant electing a new government), respondents reporting neglect were far more likely to express apathy and a degree of political nihilism. When these respondents described why they were uninterested in politics, they offered such explanations as "Eh! It's irrational. It wouldn't make a difference," "It doesn't matter who is in power," or "I do hear things on the radio, but it is all the same."[19] Other respondents had a more pernicious interpretation, making such statements as "They [the government] are just lying to us," "Politics . . . is a dirty game," and "We are just being cheated."[20] A major distinction between these descriptions and those provided by subjects who felt empowered or marginalized is that the neglected subjects were much more likely to lack efficacy. Many expressed that politics "is a waste of time"[21] and that there is no point in trying to engage with the political system. One man stated, "What do you do when you are a villager? There is nothing which you can do."[22]

Returning to typological logic, the definitional elements of neglect include exclusion from service delivery and the government's lack of awareness about needs. These elements create a specific experience that leaves respondents not only frustrated and disappointed with the government but also feeling as though they have no recourse through political participation. The essential distinction between marginalization and neglect is that the marginalized have had at least some of their needs addressed by government services, even if these policies are insufficient. The very process of interacting with government agencies through service provision creates some political efficacy. Those with marginalizing experiences feel that there is at least the prospect for positive future outcomes. The neglected, however, have no reason to hold any political efficacy whatsoever. They have no experiences to suggest that pursuing ends through politics might pay off. On average, this experience therefore diminishes political engagement.

Not all respondents react in the same way to empowering, marginalizing, burdensome, or neglectful policies. Some who reported empowering policies still lacked interest in government; some who were neglected were very interested in politics, fueled by their indignation. However, both the quantitative and the qualitative analyses suggest that these different policy experiences produce different reactions on average across populations, influencing the overall likelihood that a person—or people within a community that has a uniform experience—will express political engagement.

CONCLUSION

In Zambia, political engagement is higher for respondents who report any experience with public service delivery other than neglect. Considering policy feedback effects reported in studies in higher-capacity democracies, such a finding is surprising. Typically, one would expect positive or empowering experiences with public offices to promote political engagement, while negative or marginalizing experiences should dampen engagement. However, the low-capacity context in Zambia alters what one would generally expect by influencing respondents' expectations, which, in turn, influence their interpretations of experiences with subpar service delivery. In this analysis, political engagement was much more sensitive to the semi-subjective and fully subjective measures of government service delivery than to the objective measures, indicating that the relationship between public services and political engagement runs through interpretive pathways. This concluding section of this chapter considers several implications of this analysis. Specifically, it addresses the impact of the low-capacity context, the nature of political engagement arising from different policy experiences, and the implications for other forms of political participation.

Like the findings in chapter 4 regarding collective behavior, the present chapter's findings regarding political engagement highlight the need to adjust the policy feedback framework to take into account the low-capacity context. Particularly when considering policy feedback that runs along interpretive pathways, context is of utmost importance. The respondents with marginalizing experiences in the Zambian context reported conditions that would be unacceptable in a higher-capacity democracy: overcrowded schools with high rates of teacher absenteeism, understaffed health clinics with few medical supplies, and farming inputs arriving too late in the planting season to be useful topped the list of marginalizing experiences with public service delivery. While respondents certainly register their dissatisfaction with such government services, the context in which they live colors their interpretation of such experiences. Having an overcrowded school is certainly a reason to complain, but it is far better than being in a neighboring village with no school at all.

In many cases, in a context of inconsistent service delivery, low-quality services are better than nothing. According to the interpretive logic of policy feedback, citizens may interpret subpar services as evidence that the government is making an effort to target them for receipt of government resources—especially compared to citizens in areas with less or no government service provision. While registering their dissatisfaction with the overall level of economic development in Zambia, many respondents understand that government capacity is too low to provide universal high-quality services, and this understanding influences their interpretation of marginalizing services.

As a result of the low-capacity context, political engagement may arise from many policy experiences. As described above, political engagement was more likely for those with empowering, marginalizing, and burdensome policy experiences, compared to neglect. While political engagement is generally treated as a uniform category (interest being interest), results suggest that not all political engagement is equivalent. This observation is particularly important because political engagement is rarely an end in itself; scholars are interested in political engagement because it has such a consistent relationship to political participation. An essential question, therefore, is whether political engagement arising from such different motivations has a consistent relationship to other forms of political participation. Chapter 6 takes up this question in greater detail, but some theoretical issues merit consideration here.

An important distinction that arose from the interviews was the different way that subjects described their political interest (or lack thereof). Subjects who reported empowering and marginalizing policy experiences had an important characteristic in common: people in both groups exhibited political efficacy and spoke about using the political arena to pursue their interests—either to maintain access to resources or to lobby for change. The tone of these interviews was distinct: while empowered interview subjects tended to be more satisfied (or even complacent) with their share of government services, marginalized subjects evidenced a much greater degree of frustration. Nevertheless, subjects in both categories expressed confidence in the possibility of channeling their political energy into political participation.

Interview subjects who described neglectful policy experiences lacked the political efficacy evidenced by the empowered and marginalized. The modal reaction for this group of interview subjects was to talk about politics as a "waste of time," opining that the party and politicians in government were irrelevant. Having no expectation that the government would direct resources toward them, these subjects expressed no interest in participating in the political system. This stark contrast between the marginalized or empowered and the neglected suggests that the political engagement arising from contentment or marginalization may still be channeled into political participation, while the frustration associated with neglect is likely to generate apathy rather than political action.

The final category—burdensome policy experiences—remains puzzling. It is understandable both that the feeling of being wronged by the government would generate anger and that such anger would result in a greater likelihood of talking about or expressing interest in politics. From a theoretical perspective, however, engagement arising from the "exclusion" dimension of the typology should be unlikely to yield political participation. Unlike the frustration emerging from marginalization, those angered by burdensome experiences have little reason to hold a sense of political efficacy. In fact, they have every reason to lack political efficacy. Unfortunately, the low rate of this response among the subjects who gave in-depth interviews precludes qualitative analysis to better understand the way these citizens link their experiences to the political sphere. Whether political engagement arising from a burdensome experience translates to political participation is addressed in chapter 6.

In sum, the results presented here indicate a few conclusions. First, experiences with public policy have a dramatic impact on political engagement. Indeed, in the quantitative analysis, policy experiences were among the few characteristics that had a consistent, substantively large, and statistically significant relationship to the various elements of political engagement. Second, different experiences with public policy pique political engagement for different reasons. This finding suggests that forms of engagement arising from different types of experiences may not have an equivalent effect on other forms of political participation. Finally and perhaps most important from a governance perspective, both marginalizing and empowering experiences with public service delivery increase political engagement. In fact, the relationship between marginalizing and empowering experiences and political engagement have nearly the same magnitude. In the fully subjective measure, marginalizing assessments have a larger and more consistent relationship with the various forms of political engagement than do empowering assessments. These results indicate that to build a politically engaged citizenry, quality of service provision is less important than attempts at service delivery. Demonstrating the will to provide basic services to individuals is enough to trigger greater political interest, even if those services leave much to be desired. Indeed, these results provide strong evidence that developing state capacity and developing a democratic citizenry go hand in hand.

CHAPTER 6

From Interest to Action
Policy Experience and Formal Political Participation

Formal political participation is often the primary variable of interest for political scientists, but it is a relatively rare and costly activity. Opportunities to vote come only once every few years, few people take the time to contact their representatives directly, and only the most committed have involvement with political parties or campaigns that extends beyond the act of voting. Compared to other forms of political involvement, such as community organizing around local problems or generalized interest in political issues, political action is costly (in terms of time, money, or both), and the payoff is often remote and nontangible. Because of the intermittent nature of political participation for most people and because of its disadvantageous cost-benefit structure, experiences with public policy must be exceptional to sway the extent to which people participate in the formal political system.

In this chapter, I argue that people are more likely to participate in politics through formal channels when they have had empowering experiences with service delivery, because positive policy experiences are unique in generating a sense of efficacy and the notion that the government is likely to be responsive. This expectation contrasts with the findings of chapters 4 and 5, which demonstrated that collective behavior was linked to lower rates of objective service provision and that political engagement was related to empowering, marginalizing, and burdensome interpretations of services. These contrasting predictions are important because it is typical for collective behavior and political engagement to have a positive correlation with political participation. To reconcile my argument here with the findings of the previous chapters, it is necessary to distinguish between direct and indirect effects of public policy on political participation: public policy experiences may be directly and independently related to political participation, or their relationship to political participation may be an indirect result of their relationships with collective behavior or political engagement. This chapter considers both the direct relationship between policy and participation and the indirect relationship precipitated by policy's relationship with collective behavior and political engagement.

This chapter proceeds to review some relevant literature regarding political participation and policy feedback, to advance the hypotheses that the chapter tests. It then presents the baseline analysis of the direct relationship between public service provision and political participation. Next, it turns to an investigation of the indirect relationships between service delivery and participation, examining how collective behavior mediates the relationship between low levels of service provision and higher levels of political participation. Finally, it examines the circumstances under which political engagement leads to more political participation. This chapter demonstrates that while empowering interpretations of service delivery have a direct relationship to more political participation, service delivery is indirectly related to participation through multiple pathways, at least partially mediated by collective behavior and political engagement.

POLITICAL PARTICIPATION IN LESS-DEVELOPED DEMOCRACIES

Formal political participation includes the forms of participation most often associated with political behavior: voting, contacting officials, and supporting political parties. This dimension of political behavior is most commonly theorized in democratic contexts where participation is meaningful, particularly in advanced industrial democracies like the United States. In predicting rates of political participation in advanced democracies, studies repeatedly demonstrate that education, gender, and age are the strongest demographic predictors of participation (Verba, Schlozman, and Brady 1995). These studies show that education is generally the most important determinant of political participation, that women consistently participate less than men, and that young people are less likely to participate in politics (Marien, Hooge, and Quintellier 2010). In addition, income is a fairly consistent predictor of political participation, though the research is unclear regarding whether the significance lies in income itself or its correlates, such as education and civic skills (Pacheco and Plutzer 2008).

Examinations of political participation in African democracies have repeatedly demonstrated that these same predictors do not perform as well for those places (Bratton, Mattes, and Gyimah-Boadi 2005; M. Bratton 1999; Kuenzi and Lambright 2010; Resnick and Casale 2014). Afrobarometer data demonstrates that those who are more likely to vote in African countries include rural dwellers, men, and older people, but even these demographic characteristics have small coefficients in regression analysis and explain only a small portion of variation (Kuenzi and Lambright 2010). There is no apparent relationship between income (or other experiential measures of poverty) and participation in the African context. Contrary to what one would expect given studies in higher-capacity democracies, participation in Africa's electoral regimes is highest among the rural poor, and education is not a strong predictor of participation. These empirical trends may be a result of the patterns of political mobilization observed across African countries, in which parties use a top-down strategy, leveraging local leaders, to encourage turnout (van de Walle 2012). Because social networks are stronger in rural areas, voters there can be more easily mobilized than those in urban areas (Kuenzi and Lambright 2010). Regardless of the mechanisms driving these different results, demographics used to predict rates of political participation are not nearly as strong in African countries as in the high-capacity democracies of the West.

If demographic characteristics are less predictive, something else must account for variation in political participation. As described in earlier chapters in this book, I argue that patterns of service provision may be particularly important for explaining political participation in low-capacity democracies, because it provides citizens with valuable information about the likelihood of government responsiveness. In a low-capacity democracy with newer democratic institutions, experiences with service delivery can send important messages about the possible utility of political participation.

Formal political participation differs from other categories of independent variables considered in this book, in that it has a uniquely disadvantageous cost-benefit structure. One fundamental characteristic of political participation is that it is a costly act. Voting requires time and travel; contacting officials requires time and energy; involvement in political parties or interest groups often requires both time and monetary resources (Verba, Schlozman, and Brady 1995). Furthermore, for such a costly activity, political participation has a relatively low, often intangible payoff. Early political science literature about voting puzzles over why individuals would bother exercising their right to vote, given the time associated with the activity and the low likelihood that an individual vote would have any effect on electoral outcomes (Downs 1957). Some political scientists therefore posited that political participation reflects both material interests and the norms of civic duty (Riker and Ordeshook 1968; Schram and van Winden 1991). Regardless of the extent to which political participation reflects the rational pursuit of benefits or the personal pursuit of a principle, it stands to reason that individuals should be more likely to participate in politics if they have reason to believe that the government is likely to be responsive to their demands. The way this belief would alter the cost-benefit analysis of political participation would make participation more likely to pay off.

Belief that participation will pay off is potentially even more important in the African context than in advanced industrial democracies, because, as described in chapter 1, political participation in African countries provides few opportunities to express ideological preferences. Mr. Sakubiwa Nyambe, a young man running to become a local ward councilor in Southern Province, described his frustration with this challenge to democratic politics.[1] He was brimming with ideas to improve his ward, including such projects as improving the infrastructure of the market, regulating the shebeens (informal bars run out of private residences) to address rampant alcoholism, and starting youth employment projects such as mushroom cultivation. He had decided to run with the opposition UPND because he liked the party's manifesto, which espoused a fiscally conservative, business-minded ideology and was distilled down to 10 points and made available through pamphlets. However, when he went door-to-door to campaign, he complained that no one had any interest in understanding the differences between the manifestos of the major parties; they only wanted handouts.

They would not even ask, "What are you going to do for us?" When I am doing my campaigns, I even ask them, "You are saying you are going to give me your vote, but you have not even asked me what I am going to do for you. So if you were to give me your vote, what are you voting for? So you should ask questions, of what you want me to do." So basically people are not even aware of, uh—even to go in these households, you would not even find any party manifesto. . . . Even if you go door to door campaigning, most of them are hunger-stricken, they are not financially well-to-do, so you find that even as you are visiting them they would ask for handouts: "No, I am asking for maybe a 5 kwacha, a 10 kwacha."[2] So it is like this campaign: it is just basically people asking for things.

People see political parties as vehicles for possible material benefit and generally complain that even if there were ideological differences between parties, all parties act the same way once in office. Ideological debates around the parties are common among the educated elite in Lusaka, but outside of major cities, there is little supply of or demand for ideological content in the political parties. If political participation is most useful as a bid for resources rather than an expression of political ideology, belief that the government will actually respond to one's demands is crucial.

Unlike collective behavior (which was most closely related to material elements of service provision) and political engagement (which correlated most closely with interpretive dimensions), formal political participation may theoretically be related to both. As described above, income is not a good predictor of political participation in African democracies. However, policies that selectively distribute material benefits may influence rates of participation by conferring material resources to certain members of the polity. Those who receive more desirable resources through public service provision should theoretically be better able to undertake the costs of political participation. Such resource effects are the subject of common study in policy feedback literature (Campbell 2012). I expect that access to services may influence participation in a way distinct from income. For example, access to paved roads and markets makes it logistically easier to contact politicians; similarly, access to clinics and schools makes citizens healthier and improves the civic skills they need to engage with the political sphere. Based on this assessment, citizens on the receiving end of inclusive policies—either empowering or marginalizing—should be better equipped to participate in politics than otherwise, due to a theoretical increase in resources. Both empowering and marginalizing experiences indicate a transfer of government resources to recipients. Given the resulting increase in material resources, respondents who report policy experiences along this dimension should be better able to undertake the costs of political participation than those who report neglectful or burdensome policies, ceteris paribus.

Yet material effects are not the only pathway through which policies influence political participation. The ability to undertake the costs of political participation is essential but is unlikely to increase political participation absent motivation (Verba, Schlozman, and Brady 1995, chap. 12). Interpretive effects have the capacity to alter the extent to which citizens believe that their participation will pay off; this dimension of policy feedback is why, in the United States, certain welfare policies depress political participation, despite conferring material resources to the impoverished (Soss 1999, 2007; Bruch, Ferree, and Soss 2010). On the one hand, consider those who described a marginalized interpretation of government services: if a citizen's interpretations of policy suggest that the government does not precisely understand what he or she needs or that the government designs policies in a way that do not meet his or her needs, it may result in the sense that the government is not terribly responsive. In this case, the interpretive effects of a policy (a sense of the lack of responsiveness of government) may counteract the material effects of policy (boosting participation by conferring more resources on a group). On the other hand, consider those who described empowered interpretations of government services: if a citizen believes that the government is likely to be responsive to his or her requests, the possible payoff of political participation increases. Therefore, political participation should become more likely when citizens receive resources that reflect awareness of their needs, through empowering policies. Because empowering policies both alter the ability of individuals to undertake the cost of political participation (though material pathways) and suggest the utility of such participation (through interpretive pathways), those subject to empowering policies should be more likely to engage in formal participation, relative to those who have marginalizing, neglectful, or burdensome interpretations. This likelihood, which I expect to be true for either semi-subjective or fully subjective interpretive measures, is expressed in hypothesis 4a.

H_{4a}: Formal political participation is more likely for those with empowering policy experiences or assessments.

This hypothesis concerns the direct relationship between public policy and political participation, but indirect relationships may also exist. For these indirect relationships, I expect different processes underlying material effects (related to objective service provision) and interpretive effects (related to the subjective measures of policy experience and assessment). In chapter 4, the data demonstrated that lower levels of objective service provision were associated with higher levels of collective behavior. As the political science literature regularly demonstrates the positive relationship between collective behavior and political participation, it is possible that lower levels of objective service provision are also associated with higher levels of political participation, mediated by increased collective behavior. Such a result would be counterintuitive, as lower levels of service provision indicate fewer material resources and should therefore be associated with lower levels of service provision. However, as expressed in hypothesis 4b, such a result is possible if the link between low levels of objective service provision and higher levels of political participation is mediated by collective behavior.

H_{4b}: Mediated by collective behavior, lower levels of objective service provision will be associated with higher rates of political participation.

Similarly, with regard to subjective assessments, the results from chapter 5 regarding the relationship between marginalizing or burdensome policy interpretations and political engagement generate contradictory predictions for the present chapter. One would expect marginalizing or burdensome interpretations to dampen political participation, because they suggest that the government is unresponsive. But since they are also associated with political engagement and since political engagement is positively associated with participation, the opposite may also be true: as expressed in hypothesis 4c, it is possible that marginalizing or burdensome interpretations could precipitate an indirect relationship with political participation through political engagement.

H_{4c}: Mediated by political engagement, marginalizing or burdensome policy experiences or assessments will increase political participation.

If this is the case, such a relationship is likely to disappear once we account for the relationship between policy and political engagement. Like hypothesis 4a, I expect hypothesis 4c to be true for either semi-subjective or fully subjective interpretive measures.

The hypotheses presented in this chapter predict a variety of relationships between service delivery and participation, spanning the objective, semi-subjective, and fully subjective measures of service delivery experience. However, taking account of both the likely direct influence of service provision on participation and the indirect influence of services through their relationship to collective behavior and political engagement provides a more nuanced, holistic understanding of the relationship between service delivery and polit-

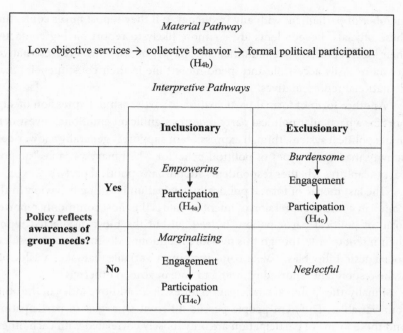

Fig. 9. Hypotheses 4a through 4c in Typological Context

ical participation. In figure 9, hypotheses 4a through 4c are represented with respect to the policy experience typology.

MEASURING AND ASSESSING POLITICAL PARTICIPATION IN ZAMBIA

To capture the relationship between service provision and political behavior, I operationalize formal political participation in several ways. These different types of behavior represent political actions that occur at different rates and require a different degree of commitment. Table 9 displays the distribution of these variables.

Contacting officials is a behavior that can occur at any time but requires intention, forethought, and more effort than something like voting. "Contact local official" and "contact MP" are binary variables that take the value of 1 if the respondent reports contacting a local government official or their member of parliament with any frequency, o if they report never contacting these officials. Respondents are far more likely to report having contacted their local representative than their MP, largely because local representatives are more easily accessible and spend more time in their constituencies than do national representatives.

Another form of formal participation is partisanship. Expression of support for a particular political party requires significant emotional investment in the political system, though expression of support is generally a lower-cost activity than other types of political behavior. The binary variable "support party" captures whether respondents support any political party.

The last metric of formal political participation is voting behavior. In the Zambian context, expression of intent to vote is the most commonly reported form of political participation. Indeed, all but the most disaffected report their intent to vote, though this measure is undoubtedly inflated as a result of social desirability bias.[3] "Vote 2016" is a binary variable that takes a value of 1 if the respondent reported planning to vote in 2016, o otherwise.[4]

Finally, the "political participation index" is an additive index of the other four variables. Different people pursue different strategies of participation, and these forms of participation are only loosely correlated with each other.[5] The index provides a measure of the intensity of an individual's commitment to political participation by capturing how many strategies of participation she or he pursues.

The results presented in table 10 demonstrate the relationship between

Table 9. Distribution of Dependent Variables Measuring Political Participation

Variable	Distribution
Contact Local Official	36.2% report contacting local officials at least occasionally
Contact MP	18.8% report contacting their MP at least occasionally
Support Party	61.1% report supporting a political party
Vote 2016	81.5% report planning to vote in 2016
Political Participation Index	None: 9.5% One: 21.6% Two: 40.1% Three: 18.2% Four: 10.5%

Table 10. Government Service Provision and Political Participation

	Contact Local Official	Contact MP	Support Political Party	Prospective Vote (2016)	Participation Index
Objective Measure					
Government Projects	0.85*	0.96	1.01	0.92	0.88*
	(0.06)	(0.08)	(0.07)	(0.08)	(0.05)
Semi-subjective Measures					
Project Experience: Empowering	1.06	1.24	1.59**	1.05	1.02
	(0.16)	(0.26)	(0.25)	(0.16)	(0.12)
Project Experience: Marginalizing	1.08	1.21	1.42**	1.06	1.00
	(0.14)	(0.22)	(0.18)	(0.14)	(0.10)
Project Experience: Neglectful	1.02	1.23	1.18	1.13	1.00
	(0.13)	(0.23)	(0.15)	(0.16)	(0.10)
Project Experience: Burdensome	1.13	1.56	1.37	1.56	1.08
	(0.28)	(0.47)	(0.36)	(0.53)	(0.26)
Subjective Measures					
Assessment: Empowering	1.50*	1.44	1.58**	1.86**	1.99**
	(0.25)	(0.30)	(0.27)	(0.38)	(0.29)
Assessment: Marginalizing	1.32	1.23	1.46*	1.87**	1.64**
	(0.20)	(0.22)	(0.22)	(0.34)	(0.21)
Assessment: Burdensome	0.83	0.81	1.48	0.89	0.70
	(0.23)	(0.27)	(0.40)	(0.27)	(0.17)
Northwestern	0.58	0.31*	1.51	0.47	0.40*
	(0.26)	(0.18)	(0.68)	(0.27)	(0.16)
Southern	0.83	0.73	1.19	1.19	1.54
	(0.24)	(0.29)	(0.37)	(0.47)	(0.40)
On-Rail	0.66	0.47*	1.36	0.78	0.57*
	(0.18)	(0.17)	(0.40)	(0.31)	(0.14)
Urban	1.23	1.04	0.67*	0.76	1.46**
	(0.22)	(0.22)	(0.13)	(0.16)	(0.21)
Male	1.19	1.30	1.51**	1.29	1.51**
	(0.14)	(0.19)	(0.18)	(0.19)	(0.15)
Age	1.39**	1.15	1.07	1.18	1.24**
	(0.11)	(0.10)	(0.09)	(0.12)	(0.08)
Education	1.02	1.02	1.05	1.10*	1.04
	(0.02)	(0.02)	(0.03)	(0.05)	(0.04)
Religiosity	1.02	1.05	1.05	1.06	1.04
	(0.04)	(0.04)	(0.04)	(0.06)	(0.03)

(continues)

Table 10.—*Continued*

	Contact Local Official	Contact MP	Support Political Party	Prospective Vote (2016)	Participation Index
Children	1.08**	1.05	1.00	1.03	1.04*
	(0.03)	(0.03)	(0.02)	(0.03)	(0.02)
Married	1.11	1.11	1.50**	1.42*	1.22
	(0.15)	(0.19)	(0.21)	(0.23)	(0.13)
Formal Employment	1.72**	1.18	0.92	1.03	1.42*
	(0.32)	(0.27)	(0.18)	(0.24)	(0.23)
Unemployed	1.00	1.01	0.66**	1.26	1.10
	(0.16)	(0.20)	(0.10)	(0.22)	(0.14)
Civil Servant	0.83	1.44	0.44**	0.82	1.01
	(0.22)	(0.43)	(0.13)	(0.31)	(0.26)
N	1,489	1,479	1,427	1,489	1,486
F	2.95	1.66	3.04	2.39	5.00
Pr > F	0.00	0.00	0.00	0.00	0.00

Note: Odds ratios for logistic and ordinal logistic regressions are reported, with standard errors parenthesized below. Statistical significance is denoted by * if $p < 0.05$, ** if $p < 0.01$.

the three different measures of policy experience and the different forms of political participation, using the same control variables and model specification as in previous chapters. A few notable trends stand out in these results. First, the objective measure of service provision has a negative relationship with several forms of political participation. Second, both empowering and marginalizing policy experiences and subjective assessments are associated with a higher degree of political participation across numerous measures. These results are consistent with all three hypotheses put forth above, but each requires a separate theoretical and methodological treatment. The following sections of this chapter assess the evidence for each hypothesis separately. The first considers the straightforward hypothesis that empowering experiences should have a direct and positive relationship to political participation. The second examines the idea that lower levels of service provision, mediated by collective behavior, may increase political participation. The third addresses the possibility that marginalizing experiences, mediated by political engagement, increase political participation. Each of these sections relies both on correlations established by the survey and on qualitative evidence from interview respondents that highlight how such experiences get translated into political behavior.

EMPOWERING EXPERIENCES AND POLITICAL PARTICIPATION

The relationship between empowering interpretations of policy experiences and political participation is the most consistent finding in the survey data. Specifically, for each additional empowering project a respondent described, that respondent's likelihood of supporting a political party increased by 59 percent. For those who had empowering subjective assessments (as compared to neglect, the base category), likelihood of contacting local officials, supporting a party, and prospective voting increased by 50, 58, and 86 percent, respectively. Empowering subjective assessments were also associated with a greater number of activities, as captured by the index. Reporting an empowering subjective assessment of government services nearly doubles the likelihood that respondents report an additional activity.

These results are consistent with hypothesis 4a. It makes sense that of all possible experiences with government service provision, those who believe the government is making an active effort to assist them are also most likely to participate. Given the uniquely negative cost-benefit structure of political participation (compared to the other forms of political behavior examined in this study), it is reasonable that individuals with more positive interactions with the government would be more likely to undertake these costs. The pattern in the data is most consistent for the subjective measure, indicating a strong interpretive dimension to this relationship. However, the primacy of subjective assessments introduces some problems for inference. The theoretical framework advanced here would suggest that actual encounters with government projects translate into positive subjective assessments and that those with positive assessments may be more likely to hold some kind of political efficacy, leading to a greater probability of political participation. Yet it is also possible that the reverse is true: that being politically active generates more positive assessments of the government, perhaps through a psychological pathway that decreases cognitive dissonance. It is more plausible that some kind of third variable, like party identification, influences both an individual's assessment of the government and his or her proclivity for participation.

This last possibility is particularly pernicious, but adding a control for support of the ruling party provides a quick check against this particular inferential challenge. Table 11 displays the coefficients for empowering experiences and assessments (for the variables that attained significance above) after controlling for party identification. The primary results are largely unchanged. The only instance in which empowering assessments lose their statistical significance is in predicting support for any political party; this change is unsurprising considering that supporting the ruling party and support for any party are inevitably closely correlated. The other change is that the coefficient for prospective voting shrinks and attains only marginal significance (p = 0.076). Despite these changes, the results remain robust: empowering assessments of the government's efforts at service provision are still positively associated with political participation.

Because the link between empowerment and participation is strongest for the fully subjective measure of policy assessment, one could interpret this data to reflect political efficacy growing out of positive experiences with the government. To support this conclusion, one would expect that those who have had positive experiences with the government through service provision would invoke a sense of government responsiveness to describe their political participation. Indeed, this type of explanation was prominent among those interview subjects who were able to describe what motivated their participation. One woman explicitly stated that the reason she planned to vote was because "the ruling party is bringing development, and [we] want the ruling party to continue providing these services."[6] This sentiment was repeated frequently for those who described empowering experiences with public services. One subject enthusiastically exclaimed that he participated because "this government is delivering through and through."[7] For some of these subjects, support for the ruling party seemed to motivate both their descriptions of empowering policy experiences and their political participation.[8] As suggested above, partisanship drives some of the relationship between policy

Table 11. Empowering Experiences, Party ID, and Political Participation

	Contact Local Official	Support Political Party	Prospective Vote (2016)	Participation Index
Support Ruling Party	1.11	4.46**	3.10**	1.60**
	(0.15)	(0.63)	(0.52)	(0.17)
Project Experience: Empowering	1.06	1.56**	0.98	1.01
	(0.16)	(0.26)	(0.16)	(0.11)
Assessment: Empowering	1.46**	1.15	1.45*	1.77**
	(0.25)	(0.21)	(0.31)	(0.26)
N	1,489	1,427	1,489	1,486
F	2.89	4.58	2.97	5.24
Pr > F	0.00	0.00	0.00	0.00

Note: Odds ratios for logistic and ordinal logistic regressions are reported, with standard errors parenthesized below. Statistical significance is denoted by * if $p < 0.10$, ** if $p < 0.05$.

experience and participation. But many subjects who reported empowering experiences were much more critical in describing the reasons for their political participation.

Many subjects who described empowering experiences with policy explained their political participation as a tool for holding the government accountable. For example, one stated that it was important to vote because "once the government says they will do something, you have to vote to make sure they follow what they say."[9] Another said that voting is an opportunity to talk to the government and that "if the government is doing well, [we] can tell the government to continue."[10] Some of these descriptions of accountability were from those who were cautiously supportive of the ruling party, making it challenging to divorce participation from tepid partisanship.

The most informative group was those who described empowering experiences, actively participated in politics, and were critical of the government. One man, an active participant in politics, described the positive changes he had experienced in infrastructure development since the ruling party came to power. When it came to his reasons for participation, however, he explained, "If I see the government is not doing well when the people are complaining, I have to vote against the government. Maybe there is no one who can come and do the right things which the people want, ok? This is why I vote. I need development in my country."[11] After another man explained his positive experiences with government service provision, he provided even more detail about his participation.

> Well a councilor is being contacted so that he knows exactly what we normally want to be done in our community. You can see like roads here. This roads, I don't know when they were last worked on. There are some schools which we need some desks. There are even clinics at times when we don't have medicine. So those things at least the councilor must be aware so he can at least take it to the chambers and see what they can do.[12]

In these cases of subjects reporting empowering experiences, their enthusiasm for participation was not purely due to their existing partisanship. Rather, they participated in politics because of a belief in government responsiveness, a belief that if they were dissatisfied with the state of development, they could pursue change through formal political channels such as voting and contacting representatives.

These descriptions of political participation based on accountability and government responsiveness are particularly remarkable when compared to the inverse: descriptions of neglect and a lack of political participation. People who described neglect were statistically much less likely to participate, and their qualitative accounts tended to reflect a sense of resignation. As one woman put it, "We don't vote, because we don't see change. It doesn't matter who is in power."[13] Others made such statements as "These people, they are too busy for commoners like us" and "It is just a waste of time. . . . Nothing would change."[14] These qualitative accounts suggest that neglect leads to decreased proclivity for participation, not the reverse. One woman described how she used to vote and spent time contacting her councilor about digging a new borehole in her area. She said that when she failed to get a response, she stopped bothering to vote.[15] Many respondents explained their frustration with the sense that nothing they could do would change their lot. When asked why she never contacted her local representatives, one woman scoffed,

> I don't even know him. . . . It is all the same. The councilor, the president, it's all the same. It's one thing. All they need is to feed themselves. When they feed themselves, they don't recognize us. We are the ones who vote for them to be there. We chose them to stand for us; now they don't. You see? Like just look for themselves in their accounts. Greed effect.[16]

Of course, these relationships between policy experiences and participation are probabilistic, not deterministic, and people vary in their responses to various policy experiences. Given these results, one particular trend identified in the quantitative analysis in the preceding section of this chapter requires further exploration. While those with neglectful assessments of the government participate less than those with empowering assessments (across multiple indicators), those with objectively less service provision are more likely to engage in some forms of participation. I hypothesized that this link may be due to the role of collective behavior in generating more political participation in a low-provision environment. The following section of this chapter explores that possibility.

TRANSLATING COLLECTIVE BEHAVIOR INTO POLITICAL PARTICIPATION IN THE ABSENCE OF THE STATE

Evident in the baseline regression was the negative relationship between objective government service provision and some forms of political participation. Specifically, access to an additional government project decreased the likelihood that a person reported contacting their local representative, by 18 percent, and the likelihood of each additional form of participation, by 14 percent. In other words, those with less objective access to services were more likely to contact their local councilor and were, on average, more politically active than those with more services. I hypothesized that this outcome, while counterintuitive, could occur due to the relationship between service provision and collective behavior. Theoretically, such an outcome would occur if collective behavior mediates the relationship between government service provision and political participation: having access to fewer government projects increases collective behavior, which, in turn, is associated with a higher degree of political participation. The results presented in table 12 lend support to this idea. Repeating the analysis above and including the collective behavior index as an independent variable completely eliminates the relationship between government projects and political participation.

These results are suggestive of mediation but are not definitive. To examine this relationship with more precision, I use Hicks and Tingley's (2011) method of causal mediation analysis to determine the extent to which each respondent's level of collective behavior mediates the relationship between lower levels of service provision and higher levels of political participation.[17] This statistical package fits models based on the observed values of the outcome and mediator variables, generates model parameters based on their distribution, and runs simulations using a quasi-Bayesian Monte Carlo

Table 12. Government Projects, Collective Behavior, and Political Participation

	Contact Local Official	Participation Index
Government Projects	0.94	0.94
	(0.07)	(0.05)
Collective Behavior Index	2.95**	2.01**
	(0.25)	(0.11)
N	1,478	1,475
F	5.65	7.92
Pr > F	0.00	0.00

Note: Odds ratios for ordinal logistic or logistic regressions are reported, with standard errors parenthesized below. Statistical significance is denoted by * if $p < 0.10$, ** if $p < 0.05$. Standard errors are clustered by ward, the level of survey stratification. A full suite of controls was included but is not reported.

approach to estimate the direct, indirect, and average causal mediation effects of the mediating variable (Hicks and Tingley 2011, 5). Applying this method to the relationship between service provision, collective behavior, and the participation index indicates that collective behavior mediates the relationship between low levels of service provision and higher levels of political participation at a mean rate of 35 percent. Because Hicks and Tingley's analysis assumes a causal relationship between the variables and because the models specified above are not causally identified, it is also necessary to examine how sensitive the results are to correlation in the error terms of the equations in the mediated model. Using their method of sensitivity analysis, the results are robust for a correlation up to 29 percent between the error terms in each model, after which the actual mediation effect is statistically zero. These results are consistent with the idea that objective measures of service provision have little direct effect on political participation but have an indirect effect through collective behavior, supporting hypothesis 4b.

Evidence from the interviews supports this interpretation, particularly as related to contacting officials. When people in more remote areas with fewer services would describe collective organizing, it was often in the form of community meetings, after which a community representative would attempt to contact the local councilor. For example, a subject in the peri-urban village of Simoonga in Kazungula District reported a community meeting about improving access to water. The village committee called and organized the meeting, then the committee leadership went to contact the local government to address these concerns.[18] Similarly, a subject in the much more remote village of Sekute in Kazungula District reported a community meeting held to discuss constructing a clinic, after which community leaders were tasked with contacting the government.[19] These examples shed some light on interview subjects in more remote areas who talked about contacting the government in the second person, stating, for instance, "We contact representatives." When pushed further, many of these respondents specified that community leaders contact officials, often after some kind of community meeting.[20]

This semantic conflation between "I" and "we" might also help explain why the survey results linked lower levels of service provision to contacting local officials but not to other outcome variables (other than the index). In the cases described above, collective behavior—particularly attendance of community meetings—seems to mediate the relationship between a lower degree of objective service provision and an increased likelihood of reporting contacting officials. At the very least, the qualitative explanations of what occurs during community meetings and the use of second-person language when describing contacting officials can help to explain why those with objectively fewer services are more likely to report contacting officials.

CHANNELING POLITICAL ENGAGEMENT INTO POLITICAL PARTICIPATION IN THE PRESENCE OF THE STATE

In this section of this chapter, I examine the finding that marginalizing assessments of the government are linked to an increase in the likelihood of party support and prospective voting and in the number of political acts a respondent reports. The baseline results indicate that each marginalizing policy experience increases the likelihood of party support by 42 percent. Similarly, holding a marginalizing subjective assessment of government services was associated with increases of 46 and 87 percent in the likelihood of supporting a party and voting, respectively. Marginalizing subjective assessments were also associated with an increase of 64 percent in the likelihood of participating in each additional form of political participation.

I hypothesized that only empowering policy experiences should be strong enough to directly precipitate political participation, but that marginalizing or burdensome experiences may increase participation indirectly, through their relationship with political engagement. The data indicate that this may be true for marginalizing (but not burdensome) experiences. Just as the preceding section of this chapter identified collective behavior as a mediator, one would expect political engagement to mediate the relationship between marginalizing experiences and party support, prospective voting, and the participation index.

In this case, there is less support for the interpretation that political engagement mediates the relationship between marginalizing experiences or assessments and political participation. As the results in table 13 demonstrate, including the political engagement index eliminates the statistical significance of marginalizing assessments in predicting party support and reduces the coefficients for marginalizing experiences and assessments in party support, prospective voting, and the index. But after controlling for political engagement, there is still a statistically significant relationship between marginalizing experiences and assessments and some forms of participation. These mixed results are consistent with the possibility for partial mediation.

Employing Hicks and Tingley's (2011) method to estimate the extent to which political engagement mediates the relationship between marginalizing subjective assessments of government service provision and the political participation index indicates (at most) partial mediation. This analysis suggests that political engagement mediates around 23 percent of the relationship between marginalizing assessments and political participation, robust to a correlation of up to about 24 percent between the error terms of the models. These results indicate that marginalizing experiences still have a substantively large and direct relationship to political participation. While this result runs counter to my initial expectations, analysis of interviews can help to explain why.

In the interview sample, as in the survey sample, respondents reporting marginalizing experiences participate in politics at approximately the same rate as those reporting empowering experiences.[21] However, they have very different explanations as to why they participate. While those reporting empowering experiences tended to explain their participation through a combination of demands for continuity or accountability and a belief in government responsiveness, those reporting marginalizing experiences overwhelmingly described their participation as a bid for change. Some were straightforward, simply justifying participation with such statements as "Maybe things, they can change."[22] Others invoked democratic principles,

Table 13. Marginalizing Experiences, Political Engagement, and Political Participation

	Support Party	Vote 2016	Participation Index
Project Experience: Marginalizing	1.31*	0.98	0.96
	(0.19)	(0.14)	(0.10)
Assessment: Marginalizing	1.19	1.55**	1.50**
	(0.19)	(0.30)	(0.19)
Political Engagement Index	2.41**	2.08**	1.59**
	(0.18)	(0.00)	(0.00)
N	1,427	1,489	1,486
F	4.85	3.35	6.36
Pr > F	0.00	0.00	0.00

Note: Odds ratios for ordinal logistic or logistic regressions are reported, with standard errors parenthesized below. Statistical significance is denoted by * if $p < 0.10$, ** if $p < 0.05$. Standard errors are clustered by ward, the level of survey stratification. A full suite of controls was included but is not reported.

giving such explanations as "I want to have my say in government. If I stay home, I shouldn't grumble when the government doesn't appeal to my specifications."[23] Others noted specific grievances they had with the government, such as lack of employment opportunities, insufficient funding for schools, or poor infrastructure.[24] Most just invoked the idea of change, often in order to achieve "development."[25]

While dissatisfaction with marginalizing experiences created political energy around change and mobilized some people to go to the polls, it had a distinctly demobilizing effect on others. A key difference between interview respondents describing empowering and marginalizing experiences was in their responses about their lack of participation. Among those describing empowering experiences, nonparticipators all failed to explain their lack of participation. They would state that they would not vote or contact officials, but then they would be unable to explain why. Most simply stated that they "just don't," indicating a degree of apathy. The nonparticipators who had marginalizing experiences gave explanations that much more closely resembled the way the neglected explained their lack of participation: not with apathy, but with a sense of hopelessness.

For the interview subjects describing marginalizing experiences and lack of participation, most explanations were variations on the theme that it would make no difference who was in charge, because all politicians are the same. "Why would I?" one respondent questioned about participating asked, adding, "Whatever I say or do doesn't matter."[26] Another explained, "I see even if I vote, it's the same. Like I said, we are still suffering just the same. . . . It doesn't matter."[27] These responses were not apathetic. Rather, they reflected a lack of efficacy and a lack of belief in government responsiveness. As one respondent explained, "I'm not even going to vote for anyone. Believe, me, I have got a voter's card, but when I look at it, I will be like, 'Who am I voting for?' And then nobody is making sense, and I just leave it."[28] Others reported that they used to participate but stopped because officials "just forget about us when they are voted in."[29]

Compared to those who report neglect, those with marginalizing and empowering assessments of government service provision are statistically more likely to participate in politics, even participating at roughly the same rates. But the qualitative data uncover very different motivations underlying these patterns of participation. Those with empowering experiences participate because of a belief in government responsiveness, while those empowered individuals who fail to participate are generally unable to articulate why, indicating general apathy. Those with marginalizing experiences are pulled in opposite directions. Some channel their frustration into political energy, evidencing even greater motivation for going to the polls to precipitate change. Others interpret their marginalization as evidence that the government—any government—is unlikely to care about them at all, making their political actions useless. This lack of political efficacy makes them far less likely to participate in politics at all.

While the quantitative analysis indicates that both empowerment and marginalization are, on average, associated with higher rates of political participation, different processes drive the aggregate results for each group. Based on the anger and frustration evidenced by interview respondents, marginalization seems to have a stronger relationship to the likelihood of political participation, but it generates countervailing tendencies. Marginalized participants appear more motivated to participate than empowered participants, but this political energy is undercut by the cynicism of marginalized nonparticipants. Meanwhile, empowerment seems to have an overall weaker but unidirectional relationship to participation.

CONCLUSION

The results presented in this chapter indicate that service delivery has the capacity to influence political participation through numerous pathways. A few trends stand out as being particularly important for political development and the cultivation of an active citizenry in developing democracies. The standard socioeconomic (or "resource") approach to understanding predictors of political participation has not fared well in African democracies. Other scholars have hypothesized that party structures and the low-information environment in African polities contribute to a situation in which the influence of top-down party mobilization on political participation is greater than the influence of individual resources (Kuenzi and Lambright 2010). The patterns of participation evident in other studies are present in my data, but the results of my survey offer an important addition: individuals' interpretations of their experiences with public service delivery are consistently important in predicting multiple varieties of political participation. Not only are these experience variables more consistently significant than the individual demographic indicators, but they also have a larger magnitude than most of these other variables. While other studies have demonstrated that African voters are mobilized by political parties from the top down, this chapter indicates that citizens' experiences with basic service delivery generate an important source of mobilization from below.

Returning to the baseline survey results, the most consistent direct predictor of the various forms of political participation is an individual's empowering subjective assessment of government service provision. Above and beyond actual objective measures of provision, citizens' interpretation that the government is trying to help them through the provision of basic services is associated with a greater likelihood of political participation. Most of these results are robust to control for partisanship, indicating that this relationship is not the spurious result of a link between partisanship, rosy assessments of the government, and participation. I theorized that empowering experiences might boost political participation because they indicate that the government is likely to be responsive, which should generate a greater degree of political efficacy for those with such experiences. The interview data support this interpretation of the survey results, demonstrating that interview respondents who described empowering experiences with government services also explained their political participation in terms of using formal political channels to communicate to their representatives, who they assumed would be responsive. These explanations of political participation were dramatically different from the explanations offered by those respondents who had not had empowering experiences with public policy.

The link between empowering experiences, political efficacy, and political participation runs primarily through interpretive pathways. Many respondents with empowering experiences had their fair share of frustrations with the objective quality of service delivery. They were responding to the perception that government officials were making genuine attempts to improve services, even in the face of significant material constraints. The results of this survey are consistent with other studies from African countries, which demonstrate that citizen evaluations of public services are contingent on the perception of responsiveness rather than objective quality (M. Bratton 2007; McLoughlin 2015). Because service delivery feeds back to influence political participation through interpretive pathways, governments could potentially boost citizen participation (and engagement) by demonstrating responsiveness to citizen demands, even if actual provision is stymied by material constraints.

The relationship between marginalizing assessments and political participation provides further evidence that expanding "inclusive" policy experiences can stimulate political participation. While my initial expectation was that any relationship between marginalizing assessments of government provision and political participation would be mediated by political engagement, my analysis of the survey data was consistent only with partial mediation (at most). The interview data indicate that in comparison to empowering experiences, marginalizing experiences can generate a stronger inclination toward political participation, but they can also make citizens dismissive of the political process. On average, those with marginalizing assessments were just as likely to report political participation as those with empowering experiences. However, qualitative analysis of the interview data demonstrated that this category of respondents includes two strong and countervailing tendencies: a greater likelihood for participation fueled by frustration, alongside a reduced likelihood for participation dampened by disaffection. Missing in this category was a clear link—evident for those who had empowering experiences—between experience with service provision and a sense of political efficacy.

The results of this analysis suggest that reorienting service delivery processes in such a way as to make citizens feel "visible" might shift their interpretation from marginalizing to empowering, even if the quality of the services does not necessarily improve. From a state-building perspective, such results suggest that small investments in the process of achieving service delivery may have a large impact on communities' political buy-in. That the link between service delivery and political participation is primarily interpretive, hinging on the degree to which people believe that the government is making an active attempt to respond to their needs, suggests that straightforward improvements to the process of service delivery might have a large impact on political participation.

Objective measures of service delivery only influenced the likelihood of contacting local officials, along with having a (substantively smaller) relationship to the political participation index. Mediation analysis suggests that this result is largely due to the relationship between lower levels of service delivery and a higher degree of collective behavior. In particular, the link between lower rates of service delivery, higher rates of collective behavior, and contacting local officials appears to be due to specific community processes related to collective organizing around bids for service improvement, as described in chapter 4. Furthermore, the interview data indicates that respondents (especially in rural communities) had a habit of conflating "I" and "we" when discussing contacting officials—a trend that appeared to grow out of the community members' practice of holding community meetings and then tasking community leaders with contacting government representatives. On the one hand, this relationship is heartening, as it illustrates how neglected areas achieve political organization. On the other hand, the survey and interview data indicate that rather than having a broader link to political participation, this outcome is probably limited to contacting officials.

In sum, the evidence presented in this chapter indicates that Zambians' interpretations of their experiences with service delivery have a consistent, substantively large, and statistically significant relationship to various forms of political participation. In the qualitative data, the most important distinction between those who described empowerment and those who described marginalization is a sense of government responsiveness leading to political efficacy. The relationship between empowering assessments and political participation is unidirectional: if empowering experiences with policy have any influence on an individual's political proclivity, it is in the direction of more participation. Furthermore, respondents with empowering experiences describe their participation in terms of the expectation of government responsiveness and the belief that their participation will make a difference. For those with marginalizing assessments, the relationship to participation is countervailing: it appears related both to frustrated mobilization and to disaffection. The marginalized tended not to believe that the government was responsive, though they differed in the degree to which they thought "throwing the rascals out" would make a difference. For this group, improving perceptions of government responsiveness could have a notable impact on rates of participation.

CHAPTER 7

Exit and Voice

Policy Experience and Alternative Modes of Interaction with the State

Some forms of political participation exist outside the realm of politics as usual. Generally speaking, participating in politics denotes a certain level of "buy-in" to the political system—belief that one's problems may possibly be solved by working through political channels. However, political actions are not confined to formal channels; some may direct their political energy outside of the "official" political realm. Alternative modes of political interaction may denote lack of belief in the efficacy of the state or in the legitimacy of the state or governing body, or may be a practical response to the state's lack of a monopoly over territorial administration. After discussing a few ways that citizens may seek alternatives to the state or alternative ways of engaging with the state, this chapter examines the relationship of such alternatives to experiences with service delivery.

A citizen seeking alternatives to the state or alternative ways of engaging the state might choose to pursue a wide array of possible behaviors, but this chapter focuses on three: (1) reliance on nonstate providers for ostensibly state-related services, (2) noncompliance with state-mandated revenue collection, and (3) protest. Each of these forms of alternative politics entails a different motivation and may be considered "alternative" for different reasons. Reliance on nonstate service providers literally involves reliance on an alternative to the state. When people view nonstate services as distinct from state-run services, reliance on nonstate providers indicates a perhaps-justified lack of faith in the government's ability to carry out its primary functions. Similarly, disgruntled citizens may evade state-mandated revenue collection (e.g., taxes or duties) as an act of subversion, undermining government authority to extract revenue to administer the polity. Finally, as an especially dramatic form of political participation, protest is distinct from "everyday politics" in its level of intensity and in the attention it draws. Unlike the other alternatives discussed above, it requires working within existing political structures, generally constituting a bid for attention from those in power.

This chapter examines these three forms of alternative politics and the relationship of each to policy experience. It begins by describing existing work that provides the political context for each of these three types of behavior in low-capacity democracies in general and in Zambia specifically. It elaborates hypotheses connecting each type of behavior to experiences with service delivery. The chapter then explains the operationalization of each variable through the survey and presents the baseline results for all the response variables. Following that presentation are separate analyses of the results from each type of behavior, using qualitative data from interview subjects to provide additional context for interpreting the results.

ALTERNATIVE AND SUBVERSIVE POLITICAL BEHAVIOR IN LESS-DEVELOPED DEMOCRACIES

The forms of political participation taken up in this chapter fall under two forms of behavior: alternative and subversive forms of political participation. I consider alternative political behavior to be the reliance on nonstate actors to perform state roles, and I regard subversive political behavior as an explicit attempt to subvert state authority. In theory, those who are unhappy with the government have two primary options through which to express their discontent: voice and exit. In his examination of dissatisfaction in organizations, Hirschman (1970) posited that disgruntled members of organizations (including citizens of states) can either voice their displeasure in the hope of initiating reform or leave altogether. This chapter uses his concepts of "voice" and "exit" to understand alternative and subversive political behaviors. Both alternative and subversive acts may be forms of exit, but they reflect different motivations, and it is useful to theorize them separately. Furthermore, while "protest behavior" is one of the response categories in this chapter, it corresponds more closely with "voice" than with "exit" and is analyzed separately herein.

Alternative Political Behavior

Hirschman posits that those dissatisfied with an organization (including a state) might choose to exit the system altogether. However, in the case of many developing countries (in Africa and elsewhere), exit can occur without change of citizenship. In Zambia, as in much of the developing world, government reach is limited. The development of precolonial polities across most of the African continent was marked by the constant struggle of asserting control over a low-density population, making it relatively easy to avoid the reach of governing bodies (Herbst 2000). Similarly, in the post-independence period, Jackson and Rosberg observed that many African governments "do not effectively control all of the important public activities within their jurisdictions" (Jackson and Rosberg 1982, 3). This problem occurs for many postcolonial states, which achieved juridical statehood without necessarily being capable of administering their entire territory—and without being the only game in town. In fact, as King and Lieberman note, "states increasingly share political primacy with nonstate entities that are bereft of territorial sovereignty but nevertheless perform some combination of governance functions, from social services to armed force, that often enjoy substantial popular support and civil-society penetration" (2009, 550). While the government's legitimacy is often contingent on its capacity for basic service provision and while communities hold the widespread expectation that the government should be responsible for service delivery, the government's failure to deliver means that communities must sometimes turn to nonstate service providers (Olivier de Sardan 2014, 400–401; M. Bratton 2006, 1989). When the "delivery state" fails to deliver, reliance on nonstate providers may be a form of "exit."

With regard to service provision, two sets of actors[1] are the primary alternative to the state: NGOs and chiefs (or local elites).[2] In Zambia, several major NGOs (e.g., World Vision and Caritas) are well known across the country, and many districts have one or two smaller NGOs working nearby. NGOs may enhance the government's ability to provide services, bolstering the relationship between citizens and their state, or they may position themselves as antithetical to the state, creating a nonstate alternative and undermining citizenship (Brass 2016; Jennings in Cammett and MacLean 2014). Anecdotally, when asked who they turn to for service provision, many respondents in this study explained reliance on NGOs due to the fact that "the government doesn't do anything," suggesting that they draw a distinction between government and NGO projects. However, NGOs and the government often work hand in hand, and Zambian politicians have a habit of claiming credit for delivering NGO projects: interview subjects from Caritas, World Vision, and Common Markets for Conservation reported that local government officials or members of parliament publicly take credit for projects the NGOs have performed.[3]

Chiefs and local elites may provide another option for service provision. The chieftaincy in Zambia encompasses a large variety of precolonial and colonial political configurations; due to the great tribal diversity of precolonial Zambia, it would be inaccurate to define a single form of chieftaincy. While most regions have a chief and some kind of hierarchical organization in which power is delegated down to subchiefs and headmen, the degree to which these relationships are powerful or hold local legitimacy varies greatly (Honig 2016). Despite variation in the extent to which chiefs are connected to their subjects, 287 chiefs are officially recognized through Zambia's House of Chiefs. These chiefs have a close connection to the political sphere, and their political power has been growing stronger since the return to multiparty democracy in 1991 (Baldwin 2015, 90; Gould 2010, chap. 5). Particularly in rural areas, chiefs are better situated than the government to organize rural populations and are often positioned to negotiate or broker service delivery in their territory (Baldwin 2015, 10, 92). Because they can play an intermediary role, some have argued that chiefs in Zambia can actually improve governance outcomes. Logan argues that in many African countries (including Zambia), the continuing political importance of traditional authorities exists alongside modern democratic institutions, not in conflict with them (Logan 2009). Similarly, Baldwin's examination of chief-state relations in Zambia indicates that chiefs broker relationships between their constituents and their members of parliament, facilitating rural dwellers' political contact with the national political system (Baldwin 2013). Therefore, chiefs may represent either a parallel system of government or simply an avenue of access to government services.

Dissatisfied with the government's ability to provide basic services, people may turn to NGOs or chiefs to either provide or broker delivery of basic services. The extent to which turning to nonstate providers constitutes "exit" depends on the relationship between the nonstate provider and the government. Cammett and MacLean convincingly argue that the political implications of reliance on nonstate service providers depend on whether the state and nonstate providers have a cooperative or conflictual relationship (2014, 32). For both NGOs and chiefs in the Zambian context, this relationship is ambiguous. However, I argue that citizens would be more likely to turn to NGOs or chiefs as providers or brokers of services when they are dissatisfied with or have limited access to state service provision. This is the case when respondents have objectively less access to services or interpret their experiences as either exclusionary (marginalizing/ burdensome) or reflecting lack of awareness of their needs (marginalizing/neglectful). This argument is captured in hypothesis 5a.

> H_{5a}: Reliance on chiefs or NGOs for service provision is more likely when respondents have less access to services or interpret government services as exclusionary or unaware.

On the one hand, such a relationship may be the result of material policy effects. Reliance on NGOs or chiefs may be a pragmatic reaction to limited service provision, leading to the expectation that it is more likely when objective rates of service provision are low. On the other hand, the decision to turn to alternative service providers may also be related to interpretation. If respondents interpret their experiences with policies as demonstrating that the government does not know enough or care enough to provide appropriate services, they may be more likely to turn to locally embedded actors like chiefs or NGOs.

Subversive Political Behavior

Another form of "exit" is the active evasion of government bodies and subversion of governmental authority. As noted by Guyer (1992) and others (e.g., Centeno 1997), many postcolonial African nations gained independence with a conundrum regarding public revenues. While taxation in Europe evolved alongside expanding state capacity to collect revenues and provide services (Tilly 1992), newly independent African states had to rely on taxation as a basis of public revenue generation without necessarily having the means—or the legitimacy—to collect them effectively. This problem is closely related to the problem of low state capacity to measure or monitor individuals' economic activity. Scott (1998) notes that one of the major projects of statehood is to make populations "legible" to governments: to rule effectively, governments must know and document who their subjects are, where they live, and what they do; meanwhile, certain portions of the population develop tactics to evade legibility, such as living in remote hard-to-reach areas, moving frequently, or otherwise evading state agents. Such behavior is possible when the capacity of the state is so low as to undermine enforcement of activities such as census taking or tax collection. As in other parts of the postcolonial world, state reach in Zambia after independence was variable: some urban centers were "legible" to the government, while parts of the rural hinterland comprised "brown spaces" in which residents could elect to avoid state control (O'Donnell 1993).

Because the government has a limited capacity to monitor and enforce revenue collection, citizens of Zambia who live in "brown spaces" can determine, to some degree, the extent to which they will adhere to or evade tax collection. Zambia's system of taxation relies on direct taxes on corporations and wage earners and on indirect value-added taxes and trade taxes. However, income taxes only effectively apply to the 11 percent of the population employed in the formal sector, while the informal sector remains difficult to tax, due to the challenge of enforcing business registration (Mwansa and Chileshe 2010, 2). Similarly, value-added taxes and customs duties are difficult to collect, due to inaccurate record keeping and outright corruption. The vast majority of Zambian citizens are therefore able to make decisions about the extent to which they will comply with taxation efforts. Revenue collection is a basic function of government, and evasion of revenue collection is a basic subversive act: if a critical mass of citizens evaded taxes, the government would be unable to function. In other work, Scott has posited that evasive behavior toward state agents comprises a "weapon of the weak," which conveys implicit rejection of the governance system (1987, 33).

To assess individuals' sentiments around subverting the government, this study examines respondents' attitudes toward evading income taxes and customs duties. While not a major act of government subversion, evasion of taxes comprises an everyday act that defies the authority and legitimacy of the government to extract revenue (Fjeldstad and Semboja 2001). Evading taxation is an illegal act, but it is also a statement about whether the individual trusts the government to invest in public goods or to act as a responsible custodian of public revenues.[4]

According to most social science treatments of state revenue collection, people pay taxes for one of two reasons: either they fear the consequences of breaking the law, or they believe that taxation is just because of what the government provides in exchange for tax revenue (Alm, McClelland, and Schulze 1992; Torgler 2005; Dhami and al-Nowaihi 2007; Luttmer and Singhal 2014). Most studies suggest that people overweigh the probability of being discovered were they to evade taxes, but even so, the decision to pay taxes is not only a matter of rational utility. Most studies suggest that paying taxes is a combination of utility and "tax morale": the decision to pay constitutes a combination of legal, moral, practical, and intellectual reasons (Lago-Penas and Lago-Penas 2010). These rationales in favor of tax compliance denote a relatively capacious government: either the government has a reasonable capacity to audit, or citizens are generally satisfied with basic public goods provision. If attitudes toward tax compliance are related to policy experiences, the relationship most likely occurs through interpretive pathways: existing studies suggest little relationship between relative material wealth and attitudes toward taxation, instead emphasizing the role of tax morale.

In Zambia, which has a limited capacity to audit, one would expect the decision to pay to hinge on individuals' tax morale. One would expect tax or customs evasion therefore to be more likely when people are dissatisfied with service provision. This may be the case with marginalizing policies but would theoretically be more pronounced with policy experiences along the exclusionary dimension of the policy typology, as expressed in hypothesis 5b.

H_{5b}: Evasion of taxes or customs duties is more likely when respondents have exclusionary interpretations of service delivery.

While those with marginalizing experiences may still be dissatisfied with service provision, they are subject to an inclusionary dimension of policies that indicates some utility in continuing to participate in the system of governance and revenue collection. Those subject to exclusionary policies are less likely to have a strong tax morale. As Kelsall (2000) observed for Tanzania, Besley and Persson (2014) note that developing countries generally have difficulty cultivating a norm of tax compliance because of issues with corruption, unfairness, and lack of perceived public return on tax payments.

Protest and Voice

Unlike the forms of "exit" described above, protest may be construed less as a subversive or alternative approach to politics and more as a dramatic expression of politics as usual.[5] Lipsky (1968, 1145) theorizes protest as a political resource for those who are relatively powerless in politics, particularly as a method for involving more-powerful third parties in various issues. In this conceptualization, the group with few political resources uses protest as a way to operate within the state, despite limited access to more formal avenues of political expression. Harris has posited that in the context of South

Africa, protest behavior is actually a complement to other forms of political participation, and protestors take to the streets "to change *what is done* by those in power rather than changing *who* is in power" (2015, 3; emphasis in original). One might construe protest as a form of "voice," a way for marginalized groups to express their dissatisfaction while still operating within the existing governance structures. Indeed, in the African context, there has been a significant increase in "valence protests" over the past decade.[6] These types of protests are less about contentious politics or symbolic dissent and more about making demands on the government for basic services. Valence protests generally do not convey new information to governments; rather, they are a way for people to indicate intensity and the degree of seriousness of bids for resources. In flawed democracies where vote choice is an inadequate avenue for expressing policy preferences, protest is a way to signal intensity of preferences, in addition to dissatisfaction (Harris and Hern forthcoming).

Based on this conceptualization of protest behavior, one might expect protest to be a more common form of voice for those with inclusionary experiences—either marginalizing or empowering. This expectation reflects the observation that protest, while more dramatic than everyday politics, is still a way of operating within the political system; it is a form of voice rather than exit. In the Zambian context, frustrated segments of the population have a long history of engaging in protest and strike behavior to air economic or political grievances (Burawoy 1976; Larmer 2011). In most cases, the protests were aimed at gaining the attention of governing bodies in order to make demands, not at undermining the regime or operating outside the political system. Therefore, unlike the other variables examined in this chapter, protest should be more likely along inclusionary dimensions, as expressed in hypothesis 5c.

H_{5c}: Protest is more likely for those who have inclusionary interpretations of service delivery.

This hypothesis rests on the assumption that people protest when they are dissatisfied with the status quo yet still believe that the government will listen to their demands. That sense of responsiveness should be limited to those who have inclusionary interpretations of government service delivery.

In figure 10, the three hypotheses examined in this chapter are represented with relation to the policy experience typology. The following section of this chapter describes how each variable is operationalized and presents the base-

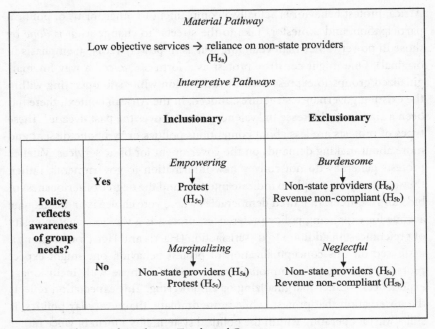

Fig. 10. Hypotheses 5a through 5c in Typological Context

line regression results linking each outcome variable to respondents' experiences with service delivery. The three subsequent sections provide separate analyses of each type of response—reliance on nonstate providers, attitudes toward revenue collection, and protest behavior. The analyses interpret the survey results alongside interview responses that illuminate the mechanisms driving the responses.

MEASURING ALTERNATIVE MODES OF INTERACTION WITH THE ZAMBIAN STATE

To operationalize the concepts described above, I rely on three different types of survey questions. The first set of variables, regarding respondents' proclivity to turn to nonstate service providers, derives from an open-ended question regarding who the respondent would turn to for help bringing a development project in the area. "NGO reliance" and "chief reliance" are binary variables that take the value of 1 if the respondent listed "NGO" or "chief" as an actor to whom they would go to ask for a development project, 0 if not. In the sample, 19.1 percent of respondents reported that they would rely on NGOs for development projects, while 16.4 percent reported that they turn to chiefs.

The next category of alternative modes of interaction with the state concerns attitudes toward compliance with revenue collection, specifically taxation and customs compliance. The variables "tax compliance" and "customs compliance" assess respondents' attitudes toward taxation and customs duties. Due to problems of social desirability bias, asking respondents directly about their attitudes toward taxation would result in a dramatic underreporting of evasive attitudes. Therefore, to elicit respondents' attitudes toward these issues, the survey presented two vignettes about otherwise sympathetic characters: one who evades taxes by failing to register his informal business, and one who skirts customs procedures. As noted above, these are very common practices in Zambia, which has limited ability to monitor taxation in the informal sector. One of the vignettes follows.

> I am going to read you a short story about a man named Isaac and ask you a question about him: Isaac is an active member of the community. He sells furniture by the roadside. He works very hard and barely makes enough money to support his family. He knows he is supposed to pay taxes on the money he makes, but because his business is not registered, it is easy for him to avoid paying taxes. He decides to skip paying taxes to buy more household goods instead. Some people say that Isaac is doing the right thing to provide for his family, while other people say that it is his duty to pay taxes no matter what. What do you think about Isaac's behavior?

Respondents are asked to provide their reactions to the vignette characters' choices, which are then coded to reflect attitudes of compliance or noncompliance. Both variables are binary, coded 1 to reflect attitudes of compliance and 0 to reflect noncompliance. In the sample, 65 percent of respondents demonstrated tax-compliant attitudes, while 80 percent demonstrated customs-compliant attitudes. Respondents were then asked why they responded the way they did.

The final category of behavior this chapter considers is protest, which I conceptualize as a particularly dramatic expression of political voice. "Protest" is a binary variable that takes the value of 1 if the respondent reports having participated in a protest or demonstration in the past year, 0 otherwise. Only 8.5 percent of the sample reported such participation. Table 14 displays the relationship between the measures of policy experience and the five response variables described above. The models are specified in the same way and use the same control variables as in previous chapters. In the table, results that are boxed but not starred were marginally significant (at p = 0.06).

Table 14. Government Service Provision and Modes of Alternative Interactions

	NGO Reliance	Chief Reliance	Tax-Compliant Attitude	Customs-Compliant Attitude	Protest
Objective Measure					
Government Projects	0.76**	0.91	1.02	0.90	0.98
	(0.07)	(0.08)	(0.08)	(0.09)	(0.13)
Semi-subjective Measure					
Project Experience: Empowering	1.02	1.66	1.35	1.13	1.26
	(0.17)	(0.51)	(0.23)	(0.22)	(0.30)
Project Experience: Marginalizing	1.08	1.93*	1.40*	1.31	1.29
	(0.16)	(0.55)	(0.20)	(0.22)	(0.28)
Project Experience: Neglectful	0.99	1.67	1.41*	1.11	1.12
	(0.15)	(0.48)	(0.21)	(0.19)	(0.26)
Project Experience: Burdensome	0.78	1.30	1.22	1.19	1.14
	(0.24)	(0.62)	(0.37)	(0.39)	(0.46)
Fully Subjective Measure					
Assessment: Empowering	0.67	1.57	2.10**	1.66*	2.13**
	(0.15)	(0.39)	(0.42)	(0.41)	(0.60)
Assessment: Marginalizing	1.29	1.02	1.52*	1.71*	1.42
	(0.25)	(0.23)	(0.26)	(0.38)	(0.40)
Assessment: Burdensome	1.13	1.63	1.33	0.81	1.64
	(0.39)	(0.50)	(0.46)	(0.37)	(0.70)
Northwestern	1.05	4.90*	1.42	1.22	1.18
	(0.54)	(3.52)	(0.68)	(0.74)	(0.79)
Southern	1.75	6.43**	1.74	1.80	1.28
	(0.54)	(3.39)	(0.55)	(0.69)	(0.68)
On-Rail	1.34	1.27	1.03	0.77	0.60
	(0.46)	(0.43)	(0.30)	(0.30)	(0.25)

Table 14.—*Continued*

	NGO Reliance	Chief Reliance	Tax-Compliant Attitude	Customs-Compliant Attitude	Protest
Urban	2.30**	0.08**	1.19	0.73	1.65
	(0.50)	(0.03)	(0.24)	(0.17)	(0.58)
Male	1.15	1.07	1.08	0.78	1.33
	(0.18)	(0.19)	(0.15)	(0.13)	(0.27)
Age	1.00	0.85	1.05	1.24*	0.93
	(0.10)	(0.09)	(0.09)	(0.13)	(0.13)
Education	1.03	0.93	1.20**	1.33**	1.07*
	(0.02)	(0.06)	(0.06)	(0.07)	(0.03)
Religiosity	0.99	1.06	1.00	0.93	0.91
	(0.04)	(0.04)	(0.07)	(0.05)	(0.09)
Children	1.01	0.99	1.00	0.98	1.05
	(0.03)	(0.03)	(0.03)	(0.03)	(0.04)
Married	1.09	0.89	1.26	1.03	1.10
	(0.18)	(0.18)	(0.19)	(0.18)	(0.25)
Formal Employment	0.99	1.42	1.09	1.16	0.96
	(0.21)	(0.45)	(0.23)	(0.30)	(0.28)
Unemployed	0.91	1.47	0.86	0.95	1.09
	(0.18)	(0.35)	(0.15)	(0.20)	(0.28)
Civil Servant	0.84	0.84	1.31	1.34	1.19
	(0.28)	(0.41)	(0.43)	(0.54)	(0.47)
N	1,486	1,384	1,299	1,240	1,334
F	3.97	5.82	4.45	4.53	2.03
Pr > F	0.00	0.00	0.00	0.00	0.00

Note: Odds ratios for logistic regressions are reported, with standard errors parenthesized below. Statistical significance is denoted by *if $p < 0.05$, **if $p < 0.01$.

Regarding nonstate service provision, the results for NGOs and chiefs trend in opposite directions. Reliance on NGOs is less likely when respondents have more objective access to services or when they have empowering assessments of government services ($p = 0.06$), while reliance on chiefs is more likely when respondents report experiences along the inclusionary interpretive dimension of service delivery ($p = 0.06$ for "empowering assessments"). These results indicate that respondents view chiefs and NGOs differently vis-à-vis service delivery and the state. While the results regarding

NGO reliance are generally in line with the expectations of hypothesis 5a, the results for reliance on chiefs suggest the opposite.

Respondents with marginalizing or empowering interpretations of service delivery are more likely to have compliant attitudes about revenue collection, though the relationship is stronger for taxes than customs. Curiously, neglectful policy experiences are also positively associated with tax compliance (as are empowering experiences, at $p = 0.06$). These results are generally supportive of hypothesis 5b but require a more nuanced analysis. Protest is only associated with empowering assessments of government services, lending some support to hypothesis 5c. The following sections of this chapter analyze the results from each set of response variables, incorporating qualitative interview data to support interpretation of the quantitative results.

SERVICE DELIVERY AND RELIANCE ON ALTERNATIVES TO THE STATE

I hypothesized that Zambians would be more likely to "exit" the state by turning to alternative service providers when they had less objective access to service provision or were subject to exclusionary or "unaware" services. The results in table 14 lend some tentative support to this hypothesis, but only as it pertains to reliance on NGOs. Contrary to expectations, of the 498 respondents reporting reliance on either chiefs or NGOs, only 34 (6.8 percent) report reliance on both, indicating that Zambians turn to chiefs and NGOs under different circumstances. The patterns in the data suggest that while turning to NGOs may be an exit from the state, reliance on chiefs is not. Reliance on NGOs was more likely for those with fewer objective services (likelihood of reliance on NGOs decreased 32 percent with each additional service) and less likely for those with empowering assessments of government service provision (likelihood of reliance on NGOs was 50 percent lower for those with empowering assessments when compared to those with neglectful assessments). These results support the idea that Zambians are more likely to turn to NGOs in the absence of state service delivery or when they interpret services as neglectful.

While turning to NGOs for service provision may be a form of exit from the state, the results for reliance on chiefs do not adhere to the same trend. Respondents were 93 percent more likely to report relying on chiefs with each additional marginalizing policy experience and 57 percent more likely to do so when they reported empowering subjective assessments of services. These results suggest that reliance on chiefs is more likely for respondents who interpret their experiences with government services along the inclusionary dimension, the opposite of what I hypothesized. These results indicate that very different circumstances precipitate reliance on chiefs versus NGOs in Zambia.[7]

To interpret these results, it is important to return to the underlying rationale that respondents would turn to nonstate providers to exit the state if they perceive the nonstate providers to be separate from the state. As described above, the relationship between chiefs or NGOs and the state is theoretically ambiguous. NGOs may provide an alternative to state provision or may work alongside state actors to coproduce services. Similarly, chiefs or other traditional authorities may form local governance structures that operate in parallel with the state or extend state reach. The results above suggest that in the Zambian context, reliance on NGOs may be a way to exit the state, while reliance on chiefs is not. This interpretation finds additional support in the qualitative interview data. In the interview sample, 52 subjects spoke at length about their perception of chiefs and/or NGOs and their relationship to the government. Of these subjects, 24 of the 37 who spoke about NGOs perceived them as being separate from the government, while 26 of 27 subjects who spoke about chiefs perceived them as being a conduit to the government. While most subjects spoke about either one or the other, 11 discussed both NGOs and chiefs. Of these subjects, 9 explicitly juxtaposed the two actors against each other—NGOs as an alternative to the government, chiefs as a gatekeeper for government services.

Subjects who discussed the role of NGOs tended to frame nonstate services as an antidote for a low-capacity government. Some were pragmatic, stating that they prefer NGOs because they "have better offices" that "respond more quickly than the government"[8] or because "the government is not 100 percent" and "does not really get to reach the target."[9] Others turned to NGOs explicitly because of their cynicism about government regard for them: "The government, they help those who are at least educated, but the poor—they don't look at [us]. [We] are barely there."[10] One man talked about how he "really needed" an NGO in his village: "These political leaders, who only come during the election, they would give [us] T-shirts, chitenges, things like that. Then, after [we] vote for them, they go and never come back."[11] Many of the respondents who expressed positive sentiments about NGOs did so explicitly because they were upset about government service provision. In these cases, turning to NGOs for services was an intentional dismissal of the state.

However, as noted above, a minority of interview respondents reported that the government and NGOs work collaboratively. One explained, "The government does not have all the finances, or rather the ways and means to overcome certain challenges. As a result, the nongovernmental organizations, they are partners."[12] Others believed that NGOs are better positioned than the average citizen to report citizens' needs to the government, suggesting that the NGOs "can tell the government that they should bring development to this country."[13] While the majority of the respondents who spoke about NGOs viewed them as alternatives to the government, this perception was by no means absolute. While, on average, reported reliance on NGOs indicated a rejection of the state's ability to provide services, some of those who turn to NGOs still view them as an extension of—rather than an alternative to—the state. Nevertheless, the results of the aggregate sample indicate that reliance on NGOs constitutes "exit" more often than not.

While some ambiguity regarding the relationship between NGOs and the state remains, there was much less ambiguity regarding the role of chiefs. The overwhelming majority of subjects who discussed chiefs (26 of 27) viewed them as directly connected to the government. Most subjects who talked about chiefs reported an inclination to turn to a chief for development projects, because "he is the one who can ask the government to come in and provide the services."[14] Many subjects talked about this feature of the chieftaincy as a positive thing, noting that "if [the chiefs] say something, the government will listen."[15] Others had a more pessimistic understanding of the relationship between chiefs and governments, stating that "the chiefs have been bought"[16] or lamenting that chiefs are just as ineffective as state agents: "They are like a part of the government, you just wait."[17] Most relevant for this study is the distinction that subjects drew between NGOs and chiefs. While many subjects viewed NGOs as distinct from and working outside the government, most subjects perceived chiefs to be either directly connected to or part of the government. Therefore, while turning to an NGO for services may constitute exit, turning to a chief would not. This distinction helps to contextualize the results above and lends support to the idea that (at least some) Zambians turn to NGOs for service provision specifically as an alternative to the state.

SERVICE DELIVERY AND ATTITUDES TOWARD
REVENUE COLLECTION

The next category of alternative modes of interaction with the state concerns attitudes toward revenue collection, specifically taxation and customs compliance. Revenue collection is a fundamental task of states, and citizens' ability to evade revenue collectors is a form of exit in its rejection of state authority. I hypothesized that Zambians would hold noncompliant attitudes toward revenue collection when they had exclusionary interpretations of their experiences with service delivery: since being excluded from basic services violates the fiscal contract that supposedly binds citizens to the state through revenue collection, such exclusion should precipitate noncompliant attitudes and a desire for exit. This hypothesis finds mixed support in the data. In general, the results were more consistent across the fully subjective policy assessments (versus the semi-subjective measures) and stronger for tax-compliant attitudes (versus customs-compliant attitudes).

Starting with attitudes toward taxation, inclusionary interpretations of policy are associated with a greater likelihood of tax-compliant attitudes for both the semi-subjective and fully subjective measures. Empowering and marginalizing policy experiences are associated with increases of 35 and 40 percent, respectively, in the likelihood of tax-compliant attitudes, while empowering and marginalizing assessments of government services are associated with increases of 110 and 52 percent, respectively. These results are consistent with my hypothesis, indicating that respondents with inclusionary experiences are much more likely to hold tax-compliant attitudes than those with exclusionary experiences. However, counter to my expectations, those with neglectful policy experiences are also more likely to hold tax-compliant attitudes. Indeed, among the semi-subjective measures, burdensome experiences are the only category not associated with tax-compliant attitudes.

Turning to attitudes toward customs, the results support the hypothesis in a more straightforward manner but are restricted to the fully subjective measures. Empowering and marginalizing assessments are associated with 66 percent and 71 percent increases, respectively, in the likelihood of customs-compliant attitudes. Respondents with inclusionary subjective assessments of government services are much more likely to support the idea that owners of small businesses should comply with customs requirements than are those with exclusionary assessments.

These results indicate that the relationship between service delivery and compliant attitudes toward revenue collection is much stronger for the fully interpretive measures. When we examine only the fully subjective measures of assessments of government services, respondents with either empowering or marginalizing assessments are far more likely than their counterparts to exhibit compliant attitudes toward both taxes and customs. The relationship between the semi-subjective measures and revenue compliance is less straightforward. There is no relationship between these measures and attitudes about customs compliance. Such a result is perhaps due to Zambians having much more uniform attitudes about customs (largely because few respondents are personally subject to customs payments). However, the positive relationship between neglectful policy experiences and attitudes toward tax compliance is more puzzling. These results indicate, first, that the semi-subjective measures are more weakly related to compliant attitudes toward revenue collection generally and, second, that only burdensome experiences are strong enough to reduce tax-compliant attitudes, as compared to other forms of policy experience.

To understand whether noncompliant attitudes toward revenue collection are actually a way of exiting the state—as opposed to simply a self-interested rational cost-benefit calculation—it is necessary to examine the reasoning that respondents provide for their attitudes. The logic underlying the initial hypothesis is based on a version of the fiscal contract, where citizens should be more likely to support revenue collection if they believe that they are likely to benefit from it (and should be likely to exit through evasion of revenue collection if they believe they will not). Respondents' explanations for compliance were coded into two categories. The first category includes respondents who gave purely legal or uncritical reasoning regarding their tax compliance ("You have to pay because it is the law / it is right"). Their explanations reflected an unquestioning response to instruction, rather than critical reasoning. The second category included respondents who gave practical reasons for tax compliance ("If people don't pay taxes, the country will never develop"). These respondents reflected an understanding of and commitment to the role of taxation. Given the logic of the fiscal contract, one would expect that those with inclusionary interpretations of state service provision would be more likely to have tax-compliant attitudes that reflect this contract. There is some evidence that this is the case: those with inclusionary subjective experiences (either empowering or marginalizing) are more likely to state that their tax-compliant attitudes are the result of practical reasoning than of uncritical legal reasoning: a simple bivariate regression indicates that the likelihood of an individual's tax compliance being driven by "fiscal contract" reasoning jumps from 36 to 46 percent if that person reported an inclusionary subjective assessment of government service provision.

Reasoning for noncompliance was also coded into two categories. The first category includes those who evidenced noncompliant attitudes on the basis of personal circumstances ("Isaac shouldn't have to pay because he is poor"). These responses did not suggest rejection of the fiscal contract so much as a myopic, individual-level assessment of ability to pay. The second category includes those who gave institutional reasons for their noncompliance, indicating a violation of the fiscal contract ("The government is corrupt / just steals the money"). These respondents described their noncompliant attitudes in terms of the fiscal contract: the government does not provide, so "Isaac" should not pay. If the fiscal contract drives noncompliant attitudes, those who have been excluded from services should be more likely to cite institutional reasons for noncompliance. The evidence for this argument is mixed: there is little difference in the rates at which the neglected provide individual or institutional explanations for their noncompliance, but those who report a burdensome assessment of government services are far more likely to cite institutional reasons for their noncompliant attitudes. The likelihood that a person reports an institutional explanation for noncompliant attitudes toward taxes jumps from 53 to 84 percent if they reported a burdensome assessment of government service provision.

Analysis of the reasoning behind compliant and noncompliant attitudes lends some support to the idea that service delivery influences attitudes toward tax compliance through a "fiscal contract" pathway, in which those with inclusionary assessments of government attempts at service see the benefit of taxation, while those with burdensome assessments see the institutions as corrupt and prefer exit. However, subjective assessments of government attempts at service provision only account for some of the variation in the reasoning behind compliant and noncompliant attitudes. Further analysis of the data indicates that educational attainment is a key factor linking interpretations of service delivery to "fiscal contract" reasoning behind attitudes toward taxation. A series of simple bivariate logistic regressions indicates that higher educational attainment is closely correlated with "fiscal contract" reasoning (either compliance based on government need for revenue or noncompliance based on institutional reasoning). With a primary education, the likelihood of "fiscal contract" reasoning is only 22 percent. This likelihood increases to 36 percent with a high school diploma, 50 to 54 percent with any postsecondary training, and 64 percent with a graduate degree.

The link between education and respondents' rationale behind either compliant or noncompliant attitudes indicates an important feature of this line of inquiry: while inclusionary interpretations of service delivery are essential for generating revenue compliance, education conditions the way people form those interpretations. Those who are more educated are far more likely to understand the importance of revenue collection at a conceptual level, while those who are less educated are far more likely to agree with individual exemptions. While inclusionary interpretations of service delivery improve attitudes of tax compliance generally, education is Janus-faced. Individuals with more education are more likely to support efforts at taxation because they understand its importance, but they are also more likely to support intentionally avoiding taxation when they believe the government is not holding up its end of the bargain.

SERVICE DELIVERY AND PROTEST BEHAVIOR

In this chapter's last hypothesis, concerning protest as a form of voice, I suggested that protest would be most likely for those with inclusionary interpretations of service delivery. The rationale behind that hypothesis is that in the Zambian context, protest is a way to amplify one's voice and make demands on the government. Those undertaking protest, a relatively high-cost behavior, are likely to be those who most strongly believe the government will be responsive to them. The results in table 14 lend some tentative support to this hypothesis: respondents who hold empowering assessments of government service provision are 113 percent more likely to report protest behavior.

To support this interpretation of the results, two things would need to be true: first, the small portion of the population who engages in protest would need to be doing so in order to make clear demands on the government (rather than engaging in symbolic or revolutionary action). Second, the protestors would need to express the belief that the government may possibly be responsive to their requests. The qualitative data provided by interview subjects on this topic is sparse but provides some insight. Of the interview subjects, only eight reported ever having participated in a protest. Of these, only four were able to explain in depth what they were protesting about and why they decided to take such action. However, these interviews were illuminating, as they all described protest as the result of inadequate government services.

One subject reported protesting when he was at university, because there was a lack of food. When asked why those involved resorted to protest as opposed to other forms of communication with the government, he reported, "There was no forum. . . . There was no other way to tell the government."[18] Another subject referenced problems with the clinics, citing protest as an effective way to relay the problem to the government, because it brought media attention.[19] One subject discussed problems with government disbursement of bursaries for university students and salaries for the lecturers, resulting in the students organizing a boycott. Reporting that they did so to "make . . . the government listen to us," he confirmed, "After some time they did. . . . It was not because we requested; it was because we took action."[20] In each of these cases, those involved in protests did so because they wanted to draw attention to a specific grievance, generally related to government service provision. They also generally had the sense that the government would be responsive to their display.

Other interview subjects who had not personally participated in protests also saw them as a way to amplify voice. Many viewed protest as effective because "when you go in a crowd, you will be heard much faster,"[21] while others referenced the role of the media in helping to draw attention to the issue.[22] Several subjects recalled successful protests in the past, including those over clean water,[23] university services,[24] salaries for civil servants,[25] or general failures in public service provision.[26] In general, these interview subjects observed that people protest to draw attention to specific grievances, and many of them noted that the government does respond, often with the desired result. These observations help to contextualize the results of the survey analysis: while protestors may not be satisfied with the state of service provision, they are more likely to believe that the government is trying to improve things and is therefore likely to be responsive to their demands. Protest is a dramatic form of voice that citizens can use to communicate with the government, and the circumstances under which it is most likely are distinct from the circumstances leading to the forms of exit discussed in this chapter.

CONCLUSION

In all organizations, those who are dissatisfied with the status quo have the option of either exiting the system or voicing their concerns. In low-capacity states like Zambia, the possibilities for exit are more easily accessible than they might be in a higher-capacity state with a better ability to monitor its citizens. Similarly, in a flawed electoral regime, citizens may need to resort to more dramatic forms of voice, like protest, when formal avenues for expressing political opinions are insufficient. Throughout this book, I have argued that citizens' experiences with basic service delivery play an integral part in influencing the way they pursue various political behaviors. This chapter has examined the relationship between these experiences and citizens' decisions to engage in various forms of exit or voice. In a low-capacity state with flawed democratic institutions, Zambians' decisions to exit the system or to voice their dissatisfaction through informal channels such as protest have the potential to influence both state and political development within the country.

This chapter first examined Zambians' decisions to exit the state by turning to nonstate service providers, considering NGOs and chiefs or traditional authorities as potential nonstate sources of basic services. The politics of nonstate service provision is a growing field of inquiry for those examining low-capacity countries, because of its potential to either bolster or disrupt the relationship between citizens and the state (Cammett and MacLean 2014). Nonstate service providers may extend the reach of a low-capacity state, allowing it to fulfill its service obligations by partnering with nonstate organizations. Alternatively, nonstate service providers may undermine relations between citizens and the state by serving as a reminder of the state's ineptitude and by providing an option for exit. Existing studies suggest that either outcome is possible, depending on the relationship between the state and the nonstate providers and on how citizens perceive that relationship. In the Zambian context, the evidence advanced in this chapter indicates that NGOs may serve as an alternative to the state, while chiefs or other traditional authorities act more as a conduit to state services. While turning to NGOs may be a form of exit from the state, reliance on traditional authorities is not.

These results have significant implications for state and political development within Zambia. If NGOs are able to act consistently as an alternative to government service provision, their ability to undermine citizen reliance on state services may disrupt the development of a politically engaged citizenry. The fiscal contract relationship between citizens and the state, marked by the exchange of income for public services, is thought to underlie modern citizenship and ensure pathways of accountability between citizens and the state. If NGOs are able to form a parallel system of service provision that allows citizens to exit the state, there is little incentive for those citizens to become more politically engaged or attempt to hold the state accountable, and there is little incentive for the state to focus energy or resources on those who have turned to external sources of services. Yet the evidence suggests that rural dwellers who would otherwise be relatively isolated from state services continue to see their chiefs as community mouthpieces or conduits to state services. This relationship—similar to Baldwin's findings about Zambian chiefs bolstering democratic accountability—indicates that chiefs may provide a countervailing force, integrating back into the state those who might otherwise exit and providing some basic (if imperfect) accountability (Baldwin 2015). In my survey sample, there was very little overlap between those who reported relying on NGOs and those who reported turning to their chiefs. While this distinction was closely related to the urban/rural divide, the divergent political implications of relying on chiefs versus NGOs indicate that understanding the source of this variation will continue to be an important line of inquiry.

Understanding the other form of exit examined in this chapter—noncompliant attitudes toward state revenue collection—requires viewing the fiscal contract from a different angle. The fiscal contract approach to understanding relations between state and society requires that the state relies on the citizenry as a source of revenue (in addition to the state providing services in exchange for that revenue). Therefore, just as turning to nonstate service providers may be a form of exit, revenue noncompliance is a way of exiting the relationship between state and society that is built around such a fiscal contract. In a low-capacity state with a limited ability to measure economic activity or monitor citizens' revenue compliance, noncompliant attitudes, which indicate a rejection of the state's authority to collect revenue, undermine the fiscal contract binding citizens to the state. The evidence in this chapter suggests that citizens' experiences with service provision—theoretically, the product of a well-functioning fiscal contract—influence the degree to which they hold compliant attitudes toward revenue collection. In general, those who interpret their experiences with service delivery as exclusionary are less likely to hold tax-compliant attitudes. Furthermore, examining the reasoning that survey respondents provided for their noncompliance indicates that those who had a more negative interpretation of their interactions with the state through service provision were more likely to provide "fiscal contract" reasoning behind their noncompliance.

These results have important implications for the ability of low-capacity states like Zambia to foster relations between citizens and the state that are based around the type of accountability implied in the fiscal contract. If the government is unable to extend services to less-developed regions of the country or less able to credibly demonstrate the intent to do so, it will be unable to cultivate a population committed to participating in the system of taxation. Theoretically, the rupture in this revenue-based relationship between citizens and the state will undermine the likelihood that the citizens demand—or that the government provides—governance based on accountability.

Finally, this chapter examined protest as a method of voicing dissatisfaction. As discussed in earlier chapters, Zambia's democracy has certain flaws—prominent among them the lack of programmatic parties—that make formal channels of political participation insufficient for expressing political preferences. Zambia is by no means unique among low-capacity states with electoral regimes, many of which have systemic features that undermine the extent to which voting or other formal behaviors are an effective way of expressing political ideas. In such a context, those who are dissatisfied may choose to express voice through alternative channels. In this chapter, I conceptualize protest as a way for citizens to amplify their voice and make specific demands on the government. This conceptualization is distinct from scholarly views of protest as part of contentious politics, social movements, or protorevolutionary behavior.

In the Zambian context, the evidence presented in this chapter indicates that protest is most likely for those who have empowering subjective assessments of government attempts at service provision. In other words, those who believed most strongly that the government was trying to help them through service provision (regardless of the material reality) were the most likely to engage in protest. This evidence, bolstered by qualitative explanations, suggests that protest behavior in Zambia is most common among those with the strongest sense of political efficacy—those who believe the government cares about them and will likely listen to them. Perceptions of service delivery play an important role in generating this sense of efficacy. However, in this analysis, the relationship between service delivery and protest was restricted to the fully subjective measure, indicating that actual material service delivery is less important than the perception that the government is putting forth its best effort.

Taken together, the evidence in this chapter paints a more complete portrait of how service delivery influences the degree to which Zambians engage in certain forms of exit and voice. Those dissatisfied with government attempts at service delivery are more likely to report forms of exit through reliance on NGOs as nonstate service providers or through noncompliant attitudes toward revenue collection, while those most satisfied with government attempts are more likely to report voice through protest behavior. This evidence indicates that citizens' experiences with service delivery do not only shape the likelihood that they participate in politics; these experiences also influence the degree to which citizens engage with the state at all. In low-capacity states with limited ability to collect revenue or administer their territory, service delivery is an essential signal to citizens, influencing the degree to which they wish to engage in the most fundamental processes of state-building.

CHAPTER 8

Conclusion

When I arrived in Lusaka in July 2016, the first thing I noticed during the drive down the Great East Road from the airport into the city was the lack of potholes that used to define that stretch of pavement. Under President Edgar Lungu, who had succeeded Michael Sata after his sudden death in October 2014, the government had prioritized infrastructure improvements, particularly along major thoroughfares in the capital. Lungu was a month away from the next election and was campaigning hard to keep his job. Posters and billboards promoting himself and his party, the Patriotic Front, lined the roads. Proclaiming that Lungu "walked the talk," they listed various projects of infrastructure and service improvement that the government had recently undertaken. The campaign was heated, triggering an unprecedented amount of electoral violence for Zambia. Even Lungu's most ardent detractors could not deny the infrastructure improvements in the capital, but many complained that those improvements fell short for those who lived outside the specific neighborhoods targeted for development.

Infrastructure development proved to be a highly mobilizing issue in the 2016 election. In urban areas, people animatedly described the improvements, expressing their support for the government, or became agitated in describing frustrations associated with incomplete service delivery that brought improvements only to other areas. Outside urban areas, improved services such as a new health clinic became a rallying point for some communities, while deteriorating services elsewhere led to political apathy. In contrast, comparisons of the policy platforms of the leading parties rarely came up. While the urban elite might compare the PF's brand of populism to the liberal economic policy platform of the opposition (the United Party for National Development) or might worry over issues of corruption and the concentration of power in Lungu's presidency, the vast majority of Zambians I talked to outside of the capital were more concerned with the government's actions (or inactions) regarding basic service delivery. Perceptions of service delivery influenced not only partisan preference but also political mobilization: many who felt wholly ignored with regard to service delivery saw little point in participating in the imminent election.

These observations underscore the principal argument of this book: in low-capacity states like Zambia, citizens' experiences with the government through basic service delivery shape their subsequent political behavior. In such states, where government presence is variable and generally low outside major cities, basic service delivery is the primary avenue through which citizens interact with the state. Therefore, the government's decisions regarding service provision signal how it regards the residents of various communities. In countries with electoral regimes that have barriers to the development of programmatic parties, experiences with basic service delivery may be stronger than ideology in motivating political behavior. Beyond partisan preference, the evidence put forth in this book indicates that experiences with basic service delivery influence both the rate and the form of the political behavior people undertake.

This concluding chapter revisits the framework I developed for this study to expand policy feedback, as a theoretical approach, beyond industrial democracies, by considering feedback loops that connect service delivery and political behavior in developing democracies. I here summarize the main findings from the study and use data from round 6 of the Afrobarometer to probe their generalizability. I then synthesize these results to form some closing arguments. Specifically, the evidence presented in this book makes the case for taking service delivery seriously as an independent variable in African politics. I argue that in countries that are developing their political systems at the same time as they are developing state capacity, the physical development of the state and the political development of citizens must be considered concurrent processes. Finally, the research presented in this book allows some conclusions but also includes some ambiguous findings and brings up additional questions related to best policy practices and possible scope conditions. The final section of this chapter considers some of these unanswered questions and identifies areas for further research.

EXPANDING POLICY FEEDBACK APPROACHES BEYOND INDUSTRIAL DEMOCRACIES

As chapter 3 elaborates, this study has relied on the theory of policy feedback to gain insights into the ways in which service delivery might influence political participation. The basic premise of policy feedback—that public policy can influence patterns of political participation—invites broad application, but this theory has been applied primarily to advanced industrial democracies. As a result, certain assumptions that have been built into the application of policy feedback limit its ready translation to low-capacity states. In particular, the growing body of literature that employs policy feedback has tended to focus on variations among "welfare states," examining the explicit (or implicit) rationale governing which citizens receive what type of entitlement or other government benefits (e.g., Esping-Andersen 1990; Orloff 1993; Gilens 1999; Kumlin 2004). Governments frame social programs as either entitlements of citizenship or "undeserved" benefits; receiving entitlements may make citizens feel more connected to their polity, while receiving stigmatized benefits may make citizens feel ashamed or embarrassed. An important feature of this scholarship, however, is its assumption that states have a high capacity to implement social policy, enabling recipients of various policies to read intention into government action. When states lack the capacity for universal basic service provision, citizens are less likely to read intentionality into their experience of social policy, and their interpretations of these experiences are likely to be different from those of citizens in a high-capacity democracy with a more consistent and evenly implemented approach to social policy.

To highlight one example, government capacity becomes particularly important in policy feedback because it influences the way that citizens may understand and interpret material neglect. Depending on the context, "material neglect" may take on many different forms. In a wealthy democracy like the United States, material neglect may manifest through overcrowded public schools, long lines and surly bureaucrats at benefits offices, or inadequate public housing. In a poor democracy like Zambia, it may manifest through a complete lack of services altogether. This illustration does not just indicate that there is a different standard for what constitutes neglect. In a wealthy democracy, where many or most citizens have reasonable access to public services, explicit neglect may feel more intentional and convey a much stronger signal about one's status in the polity. In a poor democracy, material neglect may not elicit the same interpretation. Many of my respondents reported frustration with inadequate service provision but expressed understanding that there were limits to what the government could accomplish given the economic circumstances in the country.

As a result of these different policy environments, the policy feedback framework must be adapted to take into account the realities of social policy in low-capacity countries. Because most low-capacity countries lack a robust welfare state, trying to understand how citizens are divided into categories based on the framing of social policies is less relevant. In many low-capacity countries, there is no meaningful distinction between "entitlements" and "stigmatized benefits." When the overwhelming majority of citizens in a country live in poverty, the idea that benefits from the government might be "stigmatized" is laughable. In many such states, the nuances of social policy are hardly relevant for peoples' daily lives. More immediately important is the ability to access any basic services. In a state where the government is still working toward the goal of universal basic service provision, whether or not a person has access to a basic service such as running water, a paved road, a school with teachers who attend regularly, or a staffed health clinic is the most pressing concern. Particularly since the majority of the Zambians I spoke with think the government is ultimately responsible for basic service provision, the entire spectrum of relevant social policies falls under this category of "entitlements."

In such a low-capacity environment, citizens are more likely to judge their interactions with the government based on service delivery as opposed to a more complex array of nuanced social policy. This reality requires a shift in focus to the physical presence (or not) of services and to citizens' interpretations of their experiences in gaining access to these services. As I alluded to above, this interpretive element is likely to operate differently in the context of a low-capacity state, where citizens have different expectations of what their government can reasonably accomplish. As this study demonstrates (and other studies have suggested), the way Zambians judge inadequate service provision is related more closely to their perceptions about how hard the government is trying rather than to an objective accounting of the precise array of services to which they have access.

In this study, I have therefore expanded the policy feedback framework to accomplish two things: shifting the input and providing a lens for interpreting output. First, the inputs I considered here were measures of basic service delivery rather than more complex constellations of social policy. Second, to interpret how these experiences with basic service delivery might influence citizens' perceptions of the state and their patterns of political participation, I developed a policy experience typology. This typology—categorizing service experiences as empowering, marginalizing, neglectful, or burdensome—allowed me to consider how service delivery affected peoples' perceptions of the government, while taking into account lower expectations and more flexible perceptions of government intentionality. These adaptations to the policy feedback framework allow its primary insight—that policy shapes participation—to translate to the low-capacity context.

THEMATIC OVERVIEW OF MAIN FINDINGS AND GENERALIZABILITY PROBE

In this book, I have examined the relationship between citizens' experiences with basic service delivery and the likelihood that they engage in certain forms of political behavior. Specifically, I considered various forms of collective behavior and political engagement and formal avenues of political participation. In addition, I considered the relationship between service delivery and the likelihood that citizens turn to alternatives to state providers or subvert the state by evading revenue collection. For reasons explained more fully in chapter 3, I used three different measures of service delivery: an objective measure of the number of basic services to which respondents have easy access, a semi-subjective measure in which respondents identified a certain type of service or program important to them and then described their experience with that service, and a fully subjective measure based on respondents' responses to an open-ended question asking what they thought about government attempts at service provision generally. The subjective and semi-subjective measures were coded to indicate whether the respondent received and was happy with government services (empowered), received but was unsatisfied with government services (marginalized), did not receive government services due to perceived oversight (neglected), or believed that he or she had been explicitly and intentionally excluded from government services (burdened).

The rationale for using three different measures was that service delivery may influence political participation through material pathways (with access to resources making certain forms of participation more or less feasible) or through interpretive pathways (with the experience of receiving services leading to a specific understanding of one's relationship to the government).

The various forms of political behavior considered differed in the degree that they were related to the objective, semi-subjective, or fully subjective measures of service delivery. This difference reflects the degree to which respondents' actions were related either to the material reality of receiving or being excluded from services or to the respondents' interpretations of their experiences with government services.

This study has relied solely on evidence from Zambia, but there is reason to believe that the trends identified here may generalize beyond that country. Investigating the relationship between democratization and state-building in sub-Saharan Africa, Bratton and Chang concluded that "democratization has enjoyed bright prospects only in the context of relatively effective states," and they specified that "institutional capacity and popular legitimacy" are particularly important prerequisites for a durable democracy (Bratton and Chang 2006, 1080). More recently, investigations have shed light on how important basic service delivery is for cultivating popular legitimacy. Olivier de Sardan (2014, 400–403) has argued that Africans in many countries increasingly view basic services as an entitlement that should be provided by the state, even where the state has a poor record of past delivery. Yet the physical presence of infrastructure or other basic services does not have a consistently strong relationship to perceptions of state legitimacy. Rather, perceptions of state legitimacy are bound up in interpretations of the extent to which the government is trying to provide these services. In an article reviewing a number of recent studies on the political effects of service delivery, McLoughlin (2015, 347) concluded that actual satisfaction with basic public service delivery is far less important for perceptions of state legitimacy than are "perceptions of how well the government was 'trying' to improve them." She suggests—as evidence from the present study supports—that when citizens have exceedingly low expectations of what the state can actually accomplish, the effort to improve services sends a stronger signal to citizens than the actual quality of the services.

These studies indicate that because popular legitimacy is essential for establishing democracy and because attempts at basic service delivery are, in turn, essential for popular legitimacy, the political implications of service delivery that I found in Zambia are likely to exist in other low-capacity countries with new(er) democratic or electoral institutions. This chapter proceeds to revisit the book's main findings and uses data from 31 countries in round 6 of the Afrobarometer to determine how typical or exceptional these findings are. The Afrobarometer's questions about service delivery do not map perfectly onto the framework developed here, so this analysis is necessarily approximate. Nevertheless, it provides useful insights into the generalizability of these findings.

The Afrobarometer, the Varieties of Democracy Dataset, and Methods

This probe into the generalizability of this study relies on two additional sources of data: the Afrobarometer and the Varieties of Democracy Dataset (V-Dem) (Coppedge et al. 2017). Round 6 of the Afrobarometer, carried out across 2014 and 2015, includes 31 sub-Saharan countries. To replicate my analysis as closely as possible, I rely on two measures of service delivery: an objective measure and a semi-subjective measure. The objective measure, recorded by the survey enumerators, is a count variable indicating which of the following were present in the enumeration area: a paved road, a primary school, a health clinic, and a police station.[1] The semi-subjective measure derives from questions about "how well the government is handling" the five services that were most commonly invoked in my survey: health care, education, water, roads, and electricity. I used the responses to these questions to generate the trinary variable "handle services," grouping responses into "badly," "fairly," and "well." This coding should approximate respondents who feel neglected, those who have marginal access to services, and those who likely feel empowered by access to services.[2] In the analyses below, respondents with the worst assessments of government handling of services form the base category, so the coefficients represent the differences between being in the middle or top categories, respectively, as compared to the bottom category.

Cross-country comparison also introduces the possibility of examining whether regime type or characteristics of the government have any influence on the relationship between services and political behavior. I theorized that an important feature in Africa's electoral regimes is the extent to which political parties actually represent programmatic platforms. V-Dem has produced a dataset that estimates various components of democratic governance, including the linkages that major parties within a country seek to cultivate with their citizens, along the following ordinal measure: clientelist (0), clientelist and collective (1), collective (2), collective and programmatic (3), and programmatic (4) (Pemstein et al. 2017).[3] In their estimation, Zambia's parties cultivate collective linkages. In the Afrobarometer's 31-country sample, no country has purely programmatic politics by the V-Dem measure. Therefore, the meaningful distinction is whether or not politics within the country have a clientelist component (0/1) or not (2/3), so I used this division to create the binary variable "collective." Because service delivery is a collective good by nature, one would expect the relationship between services and participation to be stronger in countries that combine collective and programmatic politics. In countries where clientelism is the dominant political mode, expectations of personal benefits may be a stronger political motivator than experiences with service provision.

Each analysis reported below includes a standard set of control variables (not reported), including the respondent's sex, age (log), residence (urban vs. rural), education, level of poverty,[4] and religiosity.[5] Coding details are available in this book's appendix. For each analysis, I used mixed-effects multilevel logistic regression, with individuals nested within countries and a random intercept for each country. This estimation strategy accounts for the likelihood that observations within countries are not independent from one another, without washing out country-level variation. It also allows the inclusion of country-level variables, like the measure of political linkages. Using these variables, the analysis below mimics my earlier chapter-by-chapter analysis as closely as possible.

Collective Behavior

In chapter 4, I explored the extent to which citizens' experiences with service delivery influence the likelihood that they undertake certain forms of collective behavior, including attending community meetings, joining with their neighbors to solve local problems, or becoming members of some kind of group. The results indicate that collective behavior is strongly linked to lower rates of objective service provision. The qualitative interview data shed light on this relationship, demonstrating that many Zambians come together with their neighbors explicitly to address challenges caused by a low degree of service provision. Interview subjects described working together to maintain roads when the government failed to or contributing labor to build schools and health clinics when the government could not provide the service outright. In this case, it was clear that the relationship between service delivery and collective behavior was primarily material: collective behavior is associated with the material conditions precipitated by a lack of service delivery. However, interpretations of service delivery were also related to some forms of collective behavior and operated in the opposite direction: those with empowering subjective assessments of service provision were more likely to engage in some forms of collective action.

The Afrobarometer similarly includes questions that measure attendance at community meetings, joining with others to raise issues, and group membership. The results in table 15 demonstrate that the same trend evident in my data occurs in the Afrobarometer's 31-country sample: objective rates of service provision are negatively associated with each measure of collective behavior. Just as in Zambia, people elsewhere in Africa are more likely to engage in collective behavior not only when they lack service provision but also when they have a more positive assessment of services, which illustrates the divergence between objective and interpretive measures of service provision. The null interaction term (column V in table 15) indicates that this relationship exists regardless of the nature of political linkages within a country. While the main results—the negative relationship between objective service provision and collective behavior—are replicated here, the magnitude of the relationship is quite small. Indeed, running the analysis by country illustrates a great deal of variation (fig. 11). While 23 of the 31 countries have a coefficient of less than 1 (indicating a negative relationship), three (Malawi, Burundi, and Lesotho) have positive, significant coefficients.[6]

Table 15. Service Delivery and Collective Behavior across Africa

	Community Meeting I	Join to Raise Issue II	Group Member III	Collective Behavior Index IV	Collective Behavior Index V
Objective Services	0.97**	0.96**	0.97*	0.97**	0.98
	(0.01)	(0.01)	(0.01)	(0.01)	(0.01)
Collective					0.81
					(0.16)
Objective Services * Collective					0.98
					(0.02)
Handle Services (1)	1.19**	1.18**	1.16**	1.20**	1.20**
	(0.03)	(0.03)	(0.03)	(0.02)	(0.02)
Handle Services (2)	1.14**	1.19**	1.23**	1.21**	1.21**
	(0.04)	(0.04)	(0.05)	(0.03)	(0.03)
N (obs)	43,705	43,634	43,661	43,425	43,425
N (countries)	31	31	31	31	31

Note: Odds ratios for multilevel logistic and ordinal logistic regressions are reported, with standard errors parenthesized below. Individuals are nested within countries, with random intercept for country. Statistical significance is denoted by *if $p < 0.05$, **if $p < 0.01$. Control variables were included but are not reported.

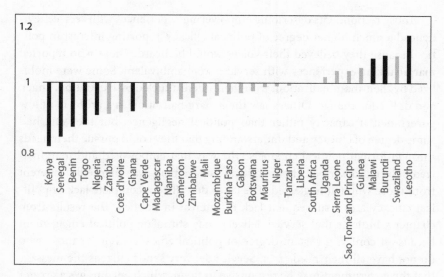

Fig. 11. Relationship between Objective Service Provision and Collective Behavior, by Country

For most of the countries in the sample, the relationship between access to services and collective behavior is negative, but this relationship is far from universal. As political linkages do not moderate the relationship, future work would do well to investigate the conditions under which communities organize in the absence of the state, as well as why they appear to organize more in the presence of the state in some places, such as Lesotho, Burundi, and Malawi.

Political Engagement

Chapter 5 took up the issue of political engagement, as measured by the degree to which respondents are interested in politics, talk about politics, or make an effort to follow current affairs in the news. I argued that because political engagement is a psychological state, it would be more closely linked to the interpretive measures of service delivery. The results indeed indicated that political engagement is unrelated to the material presence of services but strongly related to interpretations of the government's attempts to provide services. Any interpretation of government services, save outright neglect, was associated with a greater interest in and proclivity to talk about politics. However, as the qualitative data highlight, different interpretations of service delivery were associated with different forms of interest.

Those respondents describing empowering experiences with services evidenced a much higher degree of political efficacy, reporting interest in politics because they believed their voices would be heard. Those who reported marginalizing experiences with services were ambivalent. Some were mobilized by their marginalization, with their interest fueled by frustration, anger, and desire for change. Others saw their marginalization as a problem of low governmental capacity rather than political negligence, but they still had some degree of efficacy and understanding that they could pursue their needs through formal political channels. The way that empowered and marginalized subjects described their political engagement was markedly different from those who felt neglected. The latter described a complete lack of political efficacy and a subsequent lack of interest in politics. The results from chapter 5 indicate that service delivery may stimulate political engagement because it confers a certain degree of political efficacy, even for those who do not have all their needs met. Service delivery sends citizens the message that the government may be responsive to them, which encourages a greater degree of engagement in politics.

The Afrobarometer includes questions about whether respondents are "interested in politics" and whether they "talk about politics." In Zambia, where people talk about politics openly without fear of reprisal, these two measures were closely correlated. In the larger sample, comfort with discussing politics is country-dependent, and the two variables are less closely correlated. As table 16 demonstrates, interest in politics is strongly associated with the middle category of "handle services": those who think the government is doing fairly well at handling basic services have a higher degree of interest in politics than those who think the government is doing very badly or very well. The qualitative data from Zambia would suggest that this pattern reflects disengagement on the part of the poorly served and complacency for those who are best served. In that data, talking about politics has no relationship with middling interpretations of government service delivery but is negatively associated with positive interpretations of service delivery, further corroborating the idea that the best-served citizens may be more complacent. However, this variable is harder to interpret for the Afrobarometer sample, because of variation in the extent to which people feel free to talk about politics across countries. In that broader sample, objective service delivery is also associated with greater political engagement, but the magnitude of this relationship is much smaller.

The relationship between the variables "handle services" and "interest in politics" in the Afrobarometer sample depends on the political linkages in the country. While middling interpretations of service provision are nearly always associated with higher levels of political interest, positive interpretations of services are only linked to political interest in countries with collective/programmatic (rather than clientelist) politics. Figure 12 illustrates the distinction.

Panel A shows the coefficients for the relationship between the middling interpretation of service delivery and political interest for each country. The relationship is positive for 24 of the 31 countries and significant in 10, providing evidence that a middling evaluation of government performance is widely associated with greater political interest, regardless of the nature of political linkages in the country. Panel B shows the coefficients for the relationship between the positive interpretations of service delivery and political interest for each country. The relationship pulls in opposite directions: there is a strong, positive, and significant relationship between positive interpretations of service delivery and political interest in Gabon, Namibia, Cameroon, Côte d'Ivoire, and Togo but a negative and significant relationship in Guinea, Sierra Leone, and Burundi. The interaction term indicates that positive interpretations of service delivery are associated with higher political interest in

Table 16. Service Delivery and Political Engagement across Africa

	Interest in Politics I	Talk about Politics II	Interest in Politics III
Objective Services	1.04**	1.05**	1.04**
	(0.01)	(0.01)	(0.01)
Handle Services (1)	1.19**	1.01	1.12*
	(0.03)	(0.02)	(0.05)
Handle Services (2)	1.01	0.92*	0.82**
	(0.04)	(0.03)	(0.05)
Handle Services * Collective (1)			1.11
			(0.06)
Handle Services * Collective (2)			1.36**
			(0.10)
N (obs)	43,588	43,506	43,588
N (countries)	31	31	31

Note: Odds ratios for multilevel logistic regressions are reported, with standard errors parenthesized below. Individuals are nested within countries, with a random intercept for country. Statistical significance is denoted by *if $p < 0.05$, **if $p < 0.01$. Control variables were included but are not reported.

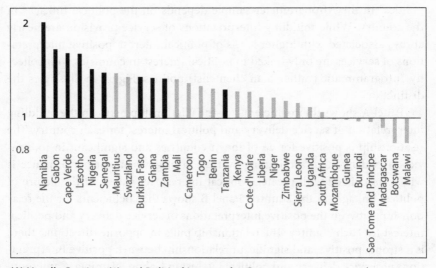

(A) Handle Services (1) and Political Interest, by Country

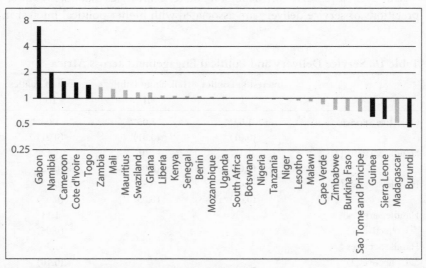

(B) Handle Services (2) and Political Interest, by Country

Fig. 12. Relationship between Interpretation of Service Provision and Political Interest, by Country

countries where politics is more programmatic and with lower political interest in countries where politics is more clientelist. This finding is logical if one considers that service delivery is linked to electoral politics in countries with collective/programmatic linkages and to personal relationships in countries with collective/clientelist linkages.

Formal Political Participation

Chapter 6 examined the extent to which service delivery influences formal political participation, as measured by contacting officials, partisan affiliation, and voting. At the most basic level of analysis, the results demonstrate that respondents who interpreted their experiences with service delivery as empowering were more likely to participate in politics, regardless of their partisan affiliation. Similar to the results regarding political engagement, the qualitative data provided by interview subjects indicates that this relationship emerges because people who have positive experiences with service delivery hold a higher degree of political efficacy, even when they are critical of the government. However, an empowering interpretation of service delivery was not a unique predictor of political participation.

The relationship between service delivery and political participation is complicated by the relationships between service delivery, collective behavior, and political engagement. Indeed, both collective behavior and political engagement mediate (at least partially) the relationship between service delivery and political participation. As a result of this mediation, lower objective rates of service provision are associated with a higher degree of political participation because they stimulate collective behavior. In particular, people living in poorly served rural communities often attend community meetings that result in attempts to contact their local representative, a trend that likely drives the relationship between low rates of service provision and more political participation. Similarly, respondents reporting marginalizing interpretations of services had higher rates of political participation. This relationship is partially mediated by the relationship between marginalization and political engagement. However, as discussed above, both marginalized and empowered interview subjects reported higher rates of political efficacy related to their experiences of receiving at least some services. Therefore, I conclude that marginalizing experiences maintain a direct relationship to political participation because citizens with these experiences have reason to believe the government may be responsive to them.

The Afrobarometer data provides additional evidence supporting the idea that either marginalizing or empowering experiences with service delivery might lead to political participation, as compared to those with negative experiences. Those with the most positive interpretation of government services were more likely to report partisan affiliation, contacting local representatives and members of parliament, and overall participation. Those with the middling interpretation of services were more likely to report voting, as well as contacting local representatives and members of parliament and overall participation. The objective measure of services is also positively associated with some forms of participation, but the magnitude of the relationship is much smaller.

The interaction term in column VI in table 17 indicates that the relationship between both levels of "handle services" and the participation index is stronger in countries with more programmatic political linkages. Figure 13 displays the strength of the relationship between the most positive interpretation of government service provision and the political participation index. While the relationship is positive for 19 of the 31 countries, there is a great degree of variation, and it is even negative and statistically significant

Table 17. Service Delivery and Political Participation across Africa

	Voted I	Partisan II	Contact Local Representative III	Contact MP IV	Participation Index V	Participation Index VI
Objective Services	0.99	1.02*	1.01	1.03*	1.03**	1.02**
	(0.01)	(0.01)	(0.01)	(0.02)	(0.01)	(0.01)
Handle Services (1)	1.08**	1.03	1.17**	1.20**	1.13**	1.00
	(0.03)	(0.03)	(0.03)	(0.04)	(0.02)	(0.04)
Handle Services (2)	0.95	1.12**	1.20**	1.16**	1.14**	0.91
	(0.03)	(0.04)	(0.05)	(0.06)	(0.03)	(0.05)
Collective						0.61*
						(0.13)
Services (1) * Collective						1.19**
						(0.05)
Services (2) * Collective						1.39**
						(0.09)
N (obs)	43,000	40,452	41,382	43,732	37,213	37,213
N (countries)	30	30	30	31	28	28

Note: Odds ratios for multilevel logistic and ordinal logistic regressions are reported, with standard errors parenthesized below. Individuals are nested within countries, with a random intercept for country. Statistical significance is denoted by *if $p < 0.05$, **if $p < 0.01$. Control variables were included but are not reported.

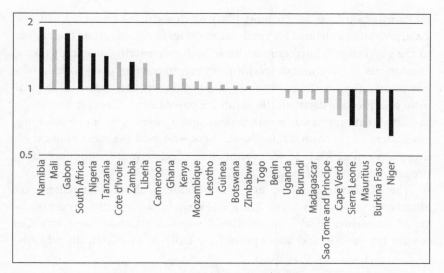

Fig. 13. Relationship between Interpretation of Service Provision and Political Participation, by Country

in Niger, Burkina Faso, and Sierra Leone. As the interaction term indicates, positive (and middling) assessments of service delivery are far more likely to precipitate political participation in countries with some degree of programmatic politics.

Alternative Modes of Interaction with the State

Chapter 7 examined how experiences with service delivery relate to some alternative modes of interaction with the state, including reliance on non-state service providers and attitudes about state revenue collection. Because taxation and state provision of services comprise the exchange at the core of the fiscal contract, a process believed to build accountability between citizens and their state, understanding when citizens turn to nonstate service providers or develop tactics to evade revenue collection is essential (particularly for low-capacity states). The evidence in chapter 7 indicates that Zambians are more likely to turn to NGOs for services when they have less objective access to state services or perceive government provision as neglectful rather than empowering. The qualitative data indicate that many Zambians understand their reliance on NGOs as a reaction to the state's abdication of its role in service delivery. Interestingly, the opposite is true of chiefs as service brokers: respondents are far more likely to view chiefs as working with the state, providing a channel for rural communities to communicate their needs to the government. Furthermore, those with empowering or marginalizing assessments of government service provision were more likely to hold tax-compliant attitudes. Chapter 7 also examined protest as a high-cost, atypical form of expressing dissatisfaction with the government. However, the results indicated that protest was most common among those with an empowering assessment of government provision: those who held the most political efficacy were more likely to see protest as an effective way of communicating preferences to the government.

The Afrobarometer does not ask respondents about their reliance on alternative service providers, but it does ask how much they trust traditional authorities. Furthermore, it asks respondents about their attitudes toward tax evasion and about protest. As table 18 illustrates, the relation-

Table 18. Service Delivery and Alternative Modes of Interaction

	Trust Traditional Authority I	Trust Traditional Authority II	Tax-Compliant Attitude III	Tax-Compliant Attitude IV	Protest V	Protest VI
Objective Services	0.96**	0.96**	1.02*	1.02	1.04*	1.22**
	(0.01)	(0.01)	(0.01)	(0.01)	(0.02)	(0.04)
Objective Services*						0.80**
Collective						(0.03)
Handle Services (1)	1.70**	1.62**	1.13**	0.98	0.94	0.95
	(0.04)	(0.07)	(0.03)	(0.04)	(0.04)	(0.04)
Handle Services (2)	2.10**	2.04**	1.23**	0.89*	1.06	1.06
	(0.08)	(0.13)	(0.04)	(0.05)	(0.06)	(0.06)
Collective		0.73		0.46**		2.17**
		(0.14)		(0.07)		(0.59)
Services (1)* Collective		1.08		1.26**		
		(0.06)		(0.06)		
Services (2)* Collective		1.05		1.64**		
		(0.08)		(0.11)		
N (obs)	38,501	38,501	41,894	41,894	43,175	43,175
N (countries)	28	28	31	31	31	31

Note: Odds ratios for multilevel logistic regressions are reported, with standard errors parenthesized below. Individuals are nested within countries, with random intercept for country. Statistical significance is denoted by *if $p < 0.05$, **if $p < 0.01$. Control variables were included but are not reported.

ship between positive interpretations of government service provision and trust in traditional authorities is positive and strikingly strong, and is not conditioned by the nature of political linkages within the country. The relationship between these two variables is positive in every country except Burkina Faso and is statistically significant in all but five (Gabon, Madagascar, Sierra Leone, Tanzania, and Liberia). While this data cannot illuminate the mechanism underlying the relationship, it is consistent with the idea that where people view traditional authorities as brokers for government services, attitudes toward those authorities are strongly associated with interpretations of those services.

Interpretation of government services is strongly associated with tax-compliant attitudes as well, but this relationship depends on the nature of political linkages within the country. As figure 14 illustrates, the relationship is positive in 21 of the 31 countries but is negative and statistically significant in Burundi, Liberia, and Gabon. In those countries, having a better interpretation of government service provision is actually associated with a lower likelihood of holding a tax-compliant attitude. While "fiscal contract" theories would predict a positive link between service provision and tax-compliant attitudes, this link depends on some degree of collective or programmatic politics in the country. Absent such politics, there is little reason for citizens to connect government service provision to taxation.

Lastly, the Afrobarometer data indicate that protest is associated with more access to services, though the relationship is not particularly strong in the overall sample. In that data, unlike in mine, proclivity to protest is related to objective access to services rather than to interpretation of services, though the relationship is in the same direction. This relationship, too, is conditioned by the nature of political linkages in the country. In this case, the link between access to services and protest is stronger in countries where the political linkages are more clientelist than programmatic. In the Afrobarometer sample, the relationship was strongest in Lesotho, Mali, and Burundi, all of which have political linkages with clientelist (rather than programmatic) elements (according to V-Dem). These results suggest that protest is a form of communicating with the government when lower-cost methods, like voting, are insufficient for communicating policy preferences. In countries without programmatic politics, such behavior may be more common among those with better access to services, because those citizens may have a greater degree of efficacy (Harris and Hern forthcoming).

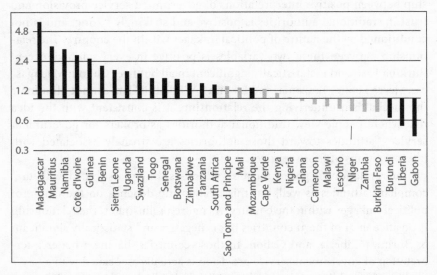

Fig. 14. Relationship between Interpretation of Service Provision and Tax-Compliant Attitudes, by Country

Analytical Conclusions

In total, the findings advanced by this study find broader support in the 31-country sample of sub-Saharan African countries included in the Afrobarometer, though there is variation in the extent to which these findings are generalizable. In some cases, the relationships described here depend on the political linkages within a country. Positive interpretations of service delivery are more likely to generate political interest, political participation, and tax-compliant attitudes in countries that have some combination of collective and programmatic political linkages. In countries with clientelist political linkages, positive interpretations of service delivery may actually undermine these same outcomes. However, regardless of political linkages, lower objective rates of service delivery increase the likelihood of collective behavior, and positive interpretations of service delivery are associated with trust in traditional authorities. While the trends I found in Zambia were strongest in countries with more programmatic linkages, 30 of the countries in the 31-country Afrobarometer sample had a coefficient that was significant and in the correct direction for at least one of the six categories of behavior (collective behavior, political interest, political participation, trust in traditional authorities, tax-compliant attitudes, and protest). Eight countries in addition to Zambia had significant coefficients in the correct direction at least half the time: Benin, Ghana, Lesotho, Namibia, Senegal, South Africa, Tanzania, and Togo. Liberia was the only country that failed to support a single one of the hypotheses tested, though its coefficients were often in the correct direction (but insignificant at the country level). The preceding analysis suggests that while the relationships established in this study are not universal, they are certainly widespread.

TAKING SERVICE DELIVERY SERIOUSLY IN AFRICAN POLITICS

This book is hardly the first effort to examine the role of service delivery in African politics. However, the overwhelming majority of such works either treat service delivery as a dependent variable to be explained by political dynamics or limit their examination of the effects of service delivery to partisan preference or voter turnout (e.g., Gottleib 2015; Jablonski 2014; Briggs 2012, 2014; Kramon and Posner 2013; Banful 2010). These works generally examine service delivery through a distributive politics framework. This body of work—multiple examples of which I describe in the introduction—is important and has much to offer. But the evidence presented in this book indicates that service delivery has political consequences that extend far beyond partisanship or voter turnout. Indeed, the evidence discussed here indicates both the importance and urgency of expanding scholarly understanding of the politics of service delivery in developing countries, beyond distributive politics.

A large number of developing countries with a low capacity for basic service provision made some kind of move toward political liberalization as part of Africa's third wave of democracy (Huntington 1991). These transitions to democracy sometimes stalled, reversed, or resulted in a persistent form of electoral authoritarianism, but almost everywhere, they resulted in the permanent installment of elections, mostly multiparty elections, even if the ruling party stands little chance of losing (Diamond 2002; Young 2012). In such countries, of which Zambia is an example, the state is in the challenging position of institutionalizing a participatory political system at the same time as it is expanding its capacity to perform the basic functions of statehood. Electoral regimes—regardless of how genuinely competitive the elections are—

rely on citizen engagement. But newer democracies in low-capacity states must cultivate such engagement with limited capacity to administer the polity. Previously, discussions of service provision and election revolved around concerns of clientelism and ethnic politics. However, the research presented in this study illustrates that governments' choices about service delivery have impacts that extend beyond winning votes. Service delivery generates different forms of political participation and engagement with the state, and the way the state extends services shapes citizenship.

The results of this study suggest that given a lack of state capacity, the related challenges around basic service delivery have serious implications for building a democratically engaged citizenry. In Zambia, people who receive basic services—even when those services are suboptimal—are far more likely to express a sense of political efficacy, be politically engaged, and translate that engagement into political participation. The high levels of political engagement and participation among respondents who deemed their access to basic services as "marginalizing" indicates that citizens in such contexts moderate their expectations; residents of low-capacity states understand how limited resources constrain the government's ability to achieve high-level service delivery. At the same time, the sense that the government is at least trying to provide basic services improves numerous measures of political engagement and participation. This finding is replicated in the Afrobarometer's broader sample, in which middling levels of satisfaction with the way the government handles services is often associated with higher rates of engagement and participation, compared to the lowest levels of satisfaction.

While this finding is encouraging, the corollary is that those who are excluded from basic service provision have a much lower degree of political efficacy and therefore have a lower proclivity for political engagement or participation. Such an outcome is deeply concerning for political development in states that face serious barriers to service extension. The results of this study would suggest that the citizenry in such contexts is less likely to become democratically engaged. This corollary may operate at two levels: within a country, those with less access to state resources may remain politically alienated, deepening existing inequality; across countries, those with a limited ability to extend basic services may also have a harder time building a politically engaged citizenry. That some of the relationships between service delivery and participation were moderated by the nature of political linkages in each country is indicative of negative feedback loops that may occur when countries have clientelist politics, poor service delivery, and a disengaged populace.

UNANSWERED QUESTIONS AND FUTURE RESEARCH

The empirical analysis included in this study provided evidence of data trends linking various service provision experiences to different forms of political participation. It also supplied qualitative evidence supporting an interpretation of those trends. A number of unanswered questions provide avenues for future research.

The data discussed in chapter 4 indicated that Zambians were more likely to engage in collective behavior—especially around service provision—when the government failed to provide those services. While this collective organizing enabled communities to obtain certain services for themselves, it was clear that the quality of the services they could provide for themselves generally fell short of what the government might have been able to produce. The status quo is an imperfect solution, and the outstanding question is whether long-term cycles of replacing government service provision with collective organizing are likely to be self-correcting or self-reinforcing.

It is easy to envision the circumstances under which such a cycle would be self-reinforcing. If the government fails to provide services, the community provides for itself, then the government may decide that scarce resources are best allocated elsewhere. Over time, as local government officials understand which communities are more likely to engage in self-help, the government may retreat from attempting provision at all. These communities may then be left with no choice but to continue engaging in collective organizing to provide for themselves. Such a self-reinforcing cycle may have tragic consequences for communities ultimately cut off from government resources.

However, there is also reason to believe that this cycle could be self-correcting, as the data show that collective behavior is also associated with higher levels of political participation. Indeed, mediation analysis supported the idea that lower rates of objective service provision increased rates of political participation. Interview subjects from villages who had engaged in these types of self-help projects described community meetings in which they designated certain leaders to take their concerns to local government officials. If the lack of services leads to collective organizing that boosts communities' civic skills, resulting in a greater frequency of contacting officials, these communities may receive more attention in the future. Ongoing research is necessary to determine whether these cycles are self-reinforcing or self-correcting, as well as the conditions under which one effect is more likely than the other.

Another unanswered question involves chapter 5's finding that those who reported marginalizing experiences with services were as and sometimes more likely to report political engagement as those with empowering experiences. Again, this finding could cut both ways: on the one hand, it is an important facet of democracy that those who are frustrated with the status quo voice their dissent; on the other hand, if the marginalized are more politically engaged than the neglected, a tendency of that engagement toward frustration could create perverse incentives for insecure democratic leaders. Considering the first, more optimistic interpretation of this data, it is encouraging that citizens who believe that the government is at least trying to provide services—regardless of its success in doing so—are more politically engaged. That bodes well for democratic citizenship in countries that are still trying to expand basic services, indicating that just making an attempt at service provision could create a more politically engaged populace.

However, chapter 5 also explored the way that people who felt marginalized and empowered explained their political engagement. While the empowered overwhelmingly described their engagement in positive or neutral terms, the marginalized were split, with a large portion of the sample expressing frustration and opposition to the government. Notably, the marginalized were more likely than the neglected to actively voice this frustration; the neglected were more likely to have disengaged from politics altogether. From the perspective of a government, this observation could create a perverse incentive: it is politically expedient to have a population of people who are either empowered or neglected, because then those who are politically engaged are more likely to be either politically neutral or generally supportive. That strategy would entail concentrating resources in fewer areas, widening the gap between those with better or worse access to services. Future research should therefore address whether having a large group of citizens who have marginalizing experiences of service delivery is better or worse for long-term democratic prospects.

Chapter 6 described how both empowering and marginalizing interpretations of service delivery were related to higher rates of political participation. As discussed above, it is encouraging that marginalizing experiences are linked to higher rates of political engagement and participation, indicating that a relatively low threshold of government service delivery can spark political interest and action. The darker corollary is that people who at least think the government is trying to provide them with services are more politically engaged and active than those who think the government is neglecting them outright. If government decisions about where to allocate resources are based partly on political consequences, it is logical to presume that the government will continue targeting areas that are the most politically active. The possible consequence is that higher rates of political participation for the empowered and marginalized could result in a reinforcing cycle that concentrates political resources in these more active areas. The historical analysis conducted in chapter 2 indicates that political activity is certainly not the only way that governments decide how to allocate resources; economic potential also plays a big role. However, if areas of high economic potential receive more resources and have a more active populace, the combination of these political and economic dynamics could encourage a long-term bias favoring investment in more active, more productive areas.

The participation patterns of those who reported marginalizing experiences requires further investigation. While those who reported marginalization participated at about the same rates as those who reported empowerment, these aggregate estimates mask the heterogeneity of the marginalized group. For some, these marginalizing experiences were mobilizing, creating political energy to demand improvements or encourage further progress. For others, marginalization was distinctly demobilizing, contributing to apathy or political nihilism. These two outcomes have distinctly different implications for the creation of a politically engaged populace in a low-capacity state, so researchers should examine what determines whether the marginalized channel their frustration into participation. Because marginalization is such a common experience in low-capacity countries that are struggling to extend service provision, the answer to this question holds much political importance.

Chapter 7 highlighted how experiences with service delivery may be related to some alternative modes of interaction with the state, including exit through reliance on nonstate service providers. The chapter demonstrated that respondents who had less access to or were dissatisfied with state service provision were more likely to turn to NGOs as service providers. If service provision forms an essential component of the fiscal contract linking citizens to the state, could reliance on NGOs as substitute service providers undermine the long-term development of the relations between the state and its citizens? While scholars have considered this question in other African countries, there remains a dearth of systematic multicountry research into the political effects of nonstate service provision. Sometimes, nonstate service providers may collaborate with the government to extend services to otherwise unreachable areas; at other times, they may serve as a symbol of state failure. Systematic future research is necessary to determine more precisely the political consequences of nonstate service provision, alongside the conditions that influence these consequences.

Finally, this study focused explicitly on the way that service delivery might incentivize people to mobilize politically around their interests in different ways, but it did not consider nonmaterial motivators of participation. While partisanship and ideology may be weak predictors of participation in African states (for the reasons discussed in chapter 1), one might expect other forms of expressive voting to be prevalent.[7] For example, people might vote out of a sense of gratitude to liberation parties (Harris 2015), due to a sense of civic duty, or as an expression of democratic identity, voting to show they are voters (Gerber et al. 2016). These expressive motivations may reinforce material incentives for participation or form countervailing pressures. While there is currently a dearth of work on this topic in the African context, future research should consider how expressive voting, especially as a result of projects to generate civic norms around political participation, may interact with material motivators to generate patterns of participation.

DEVELOPING STATE CAPACITY AND CONSTRUCTING CITIZENS AS A CONCURRENT PROCESS

In conclusion, this study has presented evidence that experiences with basic service delivery have a significant relationship with citizens' patterns of political participation in Zambia (and across sub-Saharan Africa more broadly). The theory underlying this observation is not new—many studies indicate that public policy feeds back to influence political participation in many country contexts. However, the policy feedback framework is particularly poignant when applied to low-capacity states. As described above, many low-capacity states were part of Africa's third wave of democracy, meaning that they needed to develop participatory political frameworks at the same time as they were working to expand infrastructure and basic services. In many countries, these dual processes are ongoing. Zambia, for example, has engaged in multiple processes to change its constitution—including electoral rules—since its return to multiparty democracy in 1991. Many of these changes have had a large impact on voting and electioneering, such as the recent amendment requiring that a presidential candidate receive no less than 50 percent of the vote to assume office—a change that went into place less than a year before Edward Lungu's reelection in August 2016. These ongoing changes to the participatory framework of Zambian democracy occur alongside the government's perpetual mandate to extend basic services. As the evidence in this study demonstrates, the extension of such services has clear links to various forms of political participation.

The crux of this observation is that while policy generates feedback effects across multiple contexts, the political development of citizens and physical development of the country occur in low-capacity states as concurrent processes, each likely influencing the other. As low-capacity states construct roads, health clinics, and schools, they are also constructing a citizenry. Thus, it is essential to understand patterns of service provision in low-capacity countries and citizens' understandings of government attempts to provide these services, to understand how and why citizens decide to engage or not engage with their states. In many low-capacity states, basic service provision is the most common way that people encounter the government. The messages that governments send to their citizens through service provision speak louder than bombastic campaign promises: they tell citizens how much they are valued and how likely they are to be heard. Through these powerful messages, states construct their citizens as they allocate resources for services.

Variable Operationalization and Coding

Table A1. Original Survey

Variable Name	Question Wording	Variable Coding
Age	"What is your age?"	1 = 18–35 2 = 36–50 3 = 51–65 4 = >65
Assessment: Burdensome	"In general, what do you think about government services and projects?"	1 = "government makes things harder" 0 = otherwise
Assessment: Empowering	"In general, what do you think about government services and projects?"	1 = "government usually tries to help" 0 = otherwise
Assessment: Marginalizing	"In general, what do you think about government services and projects?"	1 = "government tries but does not do enough" 0 = otherwise
Assessment: Neglectful	"In general, what do you think about government services and projects?"	1 = "government does nothing" 0 = otherwise
Chief Reliance	"If you wanted to get a development project in your community, are you likely to go to the chief or headman?"	1 = Yes 0 = No
Children	"How many children do you have?"	Count variable
Civil Servant	Respondent reports occupation as a civil servant	1 = Yes 0 = No
Collective Behavior Index	Additive index of collective behaviors, including community meetings, join to solve problems, and group member	Count variable ranging from 0 to 3
Community Meetings	"Do you ever go to community meetings?"	1 = Yes (any frequency) 0 = No

Variable Name	Question Wording	Variable Coding
Contact Local Official	"Do you contact local government officials about problems in the community?"	1 = Yes (any frequency) 0 = Never
Contact MP	"Do you contact the MP about problems in the community?"	1 = Yes (any frequency) 0 = No
Customs-Compliant Attitude	Respondents were told a vignette about an otherwise sympathetic woman who avoids customs when importing goods to sell for her small shop, then asked what they thought about her behavior	1 = Supports customs compliance 0 = Supports customs avoidance
Education	"What level of education have you completed?	1 = No school 2 = Some primary 3 = Completed primary 4 = Some secondary 5 = Completed secondary 6 = Postsecondary vocational training 7 = Some college 8 = College degree 9 = Graduate degree
Follow News	"Do you try to look at the news to follow current events?"	1 = Yes 0 = No
Formal Employment	Respondent reports being formally employed	1 = Yes 0 = No
Government Projects	Number of government projects that residents of the survey site could access, from the following list: tarred road, secondary school, health clinic, police post	Count variable ranging from 0 to 4
Group Member	"Are you a member of any groups?"	1 = Yes 0 = No or inactive
Interest in Politics	"Are you interested at all in politics?"	1 = Yes 0 = No
Join to Solve Problems	"How often do you join together with others to solve problems in your community?"	0 = Never 1 = Once every few years 2 = Once per year 3 = Several times per year
Male	Coded by researcher	1 = Male 0 = Female
Married	"Are you married?"	1 = Yes 0 = No

NGO Reliance	"If you wanted to get a development project in your community, are you likely to go to an NGO?"	1 = Yes 0 = No
Northwestern	Coded by researcher	1 = Northwestern Province 0 = Otherwise
Southern	Coded by researcher	1 = Southern Province 0 = Otherwise
On-Rail	Denotes whether respondents live along the line of rail; on-rail includes Livingstone District, parts of Kazangula District, Kabwe District	1 = Yes 0 = No
Participation Index	Additive index of political participation variables, including contact local official, contact MP, support party, and vote 2016	Count variable ranging from 0 to 4
Political Engagement Index	Additive index of political engagement variables, including interested in politics, talk about politics, and interest in news	Count variable ranging from 0 to 3
Project Experience: Burdensome	Number of government projects the respondent discussed that "make life harder"	Count variable ranging from 0 to 3
Project Experience: Empowering	Number of government projects the respondent discussed that "help"	Count variable ranging from 0 to 3
Project Experience: Marginalizing	Number of government projects the respondent discussed that "are insufficient"	Count variable ranging from 0 to 3
Project Experience: Neglectful	Number of government projects the respondent discussed that "are unavailable"	Count variable ranging from 0 to 3
Prospective Vote	"Do you plan to vote in the next election, in 2016?"	1 = Yes 0 = No
Protest	"In the past year, have you attended any protests or demonstrations (riots or strikes)?"	1 = Yes (any frequency) 0 = No
Religiosity	"How often do you attend religious events?"	0 = Never 1 = Rarely 2 = Every few weeks 3 = Once per week 4 = Multiple times per week
Support Political Party	"Do you support any political party?"	1 = Yes 0 = No

(continues)

Variable Name	Question Wording	Variable Coding
Support Ruling Party	"Which party do you support?"	1 = Ruling party 0 = Other party
Talk about Politics	"Do you talk about politics with other people?"	1 = Yes 0 = No
Tax-Compliant Attitude	Respondents were told a vignette about an otherwise sympathetic man who runs an unregistered business and avoids taxes, then asked what they thought about his behavior	1 = Supports tax compliance 0 = Supports tax avoidance
Unemployed	Respondent reports being unemployed	1= Yes 0 = No
Urban	Coded by researcher	1 = Urban 0 = Rural

Table A2. The Afrobarometer and the Varieties of Democracy Dataset

Variable Name	Source	Question Wording	Variable Coding
Age (natural log)	Afrobarometer	Q1: "What is your age?"	Natural log of response
Collective	Varieties of Democracy	Country-level variable asking, "Among the major parties, what is the main or most common form of linkage to their constituents?"	0 = Linkages are primarily clientelistic or mixed clientelistic and local collective 1 = Linkages are primarily collective or mixed local collective and programmatic
Collective Behavior Index	Afrobarometer	Community meeting + join to raise issues + group member	Count variable ranging from 0 to 3
Community Meetings	Afrobarometer	Q20A: "Here is a list of actions that people sometimes take as citizens. For each of these, please tell me whether you, personally, have done any of these things during the past year. If not, would you do this if you had the chance: attended a community meeting?"	1 = Yes (any frequency) 0 = No
Contact Local Representative	Afrobarometer	Q24A: "During the past year, how often have you contacted any of the following persons about some important problem or to give them your views: a local government councilor?"	1 = Yes (any frequency) 0 = No

(continues)

Variable Name	Source	Question Wording	Variable Coding
Contact MP	Afrobarometer	Q24B: "During the past year, how often have you contacted any of the following persons about some important problem or to give them your views: a member of parliament?"	1 = Yes (any frequency) 0 = No
Education	Afrobarometer	Q97: "What is the highest level of education you have completed?"	0 = No school 2 = Some primary school 3 = Completed primary 4 = Some secondary 5 = Completed secondary 6 = Postsecondary 7 = Some university 8 = University completed
Employed	Afrobarometer	Q95: "Do you have a job that pays a cash income? If yes, is it full-time or part-time?"	1 = Yes (part-time or full time) 0 = No
Group Member	Afrobarometer	Q19B: "Let's turn to your role in the community. Now I am going to read out a list of groups that people join or attend. For each one, could you tell me whether you are an official leader, an active member, an inactive member, or not a member: some other voluntary association or community group?"	1 = Member or leader 0 = Not a member or inactive

Handle Services	Afrobarometer	Q66G, H, I, L, M : "How well or badly would you say the current government is handling the following matters, or haven't you heard enough to say: improving basic health services, addressing educational needs, providing water and sanitation services, maintaining roads and bridges, providing a reliable supply of electricity?"	Responses added, ranging from 5 to 20, and recoded: 2 = Well (16–20) 1 = Fairly (11–15) 0 = Badly (5–10)
Interested in Politics	Afrobarometer	Q13: "How interested would you say you are in public affairs?	1 = Interested at any level 0 = Not interested
Join to Raise Issues	Afrobarometer	Q20B: "Here is a list of actions that people sometimes take as citizens. For each of these, please tell me whether you, personally, have done any of these things during the past year. If not, would you do this if you had the chance: got together with others to raise an issue?"	1 = Yes (any frequency) 0 = No
Male	Afrobarometer	Coded by researcher	1 = Male 0 = Female
Objective Services	Afrobarometer	Coded by researcher, indicating whether people have access to a paved road, a primary school, a health clinic, a police station	Count variable ranging from 0 to 4
Participation Index	Afrobarometer	Voted + contact local representative + contact member of parliament + partisan	Count variable ranging from 0 to 4

(continues)

Variable Name	Source	Question Wording	Variable Coding
Partisan	Afrobarometer	Q90A: "Do you feel close to any political party?"	1 = Yes 0 = No
Poverty	Afrobarometer	Q8A–E: "Over the past year, how often, if ever, has someone in your family gone without: enough food to eat, enough clean water for home use, medicines or medical treatment, enough fuel to cook your food, a cash income?"	Each question ranges from 0 (never) to 4 (always); responses added, ranging from 0 to 20
Protest	Afrobarometer	Q27E: "Here is a list of actions that people sometimes take as citizens when they are dissatisfied with government performance. For each of these, please tell me whether you, personally, have done any of these things during the past year. If not, would you do this if you had the chance: participated in a demonstration or protest march?"	1 = Yes (any frequency) 0 = No
Religiosity	Afrobarometer	Q98B: "How important is religion in your life?"	1 = Not at all important 2 = Not very important 3 = Somewhat important 4 = Very important
Talk about Politics	Afrobarometer	Q14: "When you get together with your friends or family, would you say you discuss political matters:"	1 = Yes (any frequency) 0 = Not at all

Tax-Compliant Attitude	Afrobarometer	Q75B: "I am going to ask you about a range of different actions that some people take. For each of the following, please tell me whether you think the action is not wrong at all, wrong but understandable, or wrong and punishable: not paying the taxes they owe on their income."	0 = Not wrong / wrong but understandable 1 = Wrong and punishable
Trust Traditional Authority	Afrobarometer	Q52K: "How much do you trust each of the following, or haven't you heard enough about them to say: traditional leaders?"	1 = Trust somewhat / a lot 0 = Trust a little / not at all
Urban	Afrobarometer	Coded by researcher	1= Urban 0.5 = Peri-urban 0 = Rural
Voted	Afrobarometer	Q21: "Understanding that some people were unable to vote in the most recent national election in [DATE], which of the following statements is true for you?"	1 = Voted 0 = Did not vote (for any reason)

NOTES

CHAPTER 1

1. Crawford Young (2012) identifies three cycles of "hope and disappointment" related to political-economic development in Africa since decolonization.

2. Poteete's 2014 article "Democracy Derailed? Botswana's Fading Halo" calls attention to mismanagement, corruption, opposition intimidation, and lack of checks on executive power in the Botswanan government.

3. Bratton, Mattes, and Gyimah-Boadi (2005) examine where patterns of participation converge and diverge from expectations generated by scholarship in Western democracies.

4. Gertzel 1984 provides an example of an exhaustive account of politics under the one-party state in Zambia. Other scholars suggest that patrimonial logic does not have such inherently negative consequences (see, e.g., Kelsall 2011; Pitcher, Moran, and Johnston 2009; Mkandiwire 2015).

5. In his 2012 article, van de Walle suggests that democratization will force political parties to engage in more mass patronage, though they will likely continue to be constrained by financial realities.

6. On retrospective economic voting, see Posner and Simon 2002; Bratton, Mattes, and Gyumah-Boadi 2005; Whitfield 2009; Hoffman et al. 2009.

7. For a brief review of such evidence, see Baldwin 2015, 69–71.

8. Posner and Simon (2002) and Baldwin (2015) make similar arguments.

9. Young (2012, chap. 5) notes that the international financial climate and the massive projects of state expansion in the 1960s created the conditions for most of the continent's countries to sink into crippling debt.

10. The 2016 election indicates this may change, but those new political dynamics were not yet in evidence during my fieldwork.

11. In the Zambian elections in 2016, there were some substantive differences between the incumbent PF and its largest challenger, the UPND. However, most voters (especially those outside the capital of Lusaka) were unaware of the differences between the parties' manifestos, and the candidates' public speeches tended to focus on valence issues.

12. I selected this time period, as opposed to one closer to the present, due to data

availability; the national and party documentation of public policy available in the National Archives of Zambia and the United National Independence Party Archives are richest during the First Republic and thin out considerably after the mid-1970s.

CHAPTER 2

1. National Archives of Zambia (hereinafter NAZ) MCI 1/1/6, "Economic Commission for Africa (ECA) Missions: Seers Mission."

2. The Zambian government has a 25-year waiting period before making internal documents available to the public through the National Archives of Zambia. During the time of my fieldwork for this study, I expected to have access to documents through 1988. However, few documents more recent than the mid-1970s are available, due, according to the archivists, to a backlog in processing documents.

3. NAZ MCI 1/1/6, "Economic Commission for Africa (ECA) Missions: Seers Mission," 3.

4. NAZ MCI 1/1/6, "Economic Commission for Africa (ECA) Missions: Seers Mission," 26.

5. NAZ Co4/4/1, Memo to all Ministers, February 19, 1965.

6. Some party cadres took this slogan very literally, calling explicitly for patronage through government credit and subsidies. United National Independence Party Archives (hereinafter UNIPA) 5/8/1/2/31, UNIP Regional HQ Broken Hill Correspondence 1967, "Mbala Resolutions: The Resolution Passed at the Provincial Regional Conference of the United National Independence Party," by J. M. Chapoloko for the national secretary, September 3–4, 1966.

7. The *Times of Zambia* was entitled *Northern News* until 1966.

8. Lusaka Province was not separated from Central Province until during the Second Republic, and Muchinga Province was delineated as the tenth province in 2011.

9. NAZ Co4/1/2, Meeting of the Provincial Development Committee, September 26, 1967.

10. NAZ Co4/1/6, Minutes of a Special Meeting of the Provincial Development Committee, September 28, 1967.

11. Notes from the Provincial Development Committee during this period of time note the centralization of mechanization schemes, removing materials from more remote areas with lower productive potential: NAZ Co4/1/2, Meeting of the Provincial Development Committee, September 26, 1967.

12. For example, NAZ CNP 1/1/148, Provincial and Local Government Division of Central Province Annual Report for the Year 1969.

13. UNIPA 5/8/1/3/11, Serenje-Mkushi Correspondence 1964–66, Tour Report by Parliamentary Secretary P. M. Kapika, undated. See also Bowen 2011.

14. NAZ Co4/1/6, Minutes of the Central Province Development Committee, July 21, 1967.

15. NAZ CNP 1/1/148, Annual Report for 1969, Provincial and Local Government, Mumbwa District.

16. UNIPA 5/8/2/1/2, "Political Assistant's Marathon Tour Report," by E. M. Lubasi, November 1967.

17. UNIPA 5/4/2/4/1, Provincial Development Committee Report, appendix A, "Speech by the Minister of State for Economic Development, Honorable U. G. Mwila, to the Provincial Development Committee at Livingstone," October 31,1966.

18. UNIPA 5/4/2/1/16, District Secretary of Sinezongwe 1973, "District Monthly Security Report, January 1973, for Gwemebe District to the Permanent Secretary."

19. For example, UNIPA SP4/2/173, "First National Development Plan Southern Province Progress Report to 30th September, 1967," by J. K. Mulwand, development officer for resident secretary.

20. For example, UNIPA 5/8/1/2/41, Regional HQ Kabwe 1969, Letter to All Regional Secretaries from National Secretary M. M. Chona, June 7, 1967.

21. NAZ C04/1/3 "My Tour Report of the North Western Province, 1st November to 9th November, 1965," by M. Sipalo, parliamentary secretary of the Office of National Development Planning.

22. Resnick (2013) notes that disappointment with the MMD almost immediately resulted in defections and the creation of new parties.

23. See Phiri 2013.

24. Sata's death occurred six months after the end of the data collection for this study. Rumors of his ill health had been circulating for a while, but based on the content of the survey interviews, I do not believe that anticipation of his death entered the public political consciousness until several months after the data collection was complete.

25. Hichilema's opposition party, the United Party for National Development, has regionally based support in the south.

26. BBC News 2015.

27. World Integrated Trade Solution, *Zambia Trade Summary 2011*, http://wits.worldbank.org/CountryProfile/Country/ZMB/Year/2011/Summary (accessed June 13, 2014).

28. Larmer and Fraser 2007, 619. Others, notably Gould (2010), argue the opposite: that Zambian economic policy continues to exhibit an urban bias at the expense of rural areas.

29. Interview with Councilor Richard Mungala of Katapazi Ward in Kazungula District, Southern Province, July 22, 2016.

30. Anonymous municipal council planning officer, July 2016.

31. Mr. Banda, acting chief health inspector for Livingstone City Council, July 21, 2016.

32. Angellah Sianjina, social and economic planner, Livingstone City Council, July 21, 2016.

33. McGiven Haketa, group accountant for expenditures and acting director of finance, Kabwe Municipal Council, July 7, 2016.

34. Anonymous muncipal council planning officer, July 2016.

35. Angellah Sianjina, social and economic Planner, Livingstone City Council, July 21, 2016.

36. Mr. Banda, acting chief health inspector for Livingstone City Council, July 21, 2016.

37. I elected to drop Luapula Province, as it would not have added additional variation into the sample. Northwestern Province voted for the outgoing MMD during the 2011 elections, so during the survey period, they had recently become an opposition region. Because all off-rail regions receive relatively little in the way of government service provision, including an off-rail province that supported the ruling party would not have added much in the way of variation in level of service provision.

38. While government ministries may have the tendency to inflate numbers, the relative provision to each province is demonstrative of relative levels of actual provision, even if the precise amounts are inaccurate.

CHAPTER 3

1. For example, Soss 1999; Campbell 2002; Kumlin 2004; Kumlin and Rothstein 2005; Mettler 2007; Sharp 2012.

2. For example, Verba and Nie 1972; Putnam 1993, 1995; Krishna 2002; Tsai 2007.

3. Due to extremely high levels of reported religious participation, designating whether respondents "belong to any religion" is not terribly meaningful, while frequency of church attendance better captures the importance of religious practice in the life of the respondent.

4. Due to problems with degrees of freedom and dropped cases, distinct tribes were only included if the category had at least 10 observations. Respondents belonging to tribes appearing fewer than 10 times in the sample were grouped into an "other" category, used as a reference group to determine the effect of specific tribal identifications as compared to a "catchall" category reflecting many tribal identities.

5. Verba, Schlozman, and Brady (1995) find these variables to have a consistent effect on various forms of political participation in the American context.

6. MacLean (2010) and Michael Bratton (2006) also note the unreliability of "income" and promote the use of "lived experiences" of poverty. In this context, education, formal versus informal employment, and rural residence were the strongest indicators of poverty. While these measures do not directly reflect income, they do reflect something of class.

7. According to Cameron and Miller (2011), clustering the standard errors for survey data (which relaxes the assumption that observations within a cluster are independent from one another) is less rigid than a random effects model (which would assign a different intercept for each cluster).

8. Particularly since different enumerators worked in different regions, it is essential not to misinterpret idiosyncrasies of an interviewer for a regional trend.

9. This strategy was more flexible in rural areas, depending on housing density. In moderately dense rural areas, enumerators were instructed to sample every third

household; in sparsely populated areas, they walked one direction and sampled every household. Daily strategy in rural areas was established upon arrival on-site.

10. This response rate is for 1,205 of the 1,500 respondents. In the remaining sites, research assistants failed to record response rates.

CHAPTER 4

1. Interview LSK-E-1, July 5, 2016.
2. See Berman 1997 for an examination of dangerous collective behavior.
3. See Fox 1994 for a similar argument regarding Mexico.
4. This variable is ordinal, rather than binary, because the strong regional trends caused collinearity in the models with a binary specification. Other dependent variables were collapsed into a binary specification to facilitate interpretation of the coefficients, but the results are largely unchanged under an ordinal specification.
5. "Groups" included clubs, youth organizations, cooperatives, church groups, unions, and various other forms of social organization with regular meetings or activities.
6. The variable "join to solve problems" collapsed into a binary variable for this index, for which any reports of "joining" were coded 1, while reports of none at all were coded 0. Due to the low inter-item covariance of these three variables, an additive index that reflects the number of behaviors in which a respondent engages is more appropriate than an alpha-scaled index.
7. The numbers reported are based on 41 respondents in New Israel (February 2, 2014), 33 in Sikaunzwe (November 4, 2013), and 25 in Waya (December 17, 2013).
8. Interviews LSK-R-1, July 5, 2016; KBW-E-7, July 8, 2016.
9. Interview KBW-E-8, July 8, 2016.
10. Ibid.
11. Interview LVS-E-16, July 21, 2016.
12. Interview LSK-E-1, July 4, 2016.
13. Interview LVS-R-11, July 19, 2016.
14. Interviews LVS-E-29, LVS-C-24, July 25, 2016.
15. Interview LVS-C-24, July 25, 2016.
16. Interviews KBW-E-19, July 12, 2016; KBW-E-25, July 13, 2016; KBW-E-34, July 14, 2016.
17. Interviews LVS-E-28, LVS-E-29, July 25, 2016; LVS-R-26, July 26, 2016.
18. Interview LVS-E-27, July 25, 2016.
19. Interview LVS-R-26, July 26, 2016.
20. Interview KBW-E-23, July 13, 2016.
21. Interview KBW-E-17, July 12, 2016.
22. Interview LVS-R-1, July 18, 2016.
23. Interview LVS-C-11, July 19, 2016.

24. Interview LVS-C-2, July 18, 2016. Other examples occur in the following interviews: KBW-E-2, KBW-R-4, July 7, 2016; KBW-C-6, July 8, 2016; LVS-E-3, LVS-C-6, July 18, 2016; LVS-E-11, July 21, 2016.

25. For example, interviews KBW-C-11, KBW-C-12, KBW-C-13, July 11, 2016.

26. Interview KBW-C-13, July 11, 2016.

27. Interviews KBW-E-31, July 14, 2016; LVS-E-31, July 25, 2016.

28. Interviews LVS-E-34, LVS-E-35, July 26, 2016.

29. Interview KBW-R-7, July 8, 2016.

30. Interviews KBW-R-7, July 8, 2016; LVS-E-40, July 26, 2016.

31. Interview KBW-E-17, July 12, 2016.

32. Interview KBW-E-16, July 12, 2016.

33. Interview KBW-E-17, July 12, 2016.

CHAPTER 5

1. Other studies have shown that civic knowledge does not necessarily correlate with interest in or proclivity to talk about politics but, rather, tends to be more closely related to level of education.

2. The binary coding of these variables reflects the nature of the responses to these survey questions: respondents tended to downplay the extent to which they talked about or were interested in politics, often claiming, "I am not a politician." When probed further ("I am not asking if you are a politician; I am asking if you ever talk about politics"), respondents would admit to discussing politics or to a general interest in politics; however, respondents' hesitance to report high levels of interest or regular discussion distorts the ordinal coding; therefore, the meaningful distinction for these responses was between those claiming no interest or discussion and those claiming at least some.

3. Interview LSK-E-1, July 4, 2016.

4. Interviews KBW-E-19, July 12, 2016; KBW-E-28, July 13, 2016; LVS-C-6, July 18, 2016.

5. Interview KBW-E-24, July 13, 2016.

6. Interview KBW-E-25, July 13, 2016.

7. Interviews LVS-E-1, LVS-C-2, July 18, 2016.

8. Interviews KBW-E-1, KBW-C-1, July 7, 2016; KBW-C-9, KBW-E-9, July 11, 2016; LVS-C-16, July 21, 2016; LVS-E-21, July 22, 2016.

9. Interviews LVS-C-16, July 21, 2016; KBW-E-9, July 8, 2016.

10. Interviews KBW-C-8, July 8, 2016; LVS-E-6, July 19, 2016.

11. Interview KBW-E-3, July 7, 2016.

12. Interview KBW-C-12, July 11, 2016.

13. Interviews LVS-C-2, July 18, 2016; KBW-E-2, July 7, 2016.

14. Interview KBW-R-10, July 11, 2016.

15. Interview LVS-R-5, July 18, 2016.

16. Interviews LVS-E-5, LVS-C-9, July 19, 2016.

17. Interview LVS-E-11, July 21, 2016.

18. Respondent 1158, interview, January 20, 2014, Solwezi.

19. Interviews KBW-R-3, July 7, 2016; LVS-C-14, LVS-C-15, July 21, 2016.

20. Interviews LVS-C-20, July 25, 2016; LVS-E-36, LVS-R-24, July 26, 2016.

21. Interviews LVS-C-18, July 21, 2016; LVS-C-21, July 23, 2016.

22. Interview LVS-R-25, July 26, 2016.

CHAPTER 6

1. Interview, July 21, 2016. Mr. Nyambe subsequently won the seat for the opposition UPND.

2. The equivalent of about 0.5–1 US dollars at the time of the interview.

3. Actual turnout in the 2016 elections, two years after the survey was completed, was approximately 56 percent of registered voters, confirming the suspicion that the prospective vote measure is inflated. But there is little reason to believe that the service delivery variables are related to the bias in the overreporting of vote intention. The results for this variable may therefore be interpreted as the relationship between service delivery and the likelihood that a person expresses an intention to vote.

4. At the time of the survey, the next regularly scheduled presidential election was in 2016. However, in October 2014, President Michael Sata died in office (from illness). Zambian law dictates that upon the president's death in office, the vice president serves as interim president for a period not exceeding 90 days, at which point an election must be held. A by-election was held in January 2015 to elect the next president. Edgar Lungu, of the ruling Patriotic Front, was elected to succeed President Sata, in a hotly contested but (by most accounts) free and fair election.

5. Calculating Cronbach's alpha for these variables reveals that the average inter-item correlation is 0.035, and the scale reliability coefficient is only 0.477, indicating that an additive index is more appropriate.

6. Interview KBW-E-28, July 13, 2016.

7. Interview LSK-E-1, July 4, 2016.

8. For example, interviews LSK-E-1, July 4, 2016; KBW-E-28, KBW-E-26, July 13, 2016.

9. Interview LVS-C-11, July 19, 2016.

10. Interview KBW-E-25, July 12, 2016 (translated).

11. Interview LSK-R-2, July 5, 2016.

12. Interview KWB-R-8, July 8, 2016.

13. Interview LVS-C-18, July 21, 2016.

14. Interviews KBW-E-6, July 8, 2016; LVS-E-9, July 19, 2016.

15. Interview LVS-E-38, July 26, 2016.

16. Interview KBW-R-3, July 7, 2016.

17. This method requires an assumption of linearity of the dependent variable. Fortunately, because the formal participation index has five categories, it can reasonably be

treated as a continuous variable, and the results are indeed robust to OLS specification. I thus performed Hicks and Tingley's mediation analysis with OLS.

18. Interview LVS-R-18, July 22, 2016.

19. Interview LVS-R-23, July 26, 2016.

20. For example, interviews KBW-C-17, July 12, 2016; KBW-R-9, July 11, 2016; KBW-R-2, July 7, 2016; KBW-E-4, July 8, 2016; LVS-R-13, July 21, 2016; LVS-E-38, July 26, 2018.

21. For each group, 76 percent report voting (only). Those who reported empowering experiences report contacting officials at the slightly higher rate of 36 percent compared to 32 percent.

22. Interview KBW-E-1, July 7, 2016.

23. Interview LVS-R-3, July 18, 2016.

24. Interviews KBW-E-2, July 7, 2016; KBW-E-7, July 8, 2016; LVS-R-6, July 18, 2016.

25. For example, interviews KBW-E-1, KBW-E-3, July 7, 2016; KBW-E-8, July 8, 2016; KBW-E-10, July 11, 2016; LVS-E-14, LVS-R-16, July 21, 2016; LVS-R-20, LVS-R-22, July 22, 2016.

26. Interview KBW-C-11, July 11, 2016.

27. Interview LVS-E-18, July 22, 2016.

28. Interview KBW-C-7, July 8, 2016.

29. Interviews LVS-C-4 (quote), LVS-R-2, July 18, 2016; LVS-E-32, July 25, 2016.

CHAPTER 7

1. The survey also asked about church groups and religious organizations, but mention of such groups was rare. Most respondents did not differentiate between NGOs and religious organizations as service providers.

2. The survey asked about chiefs as a source for public goods, but a number of respondents stated that they would first go to their village headman, who would act as an intermediary for the chief or perhaps be able to solve some smaller service provision problems himself.

3. Interviews, May 28–June 15, 2012, Lusaka and outside Serenje.

4. For example, Kelsall (2000) writes that the Arumeru Tax Revolt in 1998 in Tanzania grew directly out of dissatisfaction with service provision and the sense that the government did not have the authority or capacity to spend tax money in a way that benefited the community.

5. My use of the term *protest* denotes peaceful demonstrations, marches, sit-ins, and other such forms of political expression. Such forms of protest are distinct from revolutionary behavior intended to precipitate regime change.

6. Bond 2016.

7. Urban residence is a strong predictor of the likelihood that someone reports turning to a chief or NGO. Rural residents have much stronger ties to their chiefs than do urban residents, and NGOs have a much stronger presence in urban areas (Brass 2012). However, these divisions are not absolute: rural residents often think of NGOs in

aspirational terms, even when they have little access to them, and urban residents are often connected to chiefs through rural family members.

8. Interview KBW-C-8, July 8, 2016.
9. Interview KBW-E-30, July 13, 2016.
10. Interview KBW-E-17, July 12, 2016.
11. Interview LVS-E-10, July 19, 2016.
12. Interview KBW-E-14, July 11, 2016.
13. Interview LVS-E-22, July 22, 2016.
14. Interview LSK-E-1, July 4, 2016.
15. Interview KBW-E-4, July 8, 2016.
16. Interview KBW-R-3, July 7, 2016.
17. Interview KBW-C-17, July 12, 2016.
18. Interview LSK-E-1, July 4, 2016.
19. Interview LSK-E-2, July 4, 2016.
20. Interview KBW-E-7, July 8, 2016.
21. Interviews KBW-E-8, July 8, 2016; LVS-R-5, July 18, 2016.
22. Interview KBW-E-2, July 7, 2016.
23. Interview KBW-E-5, July 8, 2016.
24. Interviews KBW-E-8 July 8, 2016; LVS-E-15, July 21, 2016.
25. Interview KBW-E-32, July 14, 2016.
26. Interview KBW-E-37, July 14, 2016.

CHAPTER 8

1. This measure diverges from mine in that there is no indication of whether the clinics in question were actually staffed and in the use of primary schools rather than secondary ones (primary schools are far more prevalent).

2. It is essential to note the departures from my original coding scheme: these services are likely but not necessarily the ones each respondent finds most salient, and a great degree of nuance is lost when service provision is measured on a Likert scale rather than through coding open-ended responses about the experience of accessing the relevant service. Nevertheless, these two measures make it possible to compare the relationship between service delivery and political behavior across countries.

3. Clientelist linkages are those in which constituents are rewarded with material goods or jobs; collective linkages are those in which supportive communities are rewarded with collective goods such as roads or wells; programmatic goods are those in which constituents respond to a party's position on policies.

4. The poverty index measured the frequency with which respondents went without food, clean water, medicine, cooking fuel, and cash.

5. Because the overwhelming majority of survey respondents reported that they are religious, I use frequency of religious service attendance as a proxy for religiosity. Religiosity is widely believed to influence political participation, though the direction and

222 • *Notes to Pages 184–200*

nature of this relationship is context-dependent. For this study, this variable is intended strictly as a control.

6. Significant coefficients ($p < 0.1$) are shaded darker in these figures.

7. See Letsa 2017 for a discussion of nonmaterial motivations to vote in electoral authoritarian settings.

Albaugh, Ericka. 2011. "An Autocrat's Toolkit: Adaptation and Manipulation in 'Democratic' Cameroon." *Democratization* 18 (2): 388–414.

Albaugh, Ericka. 2014. *State-Building and Multilingual Education in Africa*. New York: Cambridge University Press.

Alm, James, Gary H. McClelland, and William D. Schulze. 1992. "Why Do People Pay Taxes?" *Journal of Public Economics* 48:21–38.

Arriola, Leonardo. 2013. *Multiethnic Coalitions in Africa: Business Financing and Opposition Election Candidates*. New York: Cambridge University Press.

Atkeson, Lonna Rae, and Nancy Carrillo. 2007. "More Is Better: The Influence of Collective Female Descriptive Representation on External Efficacy." *Politics and Gender* 3 (1): 79–101.

Atkeson, Lonna Rae, and Ronald B. Rapoport. 2003. "The More Things Change the More They Stay the Same: Examining Gender Differences in Political Attitude Expression, 1952–2000." *Public Opinion Quarterly* 67:492–521.

Bach, Daniel C., and Mamoudou Gazibou. 2012. *Neopatrimonialism in Africa and Beyond*. New York: Routledge.

Baldwin, Kate. 2013. "Why Vote with the Chief? Political Connections and Public Goods Provision in Zambia." *American Journal of Political Science* 57 (4): 794–809.

Baldwin, Kate. 2015. *The Paradox of Traditional Chiefs in Democratic Africa*. New York: Cambridge University Press.

Banful, Afua. 2010. "Old Problems in the New Solutions? Politically Motivated Allocation of Program Benefits and the 'New' Fertilizer Subsidies." Discussion Paper 01002. International Food Policy Research Institute, July.

Bates, Robert. 1974. *Patterns of Uneven Development: Causes and Consequences in Zambia*. Monograph Series in World Affairs 11, no. 3. Denver: University of Denver.

Bates, Robert. 1976. *Rural Responses to Industrialization: A Study of Village Zambia*. New Haven: Yale University Press.

Bates, Robert. (1981) 2014. *Markets and Tropical States in Africa*. Updated edition, Berkeley: University of California Press.

Bates, Robert, and Paul Collier. 1993. "The Politics and Economics of Policy Reform in Zambia." In *Political and Economic Interactions in Economic Policy Reform*, ed. R. Bates and A. Krueger. Oxford: Blackwell.

Bayart, Jean-Francois. 1993. *The State in Africa: Politics of the Belly*. London: Longman.

Bayart, Jean-Francois, Stephen Ellis, and Beatrice Hibou. (1999) 2009. *The Criminalization of the State in Africa*. Reprint, Bloomington: Indiana University Press.

Baylies, Carolyn. 1984. "Luapula Province: Economic Decline and Political Alienation in a Rural UNIP Stronghold." In *The Dynamics of the One-Party State in Zambia*, ed. C. Gertzel. Manchester: Manchester University Press.

Baylies, Carolyn, and Morris Szeftel. 1982. "The Rise of a Zambian Capitalist Class in the 1970s." *Journal of Southern African Studies* 8 (2): 187–213.

BBC News. 2015. "Zambia Elections: Opposition UPND Alleges Fraud." August 15.

Beckwith, Karen. 2010. "A Comparative Politics of Gender Symposium Introduction: Comparative Politics and the Logic of a Comparative Politics of Gender." *Perspectives on Politics* 8 (1): 159–68.

Berman, Sheri. 1997. "Civil Society and the Collapse of the Weimar Republic." *World Politics* 49 (3): 401–29.

Berman, Sheri. 2003. "Islam, Revolution, and Civil Society." *Perspectives on Politics* 1 (2): 257–72.

Besley, Timothy, and Torsten Persson. 2014. "Why Do Developing Countries Tax So Little?" *Journal of Economic Perspectives* 28 (4): 99–120.

Beveridge, Andrew, and Anthony Oberschall. 1979. *African Businessmen and Development in Zambia*. Princeton: Princeton University Press.

Bierschenk, Thomas, and Jean-Pierre Olivier de Sardan, eds. 2014. *States at Work: Dynamics of African Bureaucracies*. Leiden: Brill.

Bleck, Jaimie. 2013. "Islamic Schooling in Malian Democracy: Disaggregating Parents' Political Behavior." *Journal of Modern African Studies* 51 (3): 377–408.

Bodea, Christina, and Adrienne LeBas. 2016. "The Origins of Voluntary Compliance: Attitudes toward Taxation in Urban Nigeria." *British Journal of Political Science* 46 (1): 215–38.

Bogaards, Matthis. 2005. "Dominant Parties and Democratic Defects." *Georgetown Journal of International Affairs* 6 (2): 29–35.

Bond, Patrick. 2016. "Reality Check: Protests Grow as Gap Widens between Reality and 'Africa Rising' Storyline." *Mail and Guardian*, May 15.

Boone, Catherine. 2009. "Electoral Populism Where Property Rights Are Weak: Land Politics in Contemporary Sub-Saharan Africa." *Comparative Politics* 41 (2): 183–201.

Bowler, Shaun, Todd Donovan, and Robert Hanneman. 2003. "Art for Democracy's Sake? Group Membership and Political Engagement in Europe." *Journal of Politics* 65 (4): 1111–29.

Brady, Henry E., Sidney Verba, and Kay Lehman Schlozman. 1995. "Beyond SES: A Resource Model of Political Participation." *American Political Science Review* 89 (2): 271–94.

Brass, Jennifer. 2012. "Blurring Boundaries: The Integration of NGOs into Governance in Kenya." *Governance* 25 (2): 209–35.

Brass, Jennifer. 2016. *Allies or Adversaries: NGOs and the State in Africa*. New York: Cambridge University Press.

Bratton, Kathleen. 2005. "Critical Mass Theory Revisited: The Behaviour and Success of Token Women in State Legislatures." *Politics and Gender* 1 (1): 97–125.

Bratton, Michael. 1980. *The Local Politics of Rural Development: Peasant and Party-State in Zambia*. Hanover, NH: University Press of New England.

Bratton, Michael. 1989. "The Politics of Government–NGO relations in Africa." *World Development* 17 (4): 569–87.

Bratton, Michael. 1999. "Political Participation in a New Democracy: Institutional Considerations from Zambia." *Comparative Political Studies* 32 (5): 549–88.

Bratton, Michael. 2006. "Poor People and Democratic Citizenship in Africa." Working Paper 56, Afrobarometer.

Bratton, Michael. 2007. "Are You Being Served? Popular Satisfaction with Health and Education Services in Africa." Working Paper 65, Afrobarometer.

Bratton, Michael, Ravi Bhavnani, and Tse-Hsin Chen. 2012. "Voting Intentions in Africa: Ethnic, Economic, or Partisan?" *Commonwealth and Comparative Politics* 50 (1): 27–52.

Bratton, Michael, and Eric C. Chang. 2006. "State Building and Democratization in Sub-Saharan Africa: Forwards, Backwards, or Together? *Comparative Political Studies* 39 (9): 1059–83.

Bratton, Michael, and Carolyn Logan. 2006. "Voters but Not Yet Citizens: The Weak Demand for Vertical Accountability in Africa's Unclaimed Democracies." Working Paper 63, Afrobarometer.

Bratton, Michael, Robert Mattes, and E. Gyimah-Boadi. 2005. *Public Opinion, Democracy, and Market Reform in Africa*. New York: Cambridge University Press.

Bratton, Michael, and Daniel Posner. 1999. "A First Look at Second Elections in Africa, with Illustrations from Zambia." In *State, Conflict, and Democracy in Africa*, ed. R. Joseph. Boulder, CO: Lynne Rienner.

Bratton, Michael, and Nicolas van de Walle. 1997. *Democratic Experiments in Africa: Regime Transitions in Comparative Perspective*. New York: Cambridge University Press.

Brehm, John, and Wendy Rahn. 1997. "Individual-Level Evidence for the Causes and Consequences of Social Capital." *American Journal of Political Science* 41 (3): 999–1023.

Briggs, Ryan. 2012. "Electrifying the Base? Aid and Incumbent Advantage in Ghana." *Journal of Modern African Studies* 50 (4): 603–24.

Briggs, Ryan. 2014. "Aiding and Abetting: Project Aid and Ethnic Politics in Kenya." *World Development* 64:194–205.

Bruch, Sarah K., Myra Marx Ferree, and Joe Soss. 2010. "From Policy to Polity: Democracy, Paternalism, and the Incorporation of Disadvantaged Citizens." *American Sociological Review* 75 (2): 205–26.

Burawoy, Michael. 1976. "Consciousness and Contradiction: A Study of Student Protest in Zambia." *British Journal of Sociology* 27 (1): 78–98.

Burgess, Robin, Remi Jedwab, Edward Miguel, Ameet Morjaria, and Gerard Padró i Miquel. 2015. "The Value of Democracy: Evidence from Road Building in Kenya." *American Economic Review* 105 (6): 1817–51.

Burke, William, Thomas Jayne, and Nicholas Sitko. 2012. "Can the FISP More Effectively Achieve Food Production and Poverty Goals?" Policy Synthesis 51, Food Security Research Project, Lusaka.

Burnell, Peter. 2001. "The Party System and Party Politics in Zambia: Continuities Past, Present, and Future." *African Affairs* 100 (399): 239–63.

Burns, Nancy, Kay Lehman Schlozman, and Sidney Verba. 2000. *The Private Roots of Public Action: Gender, Equality, and Political Participation.* Cambridge, MA: Harvard University Press.

Callaghy, Thomas. 1984. *The State-Society Struggle: Zaire in Comparative Perspective.* New York: Columbia University Press.

Callaghy, Thomas. 1990. "Lost between State and Market: The Politics of Economic Adjustment in Ghana, Zambia, and Nigeria." In *Economic Crisis and Policy Choice: The Politics of Adjustment in the Third World*, ed. J. Nelson. Princeton: Princeton University Press.

Cameron, A. C., and D. L. Miller. 2011. "Robust Inference with Clustered Data." In *Handbook of Empirical Economics and Finance*, ed. A. Ullah and D. E. Giles. Boca Raton, FL: CRC Press.

Cammett, Melani, and Lauren MacLean. 2014. *The Politics of Non-State Social Welfare.* Ithaca: Cornell University Press.

Campbell, Andrea Louise. 2002. "Self-Interest, Social Security, and the Distinctive Participation Patterns of Senior Citizens." *American Political Science Review* 96 (4): 565–74.

Campbell, Andrea Louise. 2012. "Policy Makes Mass Politics." *Annual Review of Political Science* 15:333–51.

Centeno, Miguel. 1997. "Blood and Debt: War and Taxation in Nineteenth-Century Latin America." *American Journal of Sociology* 102 (6): 1565–1605.

Chabal, Patrick, and Jean-Pascal Daloz. 1999. *Africa Works: Disorder as a Political Instrument.* Bloomington: Indiana University Press.

Cheeseman, Nic, and Marja Hinfelaar. 2009. "Parties, Platforms, and Political Mobilization: The Zambian Presidential Elections of 2008." *African Affairs* 109 (434): 51–76.

Coppedge, Michael, John Gerring, Staffan I. Lindberg, Svend-Erik Skaaning, Jan Teorell, David Altman, Michael Bernhard, et al. 2017. V-Dem Data, Version 7.1. Varieties of Democracy (V-Dem). https://www.v-dem.net/en/data/data-version-7-1/

Craig, John Robert. 1999. "State Enterprise and Privatisation in Zambia 1968–1998." PhD diss., University of Leeds.

Dalton, Russell, and Martin Wattenberg. 2000. *Parties without Partisans: Political Change in Advanced Industrial Democracies.* Oxford: Oxford University Press.

Dhami, Sanjit, and Ali al-Nowaihi. 2007. "Why Do People Pay Taxes? Prospect Theory versus Expected Utility Theory." *Journal of Economic Behavior and Organization* 64:171–92.

Diamond, Larry. 2002. "Thinking about Hybrid Regimes." *Journal of Democracy* 13 (2): 21–35.

Downs, Anthony. 1957. *An Economic Theory of Democracy*. New York: HarperCollins.

Dresang, Dennis, and Ralph A. Young. 1979. "The Public Service." In *Administration in Zambia*, ed. W. Tordoff. Manchester: Manchester University Press.

Eifert, Benn, Edward Miguel, and Daniel N. Posner. 2010. "Political Competition and Ethnic Identification in Africa." *American Journal of Political Science* 54 (2): 494–510.

Ekeh, Peter P. 1975. Colonialism and the Two Publics in Africa: A Theoretical Statement. *Comparative Studies in Society and History* 17 (1): 91–112.

Englebert, Pierre. 2000. *State Legitimacy and Development in Africa*. Boulder, CO: Lynne Rienner.

Esping-Andersen, Gøsta. 1990. *The Three Worlds of Welfare Capitalism*. Princeton: Princeton University Press.

Fatton, Robert. 1992. *Predatory Rule: State and Civil Society in Africa*. Boulder, CO: Lynne Rienner.

Ferree, Karen E. 2006. "Explaining South Africa's Racial Census." *Journal of Politics* 68 (4): 803–15.

Fjeldstad, Odd-Helge, and Joseph Semboja. 2001. "Why People Pay Taxes: The Case of the Development Levy in Tanzania." *World Development* 29 (12): 2059–74.

Fox, Jonathan. 1994. "The Difficult Transition from Clientelism to Citizenship: Lessons from Mexico. *World Politics* 46 (2): 151–84.

Franck, Raphael, and Ilia Rainer. 2012. "Does the Leader's Ethnicity Matter? Ethnic Favoritism, Education, and Health in Sub-Saharan Africa." *American Political Science Review* 106 (2): 294–325.

Frimpong-Ansah, Johnathan H. 1991. *The Vampire State in Africa: The Political Economy of Decline in Ghana*. London: James Currey.

Gerber, Alan D., Gregory Huber, David Doherty, and Conor Dowling. 2016. "Why People Vote: Estimating the Social Returns to Voting." *British Journal of Political Science* 46 (2): 241–64.

Gerring, John. 2008. "Case Selection for Case Study Analysis: Qualitative and Quantitative Techniques." In *The Oxford Handbook of Political Methodology*, ed. J. M. Box-Steffensmeier, H. E. Brady, and D. Collier. Oxford: Oxford University Press.

Gertzel, Cherry. 1984. *The Dynamics of the One-Party State in Zambia*. Manchester: Manchester University Press.

Gilens, Martin. 1999. *Why Americans Hate Welfare: Race, Media, and the Politics of Antipoverty Policy*. Chicago: University of Chicago Press.

Gottlieb, Jessica. 2015. "The Logic of Party Collusion in a Democracy: Evidence from Mali." *World Politics* 67 (1): 1–36.

Gould, Jeremy. 2010. *Left Behind: Rural Zambia in the Third Republic*. Lusaka: Lembani Trust.

Govereh, Jones, Emma Malawo, Tadeyo Lungu, Thom Jayne, Kasweka Chinyama, and Pius Chilonda. 2009. "Trends and Spatial Distribution of Public Agricultural Productivity Growth." Working Paper 36, Food Security Research Project, Lusaka.

Guyer, Jane. 1992. "Representation without Taxation: An Essay on Democracy in Rural Nigeria, 1952–1990." *African Studies Review* 35 (1): 41–79.

Harris, Adam. 2015. "To Protest and Vote: The Complementarity of Protesting and Voting." Paper presented at the Annual Meeting of the Midwest Political Science Association, Chicago, April.

Harris, Adam, and Erin Hern. Forthcoming. "Taking to the Street: Protest as an Expression of Political Preference in Africa." *Comparative Political Studies*.

Herbst, Jeffrey. 2000. *States and Power in Africa: Comparative Lessons in Authority and Control*. Princeton: Princeton University Press.

Hern, Erin. 2015. "Plus Ça Change: Rural Development Policy and the Persistence of Rural Poverty in Zambia." In "Rural Development and Poverty Reduction in South Africa: Experiences from Zambia and Malawi," special issue, ed. Davide Chinigò and Arrigo Pallotti, *Afriche e Orienti*.

Hern, Erin. 2017. "Better than Nothing: How Policies Influence Political Participation in Low-Capacity Democracies." *Governance* 30 (4): 583–600.

Hicks, Raymond, and Dustin Tingley. 2011. "Causal Mediation Analysis." *Stata Journal* 11 (4): 1–15.

Hirschman, Albert O. 1970. *Exit, Voice, and Loyalty: Responses to Decline in Firms, Organizations, and States*. Cambridge, MA: Harvard University Press.

Hoffman, Barak, Clark Gibson, Karen E. Ferree, and James D. Long. 2009. "Explaining the African Vote." Paper presented at the Annual Meeting of the American Political Science Association, Toronto, September.

Holzner, Claudio A. 2010. *Poverty of Democracy: The Institutional Roots of Political Participation in Mexico*. Pittsburgh: University of Pittsburgh Press.

Honig, Lauren. 2016. "Land, State-Building, and Political Authority in Africa." PhD diss., Cornell University.

Hunter, Wendy, and Natasha Borges Sugiyama. 2014. "Transforming Subjects into Citizens: Insights from Brazil's Bolsa Familia." *Perspectives on Politics* 12 (4): 829–45.

Huntington, Samuel. 1991. *The Third Wave: Democratization in the Late Twentieth Century*. Norman: University of Oklahoma Press.

Hutchful, Eboe. 1996. "The Civil Society Debate in Africa." *International Journal* 51 (1): 54–77.

Ichino, Nahomi, and Noah L. Nathan. 2013. "Crossing the Line: Local Ethnic Geography and Voting in Ghana." *American Political Science Review* 107 (2): 344–61.

Jablonski, Ryan. 2014. "How Aid Targets Votes: The Impact of Electoral Incentives on Foreign Aid Distribution." *World Politics* 66 (20): 293–330.

Jackson, Robert, and Carl Rosberg. 1982. "Why Africa's Weak States Persist." *World Politics* 35 (1): 1–24.

Johns, Sheridan. 1979. "The Parastatal Sector." In *Administration in Zambia*, ed. W. Tordoff. Manchester: Manchester University Press.

Joseph, Richard, ed. 1999. *State, Conflict, and Democracy in Africa*. Boulder, CO: Lynne Rienner.

Kasara, Kimuli. 2007. "Tax Me If You Can: Ethnic Geography, Democracy, and the Taxation of Agriculture in Africa." *American Political Science Review* 101 (1): 159–72.

Kelsall, Tim. 2000. "Governance, Local Politics and Districtization in Tanzania: The 1998 Arumeru Tax Revolt." *African Affairs* 99 (397): 533–51.

Kelsall, Tim. 2011. "Going with the Grain in African Development?" In "Aid, Institutions and Governance: What Have We Learned?," ed. David Booth, special issue, *Development Policy Review* 29:223–51.

King, Desmond, and Robert Lieberman. 2009. "Ironies of State Building: A Comparative Perspective on the American State." *World Politics* 61 (3): 547–88.

Kramon, Eric, and Dan Posner. 2013. "Who Benefits from Distributive Politics? How the Outcome One Studies Affects the Answer One Gets." *Perspectives on Politics* 11 (2): 461–74.

Krasner, Stephen, and Thomas Risse. 2014. "External Actors, State-Building, and Service-Provision in Areas of Limited Statehood: Introduction." *Governance* 27 (4): 545–67.

Krishna, Anirudh. 2002. *Active Social Capital: Tracing the Roots of Development Democracy*. New York: Columbia University Press.

Kuenzi, Michelle, and Gina M. S. Lambright. 2005. "Party Systems and Democratic Consolidation in Africa's Electoral Regimes." *Party Politics* 11 (4): 423–46.

Kuenzi, Michelle, and Gina M. S. Lambright. 2010. "Who Votes in Africa? An Examination of Electoral Participation in 10 African Countries." *Party Politics* 17 (6): 767–99.

Kumlin, Staffan. 2004. *The Personal and the Political: How Personal Welfare State Experiences Affect Political Trust and Ideology*. New York: Palgrave Macmillan.

Kumlin, Staffan, and Bo Rothstein. 2005. "Making and Breaking Social Capital: The Impact of Welfare-State Institutions." *Comparative Political Studies* 38 (4): 339–65.

Lago-Penas, Ignacio, and Santiago Lago-Penas. 2010. "The Determinants of Tax Morale in Comparative Perspective: Evidence from European Countries." *European Journal of Political Economy* 26:441–53.

Larmer, Miles. 2006. "The Hour Has Come at the Pit: The Mineworkers' Union of Zambia and the Movement for Multi-Party Democracy, 1982–1991." *Journal of Southern African Studies* 32 (2): 293–312.

Larmer, Miles. 2011. *Rethinking African Politics: A History of Opposition in Zambia*. Surrey, UK: Ashgate.

Larmer, Miles, and Alastair Fraser. 2007. "Of Cabbages and King Cobra: Populist Politics and Zambia's 2006 Election." *African Affairs* 106 (425):611–37.

Letsa, Natalie Wenzell. 2017. "Voting for the Devil You Know: Understanding Electoral Behavior in Authoritarian Regimes." PhD diss., Cornell University.

Levi, Margaret. 1988. *Of Rule and Revenue*. Berkeley: University of California Press.

Lipsky, Michael. 1968. "Protest as a Political Resource." *American Political Science Review* 62 (4): 1144–58.

Logan, Carolyn. 2009. "Selected Chiefs, Elected Councillors, and Hybrid Democrats: Popular Perspectives on the Co-Existence of Democracy and Traditional Authority." *Journal of Modern African Studies* 47 (1): 101–28.

Lowi, Theodore. 1972. "Four Systems of Policy, Politics, and Choice." *Public Administration Review* 32 (4): 298–310.

Luttmer, Erzo F. P., and Monica Singhal. 2014. "Tax Morale." *Journal of Economic Perspectives* 28 (4): 149–68.

MacLean, Lauren. 2010. "State Retrenchment and the Exercise of Citizenship in Africa." *Comparative Political Studies* 44 (9): 1238–66.

Macola, Giacomo. 2006. "'It Means as if We Are Excluded from the Good Freedom': Thwarted Expectations of Independence in the Luapula Province of Zambia, 1964–6." *Journal of African History* 47:43–56.

Mamdani, Mahmood. 1996. *Citizen and Subject: Contemporary Africa and the Legacy of Late Colonialism*. Princeton: Princeton University Press.

Marien, Sophie, Marc Hooge, and Ellen Quintellier. 2010. "Inequalities in Non-Institutionalized Forms of Political Participation: A Multi-Level Analysis of 25 Countries." *Political Studies* 58:187–213.

Mason, Nicole, Thomas Jayne, and R. Mofya-Mukuka. 2013. "A Review of Zambia's Agricultural Input Subsidy Programs: Targeting, Impacts, and the Way Forward." Working Paper 77, Indaba Agricultural Policy Research Institute, Lusaka.

Mason, Nicole, Thomas Jayne, and Nicolas van de Walle. 2017. "The Political Economy of Fertilizer Subsidy Programs in Africa: Evidence from Zambia." *American Journal of Agricultural Economics* 99 (3): 705–31.

McDonagh, Eileen. 2010. "It Takes a State: A Policy Feedback Model of Women's Political Representation." *Perspectives on Politics* 8 (1): 69–91.

McLoughlin, Claire. 2015. "When Does Service Delivery Improve the Legitimacy of a Fragile or Conflict-Affected State?" *Governance* 28 (3): 341–56.

Mettler, Suzanne. 2007. *Soldiers to Citizens: The G.I. Bill and the Making of the Greatest Generation*. Oxford: Oxford University Press.

Mettler, Suzanne. 2011. *The Submerged State: How Invisible Government Policies Undermine American Democracy*. Chicago: University of Chicago Press.

Mettler, Suzanne, and Joe Soss. 2004. "The Consequences of Public Policy for Democratic Citizenship: Bridging Policy Studies and Mass Politics." *Perspectives on Politics* 2 (1): 55–73.

Mettler, Suzanne, and Jeffrey Stonecash. 2008. "Government Program Usage and Political Voice." *Social Science Quarterly* 89 (2): 273–93.

Michelitch, Kristin. 2015. "Does Electoral Competition Exacerbate Interethnic or Interpartisan Economic Discrimination? Evidence from a Field Experiment in Market Price Bargaining." *American Political Science Review* 109 (1): 43–61.

Mkandawire, Thandika. 1999. "Crisis Management and the Making of Choiceless Democracies." In *State, Conflict, and Democracy in Africa*, ed. R. Joseph. Boulder, CO: Lynne Rienner.

Mkandawire, Thandika. 2015. "Neopatrimonialism and the Political Economy of Economic Performance in Africa: Critical Reflections." *World Politics* 67 (3): 563–612.

Mwansa, Sydney, and Chilufya Chileshe. 2010. *Zambia's Tax System: Need for Equity and Efficiency*. Lusaka: Jesuit Center for Theological Reflection. Available at http://www. saipar.org:8080/eprc/handle/123456789/101

Nugent, Paul. 2001. "Winners, Losers, and Also Rans: Money, Moral Authority, and Voting Patterns in the Ghana 2000 Election." *African Affairs* 100 (400): 405–28.

O'Donnell, Guillermo. 1993. "On the State, Democratization and Some Conceptual Problems." Working Paper 192, Kellogg Institute.

Olivier de Sardan, Jean-Pierre. 2014. "The Delivery State in Africa: Interface Bureaucrats, Professional Cultures, and the Bureaucratic Mode of Governance." In *States at Work: Dynamics of African Bureaucracies*, ed. T. Bierschenk and T. J. P. Olivier de Sardan. Leiden: Brill.

Olson, Mancur. 1965. *The Logic of Collective Action: Public Goods and the Theory of Groups*. Cambridge, MA: Harvard University Press.

Orloff, Ann Shola. 1993. "Gender and the Social Rights of Citizenship: The Comparative Analysis of Gender Relations and Welfare States." *American Sociological Review* 58 (3):303–28.

Ostrom, Elinor.1990. *Governing the Commons: The Evolution of Institutions for Collective Action*. New York: Cambridge University Press.

Pacheco, Julianna Sandell, and Eric Plutzer. 2008. "Political Participation and Cumulative Disadvantage: The Impact of Economic and Social Hardship on Young Citizens." *Journal of Social Issues* 64 (3): 571–93.

Pemstein, Daniel, Kyle L. Marquardt, Eitan Tzelgov, Yi-ting Wang, Joshua Krusell, and Farhad Miri. 2017. "The V-Dem Measurement Model: Latent Variable Analysis for Cross-National and Cross-Temporal Expert-Coded Data." Working Paper 21, 2nd ed., University of Gothenburg, Varieties of Democracy Institute.

Phiri, Chris. 2013. "NGO Group Complains of Crackdown on Rights." *Zambia Reports*, February 9.

Pierson, Paul. 1993. "When Effect Becomes Cause: Policy Feedback and Political Change." *World Politics* 45 (4): 595–628.

Pierson, Paul. 2000. "Increasing Returns, Path Dependence, and the Study of Politics." *American Political Science Review* 94 (2): 251–67.

Pitcher, Anne, Mary Moran, and Michael Johnston. 2009. "Rethinking Patrimonialism and Neopatrimonialism in Africa." *African Studies Review* 52 (1): 125–56.

Posner, Daniel. 2005. *Institutions and Ethnic Politics in Africa*. New York: Cambridge University Press.

Posner, Daniel, and David J. Simon. 2002. "Economic Conditions and Incumbent Support in Africa's New Democracies: Evidence from Zambia." *Comparative Political Studies* 35 (3): 313–36.

Poteete, Amy. 2014. "Democracy Derailed? Botswana's Fading Halo." *Washington Post*, November 4.

Putnam, Robert. 1993. *Making Democracy Work: Civic Traditions in Modern Italy*. Princeton: Princeton University Press.

Putnam, Robert. 1995. "Bowling Alone: America's Declining Social Capital." *Journal of Democracy* 6 (1): 65–78.

Rakner, Lise. 2001. "The Pluralist Paradox: The Decline of Economic Interest Groups in Zambia in the 1990s." *Development and Change* 32:507–29.

Rakner, Lise, Nicolas van de Walle, and Dominic Mulaisho. 2001. "Zambia." In *Aid and Reform in Africa*, ed. D. Shatayanan, D. Dollar, and T. Holmgren. Washington, DC: World Bank.

Rasmussen, Thomas. 1974. "The Popular Basis of Anti-colonial Protest." In *Politics in Zambia*, ed. W. Tordoff. Manchester: Manchester University Press.

Reingold, Beth, and Jessica Harrell. 2010. "The Impact of Descriptive Representation on Women's Political Engagement: Does Party Matter?" *Political Research Quarterly* 63 (2): 280–94.

Reno, William. 1996. *Corruption and State Politics in Sierra Leone*. New York: Cambridge University Press.

Republic of Zambia. 1966. "First National Development Plan." Office of National Development and Planning, Lusaka.

Republic of Zambia. 1971. "Second National Development Plan." Ministry of Development Planning and National Guidance, Lusaka.

Republic of Zambia. 2010. "2010 Population and Housing Census." Central Statistical Office, Lusaka.

Republic of Zambia. 2011. "Sixth National Development Plan." Lusaka.

Resnick, Danielle. 2013. *Urban Poverty and Party Populism in African Democracies*. New York: Cambridge University Press.

Resnick, Danielle, and Daniela Casale. 2014. "Young Populations in Young Democracies: Generational Voting Behaviour in Sub-Saharan Africa." *Democratization* 21 (6): 1172–94.

Riker, William H., and Peter C. Ordeshook. 1968. "A Theory of the Calculus of Voting." *American Political Science Review* 62 (1): 25–42.

Sacks, Audrey. 2011. *The Antecedents of Approval, Trust, and Legitimating Beliefs in Sub-Saharan Africa, Latin America, and Six Arab Countries*. Washington, DC: World Bank.

Sartori, Giovanni. 1976. *Parties and Party Systems: A Framework for Analysis*. New York: Cambridge University Press.

Schedler, Andreas. 2002. "The Menu of Manipulation." *Journal of Democracy* 13 (2): 36–50.

Schneider, Ann, and Helen Ingram. 1993. "Social Construction of Target Populations: Implications for Politics and Policy." *American Political Science Review* 87 (2): 334–47.

Schram, Arthur, and Frans van Winden. 1991. "Why People Vote: Free Riding and the Production and Consumption of Social Pressure." *Journal of Economic Psychology* 12 (4): 575–620.

Schram, Sanford F., Joe Soss, Richard C. Fording, Linda Houser. 2009. "Deciding to Discipline: Race, Choice, and Punishment at the Frontlines of Welfare Reform." *American Sociological Review* 74 (3): 398–422.

Scott, James. 1987. *Weapons of the Weak: Everyday Forms of Peasant Resistance*. New Haven: Yale University Press.

Scott, James. 1998. *Seeing Like a State: How Certain Schemes to Improve the Human Condition Have Failed*. New Haven: Yale University Press.

Sharp, Elizabeth. 2012. *Does Local Government Matter? How Urban Policies Shape Civic Engagement*. Minneapolis: University of Minnesota Press.

Skocpol, Theda, Marshall Ganz, and Ziad Munson. 2000. "A Nation of Organizers: The Institutional Origins of Civic Voluntarism in the United States." *American Political Science Review* 94 (3): 527–46.

Smith, Daniel. 2007. *A Culture of Corruption: Everyday Deception and Popular Discontent in Nigeria*. Princeton: Princeton University Press.

Soss, Joe. 1999. "Lessons of Welfare: Policy Design, Political Learning, and Political Action." *American Political Science Review* 93 (2): 363–80.

Soss, Joe. 2007. "A Public Transformed? Welfare Reform as Policy Feedback." *American Political Science Review* 101 (1): 111–27.

Sunshine, Jason, and Tom R. Tyler. 2003. "The Role of Procedural Justice and Legitimacy in Shaping Public Support for Policing." *Law and Society Review* 37 (3): 513–47.

Tarrow, Sidney. 1996. "Making Social Science Work across Space and Time: A Critical Reflection on Robert Putnam's *Making Democracy Work*." *American Political Science Review* 90 (2): 389–97.

Terray, Emmanuel. 1986. "Le climatiseur at la veranda." in *Afrique plurielle, Afrique actuelle: Hommage a Georges Bandalier*. Paris: Karthala.

Tilly, Charles. 1992. *Coercion, Capital, and European States, AD 990–1992*. Oxford: Blackwell.

Tordoff, William, ed. 1974. *Politics in Zambia*. Manchester: Manchester University Press.

Tordoff, William. 1977. "Zambia: The Politics of Disengagement." *African Affairs* 76 (302): 60–69.

Tordoff, William, ed. 1979. *Administration in Zambia*. Manchester: Manchester University Press.

Tordoff, William, and Richard Molteno. 1974. "Government and Administration." In *Politics in Zambia*, ed. W. Tordoff. Manchester: Manchester University Press.

Torgler, Benno. 2005. "Tax Morale and Direct Democracy." *European Journal of Political Economy* 21:525–31.

Tsai, Lily. 2007. "Solidary Groups, Informal Accountability, and Local Public Goods Provision in Rural China." *American Political Science Review* 101 (2): 355–72.

van de Walle, Nicolas. 2001. *African Economies and the Politics of Permanent Crisis*. New York: Cambridge University Press.

van de Walle, Nicolas. 2003. "Presidentialism and Clientelism in Africa's Emerging Party Systems." *Journal of Modern African Studies* 41 (2): 297–321.

van de Walle, Nicolas. 2012. "The Path from Neopatrimonialism: Democracy and Clientelism in Africa Today." In *Neopatrimonialism in Africa and Beyond*, ed. D. C. Bach and M. Gazibou. New York: Routledge.

van de Walle, Nicolas, Nicole Ball, and Vijaya Ramachandran, ed. 2003. *Beyond Structural Adjustment: The Institutional Context of African Development*. New York: Palgrave Macmillan.

Verba, Sidney, and Norman Nie. 1972. *Participation in America*. New York: Harper and Row.

Verba, Sidney, Kay Lehman Schlozman, and Henry Brady. 1995. *Voice and Equality: Civic Voluntarism in American Politics*. Cambridge, MA: Harvard University Press.

Vickery, Kenneth. 1986. *Black and White in Southern Zambia: The Tonga Plateau Economy and British Imperialism*. Westport, CT: Greenwood Press.

Wantchekon, Leonard. 2003. "Clientelism and Voting Behavior: Evidence from a Field Experiment in Benin." *World Politics* 55 (3): 399–422.

Wedeen, Lisa. 2009. *Peripheral Visions: Publics, Power, and Performance in Yemen*. Chicago: University of Chicago Press.

Weghorst, Keith, and Michael Bernhard. 2014. "From Formlessness to Structure? The Institutionalization of Competitive Party Systems in Africa." *Comparative Political Studies* 47 (12): 1707–37.

Weghorst, Keith, and Staffan Lindberg. 2013. "What Drives the Swing Voter in Africa?" *American Journal of Political Science* 57 (3): 717–34.

Weinstein, Laura. 2011. "The Politics of Government Expenditures in Tanzania, 1999–2007." *African Studies Review* 54 (1): 33–57.

Whitfield, Lindsay. 2009. "Change for a Better Ghana: Party Competition, Institutionalization and Alternation in Ghana's 2008 Elections." *African Affairs* 108 (433): 621–41.

Wolbrecht, Christina, and David Campbell. 2007. "Leading by Example: Female Members of Parliament as Political Role Models." *American Journal of Political Science* 51 (4): 921–39.

Young, Crawford. 2012. *The Post-Colonial State in Africa: Fifty Years of Independence, 1960–2010*. Madison: University of Wisconsin Press.